Secret Doctrines of the Tibetan Books of the Dead

Secret Doctrines of the Tibetan Books of the Dead

DETLEF INGO LAUF

Translated by Graham Parkes

SHAMBHALA
Boulder & London
1977

Shambhala Publications, Inc.
1123 Spruce Street
Boulder, Colorado 80302

Published by arrangement with Aurum Verlag, Erwinstrasse 58-60,
D-7800 Freiburg i. Br., West Germany

ISBN 0-87773-102-0 (cloth)
0-87773-103-9 (paper)
LCC 76-53363

Distributed in the United States by Random House
and in Canada by Random House of Canada Ltd.

Distributed in the Commonwealth by Routledge & Kegan Paul Ltd.,
London & Henley-on-Thames

Printed in the United States of America

Contents

Plates appear between pages 100–101.

Introduction

AMONG the secret traditions of Tibetan Buddhism we find certain doctrines that deal with the central problems of human existence, with the advanced paths to self-knowledge, and with death. To these secret traditions belong the Tibetan Books of the Dead, which were for the most part found by "treasure discoverers" and thereby brought to our attention. Even though there is a definite and clearly developed basic structure peculiar to the Tibetan Book of the Dead, there are so many different works that build on this structure and elaborate various aspects of it, that we must talk of several Tibetan Books of the Dead rather than of one.

The Tibetans consider that it is a task of the utmost importance to confront the problem of death and of a possible transformation beyond the so called bardo state which leads to a new incarnation. Ultimately, this task must be resolved or at least suitably prepared for in this life. The visions of deities experienced in the bardo are the reflections of spiritual processes and experiences in this life, which then work autonomously on the higher plane of the disembodied state. Therefore, the lamas who direct the death ritual admonish the dead person again and again to remind himself of all those teachings and of the meanings of the visionary deities which in his earthly life should have been the patterns and exemplars of the spiritual and religious way of life.

The primary aim is to grasp the essence of the deities and their various attributes in relation to transformations of awareness and to integrate them into one's own conscious mind. This, however, is a significant psychic achievement rooted in the practice of meditation, which must be attained in this earthly existence, since speculations about a better life after death would constitute a dangerous illusion and a renewed bond to the ego.

The Bar-do thos-grol, or Tibetan Book of the Dead, deals with the events of death and the experiences to be expected on the other side, which take place between total liberation and renewed incarnation. But all this, in spite of Buddhist psychology's considerable experience of the paranormal, can be conveyed in the texts of the Tibetan Books of the Dead so convincingly only because their doctrines are always oriented towards the reality of earthly life. Only that which can be the genuine experiential content of our knowledge on earth, the empirical experience of consciousness, is used in the Tibetan Book of the Dead to portray the contents of the bardo that transcend consciousness.

To this extent the Tibetan Book of the Dead is applicable only in its close relation to Buddhist philosophy and practice and without this would have sunk to the level of pure speculation. Since experience of life, knowledge of reality, and perfection of awareness also constitute the doctrinal basis of the transcendent states of the bardo, we may characterize the Tibetan Book of the Dead as a book of *life* a priori. The value of the psychic individuation attained by the individual human life in its earthly body will be received again in the bardo realm beyond, nothing more and nothing less—that is the unequivocal law of karma.

In the knowledge that there is not just one single Tibetan Book of the Dead but a whole group of various writings of this kind, and that outside of Tibet there was a rich tradition of the *ars moriendi* that can also be related to ancient Indian teachings, we have chosen a different form for the development of our theme. Given the abundance of various texts of the Bar-do thos-grol and related writings, we have attempted a synopsis of various traditions and have focused on the central points of certain buddhological and psychological questions about the nature of the bardo and its visions. In considering these issues, basic questions about understanding the bardo will be explained, the solution to which can be found only by referring to various different sources and commentaries. Among the indispensable Tibetan secret doctrines are the traditions of the bKa'-brgyud-pa sect, which has preserved the teachings of the Indian guru and siddha Nāropa.

We have drawn for comparison from works of the Shangs-pa, 'Brug-pa, and Kaṃ-tshang sects, in order to assess the significance of the Tibetan Book of the Dead "from the inside" as it were; that is, from the Tibetan point of view. But all of this would have been unthinkable without my teacher, Vairocana Tulku, the sixteenth incarnation of the great translator Vairocana of the east Tibetan monastery of Ka-thog rdo-rje-gdan, who revealed to me the mysteries of the Bar-do thos-grol. I am grateful also to my Tibetan teachers in Ladakh, Sikkim, and Bhutan, for their assistance and support in providing many original Tibetan texts dealing with the bardo problems that lie at the core of this work.

In order to place the doctrines of the Tibetan Books of the Dead in a broader perspective for the Western intellectual and spiritual worlds, we have drawn a comparison with the problem of the guidance of souls after death as it appears in other cultures. Although this comparison could only be carried out on a small scale, we felt it necessary to attempt, after the purely Tibetan section of the book, to draw certain parallels which would show that comparable symbols and contents are not confined to Asia but appear quite familiar and comprehensible to us in other forms. Psychology also offers us proof that the handling of the most primordial problems of human being and death follows universal forms and patterns of spiritual expression; through these we can enhance our understanding of the Tibetan Book of the Dead and its secret doctrines. Thus, the concluding psychological commentary attempts to understand from a psychological perspective the Tibetan path through the bardo with all its symbols and visions, in order to compare it with Western manifestations of consciousness. Perhaps it will thereby become possible to attain a better understanding of the essential experiences of the Tibetan Book of the Dead, in order to integrate them into our own knowledge and experience. In our world it is proving more and more necessary to bring oriental wisdom and occidental thinking into a synthesis on a higher plane of awareness. This book should be a small contribution to this end.

The diagrams and works of art portrayed here for the initiation into the visionary world of the bardo deities come from Tibet, Ladakh, Sikkim, and Bhutan. A number of the block prints have already reached the West, and we here acknowledge our gratitude to those who have loaned rare pictorial material, in particular to Professor F. Spiegelberg for six of the reproductions. We owe the same gratitude to valuable unnamed help and to the publisher who spared no trouble to support and encourage such a difficult book.

I
The Traditions of the Tibetan Books of the Dead

Purity of the soul depends on her being clarified by a life that is divided, and on her entering into a life of unity.

MEISTER ECKHART, *On Death*

THE DOCTRINES of the Tibetan Book of the Dead, with their directions for passing through the visionary and (in the deepest sense) symbolic worlds of the intermediate state or of the after-death realm, rest upon a broad foundation of the most ancient Tibetan and also Indian traditions. It would not, in general, be appropriate to talk of only one Tibetan Book of the Dead, for our present knowledge of the written traditions shows that a highly developed and extensive system of "soul guidance" for the dead has long flourished in Tibet. The sources listed in the Tibetan bibliography (see below, chapter VIII, 1, A, B), which are primarily texts on "experience after death," or simply "Books of the Dead," are by no means exhaustive and represent only a portion of the extant literature of this kind. Let us think, for example, of *The Tibetan Book of the Dead* published by Evans-Wentz.[1] In this work, which has already become a classic, only seven of the seventeen chapters of the Tibetan Book of the Dead (those chapters most important for the understanding of the whole) were translated.

But there are also works in which we find, for example, 38 sections,[2] as well as essentially shorter versions of various kinds, which come from different traditions and will be discussed further below. A large part of these writings is concerned with instructions for ritual and the performing of initiations, or else consists of mantric books. Concerning these last, there are certain books which belong to the ritual texts that are read at the ceremony for the dead person, and these contain almost nothing but mantras. These mantras are series of mystical syllables that are to be understood as esoteric invocations for the deities. In Vajrayāna Buddhism, mantras and their correct recitation form an essential part of those esoteric doctrines that are transmitted from teacher to pupil in generally secret rites of initiation. Thus, even within the Tibetan Books of the Dead, we have mantric texts that contain the whole cycle of the deities of the bardo, or intermediate state. Only one who knows those mantras is thereby in a position to use them correctly and to assign them to the corresponding deities during meditative invocations. These mantric texts are also very condensed, and they can contain, for example, in only a few pages of mantric "shorthand" the whole Tibetan Book of the Dead with its hundred deities and their meanings. The knowledge and transmission of these mantras is one of the secret and particular aspects of initiation by the guru, and it is then the duty of the pupil to preserve them in a similar way.

We should at this point indicate a peculiarity of these mantric texts within the Tibetan Book of the Dead. There is a certain group of short mantric texts compiled in such a way that one can always carry a copy on one's person. For this purpose they are produced as small foldable books or in the form of maṇḍalas printed on paper.[3] The texts are printed in small print on square blocks, the maṇḍalas in the form of larger, articulated lotus blossoms on the leaves of which the mantras are printed in cosmological order.[4] These writings or diagrams are folded small and sewn into cloth in a particular order, bound with silk thread of the five colors of the Buddhas (or Tathāgatas),[5] and then placed in a metal amulet-holder (T. Ga'u), like those carried by most Tibetans. Often the texts are bound in cloth and worn around the neck. They thus afford the wearer a lifelong magical protection in all places and on long journeys of pilgrimage in Tibet.

In discussing the traditional Buddhist texts and those that we can characterize as Books of the Dead, it must be remarked that we already possess an inexhaustible reservoir of Tibetan writings that, when translated with commentary, would fill a dozen volumes. However, we are here concerned with extracting the essence of these texts by means of a synoptic overview, trying to make it as multifaceted and yet concise as possible in order to reveal the broad significance of the Tibetan doctrines of the bardo state. This is of course a two-fold task, in that we have before us in these works, not only doctrines about the bardo, but also the whole philosophical and ethico-religious system of Mahāyāna Buddhism upon which these doctrines are founded. So we also encounter in the Tibetan Book of the Dead a quintessence of Buddhism, out of which the maṇḍalas of the symbolic deities related to the bardo develop. Underlying all the deities of the bardo are one or more fixed meanings that have been taken from the Buddhist framework or are closely related to it. Thus we must also take into account works written by various Indian and Tibetan Vajrayāna Buddhist scholars which have contributed essential texts or doctrines about the bardo to the Book of the Dead.

The bardo (S. antarābhava), the "intermediate state" after death or between two forms of existence, receives its foundational discussion primarily in three groups of texts. The first group to be described includes the Bar-do thos-grol chen-mo, the "Great Liberation through Hearing in the Bardo," set down in books of several volumes or in collections of texts which are for the most part attributable to several authors.[6]

This group of Book of the Dead writings is associated in a striking way with the well known name of the Indian tantric sage and guru Padmasambhava, to whom the origination of the Bar-do thos-grol is attributed. Padmasambhava came to Tibet in the 8th century (around 750 A.D.) in order to spread the tantric doctrines of Indian Mahāyāna Buddhism. This tantric form of Mahāyāna is also called Vajrayāna, the "Diamond Vehicle" (T. rDo-rje theg-pa). As mentioned already, not only were several authors involved in the compiling of the Tibetan Books of the Dead, but also several generations, so that it must have reached the form with which we are familiar today in about the 14th or 15th century. This form was particularly influenced by the work of the so-called "treasure discovers" (T. gTer-ston), who for centuries exerted a great influence on the spiritual life of the rNying-ma-pa sect. This sect, also more generally known as the non-reformed Red-Cap sect, is the institutionalized successor to the great guru Padmasambhava (T. mTsho-skyes rdo-rje). One of the Books of the Dead[7] draws up a spiritual lineage from which the after-death doctrines could be derived. Such lineages are popular in many Tibetan texts, but often show the successions in a different order depending on the personal tradition of the author. In our text the spiritual heritage is characterized as the "tree of life of the doctrine that originated in

India,"[8] and we read further how "the light of the doctrine came to be lit in the Land of Snows (Tibet)."[9]

The first guru is the tantric Padmasambhava; his successors were Śāntarakṣita (T. mKhan-chen zhi-ba-mtsho, 705-762), who was the first abbot of the great Tibetan monastery of bSam-yas,[10] and the king Khri-srong Lde-btsan, who ruled Tibet in Lhasa from 755 until 797. The accepted order of transmission, corresponding to the Indian principle of the spiritual hierarchy of guru and pupil, represents those two as being followed by the gurus Ākāśagarbha (T. Nam-mkha' snying-po), Buddhajñāna (T. Sangs-rgyas ye-shes), rGyal-mchog-dbyangs, and Ye-shes mtsho-rgyal, this last being one of the two important female pupils of Guru Padmasambhava. Other Tibetan sages of the 8th and 9th centuries appear in the succession, namely, 'Brog-mi dpal-gyi ye-shes, dPal-gyi seng-ge, Vairocana of sPa-gor, and the 25 tantric gurus (T. rJe-dbang nyer-lnga) who in the 9th century became known as yogis because of their supernatural powers.

Another lineage shows the doctrines of the Tibetan Book of the Dead as a revelation of the principle of the mystical Ādibuddha Samantabhadra (T. Kun-tu bzang-po), who resides in the highest state of the dharmakāya (T. Chos-sku).[11] The lineage emanates from him in the mystical visionary body (sambhogakāya[12]) of the white Buddha Vajrasattva (T. rDo-rje sems-dpa') and then in the earthly incarnation of the guru dGa'-rab rdo-rje. He is succeeded by the Indian mahāsiddha Śrī Siṃha, Guru Padmasambhava, his Tibetan female pupil mKhar-chen mtsho-rgyal, the Tibetan sage and translator Klu'i rgyal-mtshan, and then the great Tibetan "treasure discoverer," Karma gling-pa (in about the 14th century). The "treasure discoverers" were Tibetan scholars who found treasure (T. gTer-ma) in the form of certain uncanonized writings of Buddhism in secret places where they had been concealed by earlier gurus, by Padmasambhava in particular. The particular circumstances of the discoveries (the writings were found under rocks, buildings, stupas, etc.,) and the prediction of their rediscovery can be found in the biography of Padmasambhava.[13] These texts are not included in the Tibetan Buddhist Canon of bKa'-'gyur and bsTan-'gyur but were, like most gTer-ma, collected

Fig. 1. The tantric guru, Padmasambhava, with his two female pupils. Tibetan block print.

in the great compilation of the Rin-chen gter-mdzod of the rNying-ma-pa sect. We see, then, that there are very complicated connections within the Tibetan tradition of Books of the Dead and that several scholars developed the foundations of the Bar-do thos-grol. Of these the most important are Śrī Siṃha, Padmasambhava, Vimalamitra, Vairocana, and Karma gling-pa. The great discoverer of treasure, Rig-'dzin Karma gling-pa, is known as the discoverer of the Bar-do thos-grol, which he found on the mountain sGam-po-dar. He also contributed considerable additions, so that we have today in the collection "Kar-gling zhi-khro" ("the peaceful and wrathful deities according to Karma gling-pa") not only the entire Bar-do thos-grol but also a series of ritual texts and prayers (in 38 parts) that are of great importance for the initiation into the maṇḍalas of the visionary deities. These texts are particularly illuminating for our inquiry.

In the tradition of the rNying-ma-pa sect we find a second group of Book of the Dead writings which, while related to the first group, display various iconographic differences. This second group is composed of texts from the cycle of the Nāraka deities (T. Zhi-khro na-rag dong-sprugs) who are described in comprehensive books and rituals (T. Na-rag dong-sprugs)[14] and are also included in part in the famous collection "Klong-chen snying-thig," collated from the work of the Tibetan master Klong-chen rab-'byams-pa.[15] The sNying-thig literature in general is a rich source of information about bardo doctrines. Much is to be learned about the various bardo states and the signs of approaching death as well as the transformation of awareness in the six worlds from the following works: the "Ye-shes bla-ma,"[16] the "bsKyed-rim lha-khrid,"[17] the "Shes-rig rdo-rje rnon-po,"[18] the important "Lam-rim ye-shes snying-po" on fundamental principles,[19] the encyclopedic "Kun-bzang bla-ma'i zhal-lung,"[20] the collected works of gTer-ston Padma gling-pa,[21] the ritual work "rDo-rje theg-pa sngags-kyi gso-sbyong,"[22] and the "Maṇi bka'-'bum" attributed to the Tibetan king Srong-btsan sgam-po.

Further contributions to the doctrines of the bardo are to be found in a third group of texts, the "Six Doctrines of Nāropa" (T. Nā-ro chos-drug), which constitute a pivotal point in the tradition of the bKa'-brgyud-pa sect of Tibet. The "Six Doctrines of Nāropa"[23] provide important information for the understanding of the bardo doctrines, the awareness principle, the trikāya doctrine, and meditation on the light, all of which play an important role in the Tibetan Book of the Dead.

Nāropa (who lived from 1016 to 1100 in India and Kashmir[24]) is the second guru in the bKa'-brgyud-pa tradition of Tibet.[25] There are two versions of his "Six Doctrines" extant, one by him and the other by his sister Niguma (T. Ni-gu chos-drug). Nāropa's teachings reached Tibet through his pupil Mar-pa of Lho-brag (1012 to 1097), the great Tibetan translator. Mar-pa is the founder of the bKa'brgyud-pa sect, the line of "oral tradition." The "Six Doctrines of Niguma" came through the ḍākinī Sukhasiddhi (a pupil of Virūpa) to the Tibetan scholar Shangs-pa Khyung-po rnal-'byor (born 1086), in a tradition named the Shangs-pa sect after its founder. Its founder transmitted the "Six Doctrines" to Chos-kyi seng-ge, Shangs-ston rig-pa'i rdo-rje (1234–1309), and further successors.[26]

What then are the "Six Doctrines" of Nāropa and Niguma? They are doctrines founded upon Yoga and tantric Buddhist experience that discuss "the mystical heat" (S. caṇḍa; T. gTum-mo), the "Illusory body" (S. mahāmāyā; T. sGyu-lus), the "dream state" (S. svapnadarśana; T. rMi-lam), the "clear light" (S. ābhāsvara; T. 'Od-gsal), the "intermediate state" (S. antarābhava; T. Bar-do), and the "transmission of consciousness" (S. saṃkrānti; T. 'Pho-ba).

For our purposes, the last three doctrines, those of the "clear light," the "bardo," and "transmission of consciousness" are the most important, and we can draw from several sources[27] that developed these basic concepts of the Bar-do thos-grol. Another highly esoteric doctrine called Grong-'jug (S. parakāyapraveśana) belongs to the doctrine of transmission of consciousness, the living transmission of which was curtailed by the death of Mar-pa's son in the 11th century. Grong-'jug has a metaphorical meaning equivalent to "the re-animating of a dead person" and forms a part of the Ārya-Catuṣpīṭha-Tantra. Several theoretical and practical directions connected with it are to be found in the sNying-thig literature. The "Six Doctrines" were transmitted from the Tibetan translator Mar-pa to his great pupil, the poet and yogi Mi-la raspa, who is held to be Tibet's most important mystic. In his "Hundred Thousand Songs," as in the collection "Six Songs,"[28] we are given wonderful detailed descriptions of the bardo and

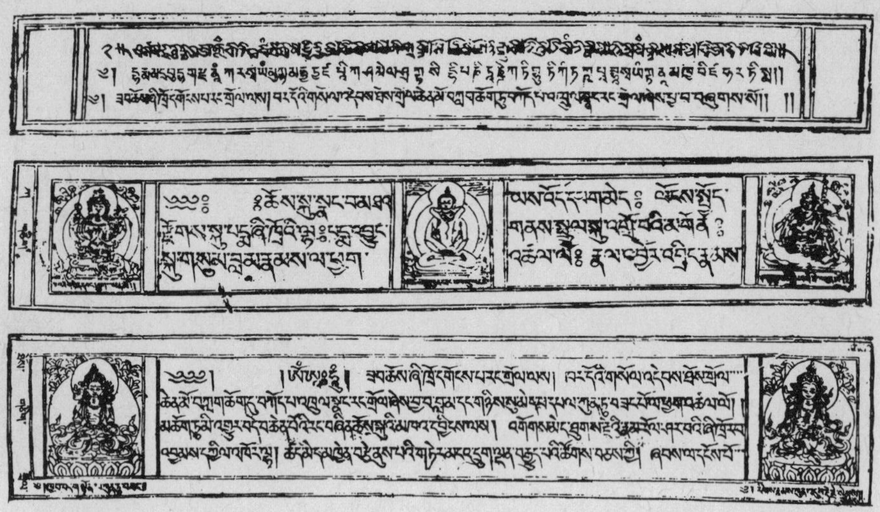

Fig. 2. Block print editions of the Tibetan Book of the Dead; above: title page and (middle) first page of a work from Bhum-thang; below: the first page of a block print from Punakha (Bhutan). The vignettes show the Bodhisattva Avalokiteśvara, the Ādibuddha Samantabhadra, Padmasambhava, Samantabhadra, and the Buddha Vajrasattva. The title page (above) shows the title of the book in Sanskrit Lantshascript, in Tibetan transliteration, and in Tibetan.

therewith of everything characterizable as an intermediate state. We find that many of the gaps in our understanding of the bardo from the Tibetan Book of the Dead are here filled.

The secret knowledge of the wanderings of the dead person's awareness-principle belongs to the most ancient heritage of Tibetan and central Asian culture. So we find these books of the dead, not only in the Buddhist tradition of Tibet, but already in the pre-Buddhist Bon religion of the Land of Snows beyond the Himalayas, which can be characterized in its various forms as the authentic, indigenous religion of Tibet. Mahāyāna Buddhism and its tantric form, Vajrayāna, did not reach Tibet until the early 7th century.

The teachings of the Tibetan Bon religion, as propounded by its almost mythical founder gShen-rab, portray a comprehensive system of which we have only recently come to have any concrete knowledge. Only slowly are some of the texts of the Bon-po tradition being published, and until now they have been accessible only to the experts.[29] So in discussing the Tibetan Books of the Dead and related works, we should, from the chronological point of view, have mentioned those of the Bon religion first, which probably reflect the oldest transmitted forms. This is perhaps also recognizable from the fact that the few known and as yet untranslated texts do not display that systematic richness of cosmological and psychological relationships and meanings of the visionary deities that we find in the Buddhist texts of the Tibetan tradition.

But the Buddhist texts of the Book of the Dead tradition are without doubt founded upon these very ancient experiences of the Tibetan religion. The wrathful deities that are to be found there, above all the theriomorphic ḍākinīs and the blood-drinking guardians of the four gates of the maṇḍalas, are not of exclusively Buddhist origin from the Indian tantras, but stem from much older layers of the magical-mythical religions of central Asia. One must not overlook the similarities in symbolism, ritual, and content to certain central Asian and shamanistic forms of religion. For a few parallels to this question, the reader is referred to the section on comparative religious studies (chapter V). A detailed discussion of the Book of the Dead tradition of the Bon religion must wait for the future. However, in this book (chapter III, 3) we shall discuss briefly two important texts,[30] in order to make possible a preliminary comparative overview of the Buddhist texts. One text is the Bar-do thos-grol gsal-sgron chen-mo from the canonical collection of the Bon-po bstan-'gyur (T. 124), and the other important work is the Na-rag pang-'gong rgyal-po, which belongs to the gTer-ma tradition of the Bon-po "treasure discoverers" and was found by 'Or-sgom phug-pa (in around the 11th or 12th century).[31]

In the Bon religion too, we have the esoteric "treasure discoverer" (T. gTer-ston) system, which brought us such an abundance of important works in the Buddhist rNying-ma-pa sect, unavailable in the canonical tradition. It is interesting that some "treasure discoverers" have found gTer-ma texts of both the Bon-po and the Buddhist tradition of Padmasambhava. So there were clearly quite deep connections and spiritual interactions between the ancient Bon religion and the Buddhism of Tibet. We can infer from the detailed historical work of the Bon religion, the Legs-bshad-mdzod,[32] that here too the bardo doctrines are associated with an extensive tradition that has been collated in many texts, books of ritual, and commentaries.[33] Just as in the Buddhist tradition, we find in the Bon-po religion important contributions to knowledge about the bardo, the visionary deities, and the six realms of existence, in writings other than those specifically called Books of the Dead. And so, for example, the doctrines of the rDzogs-chen tradition of Zhang-zhung constitute an indispensable supplement to our knowledge of the Bon-po Bar-do thos-grol. Zhang-zhung is that western Tibetan region which can be seen as an ancestral home of the spiritual culture of the Bon religion. We shall return to the doctrines of the Bon-po Niṣpanna-Yoga of this school and its statements about the bardo when we come to discuss the deities of the Bon tradition.

Further empirical experiences relating to the problem of death, which are discussed in detail in the Buddhist tradition of Books of the Dead, must certainly have come from the Indian Vedic tradition. Or rather, there were for a long time definite descriptions of the process of dying and of the path of the soul after death which were generally current in India and were formulated in the Vedas and the Upaniṣads. The extant texts for the most part display considerable similarities with the content of Buddhist writings, and in this context the reader is referred in particular to the Bṛhadāranyaka Upaniṣad IV. 4, 1–2; the Aitareya Āranyaka III. 2, 4; the Śatapatha Brāhmaṇa; and the Pretakalpa of the Garuḍa Purāṇa.

II

Basic Elements of Wisdom about Life and Knowledge about the After-Death State and Rebirth

1. Life, Karma, Death, and Rebirth

> Life is only another death. The birth of life, not its end, is death.
>
> FR. HEBBEL, *Journals*

THE INTRODUCTORY quotation from Hebbel is perhaps the best introduction to Asiatic thought in general and Buddhist teachings in particular. We have already mentioned that the Tibetan Books of the Dead not only attempt to answer questions about dying and transformation in the bardo but that they also presuppose acquaintance with the whole course of life and the Buddhist doctrine of salvation and so communicate this latter in their texts in the form of a self-contained compendium.

Condensed into a short formula, this means: life, knowledge of life, and correct transformations in life are the true prerequisites for proper dying and for the possibility of determining one's fate beyond death. It is precisely this problem that the Tibetan Book of the Dead attempts to resolve. Although we cannot here give a complete outline of the Buddhist teachings, which will appear again and again in the texts and clarificatory remarks in the course of this book, we must nevertheless sketch some typical thoughts which lie at the core of the Buddhist spiritual and intellectual worlds. For only from this foundation is the meaning and purpose of the Tibetan writings about the bardo comprehensible.

Buddhism regards life in all its forms as an inviolable blessing that should never be intentionally harmed or destroyed. But life in human form is something "precious and difficult to attain," since only man, thanks to thinking and discriminating awareness, is able to influence and guide the processes of life and conditions of existence from his own experience and intuition. The great Tibetan scholar, sGam-po-pa (1079–1153), offers in his 28 instructions for yogis[34] the following admonitions:

> If one has reached this human body, pure and hard to attain, it would be regrettable to die an unreligious and ordinary person.
>
> Since human life in the Kali Yuga (i.e., our contemporary age of darkness through ignorance) is brief and uncertain, it would be regrettable to squander it in meaningless activity.

Since one's own spirit partakes of the uncreated nature of the dharmakāya, it would be regrettable if it were led into the mire of the worldly illusions.

Thus Buddhism places life and existence at the unconditioned center of meaning-giving. The question of the whence and whither of human life is secondary in comparison to earthly existence and its mastery. If the here and now of being born human is resolved as a problem of existence, there is no longer fear of the future, and paths of liberation open up. The Buddha saw through life and the processes of existence by means of a practical method of knowledge oriented to reality, and from this came his important dictum: all life is ultimately suffering, the opposite of freedom and salvation. The path from suffering to liberation, which involves the recognition of the causes of suffering and the overcoming of it, is long. Suffering is one's enduring of all forms of opposites, in view of the knowledge of an indescribable absolute, of something deathless, called nirvāṇa. Suffering is "to be separated from the agreeable and bound to the unpleasant." Suffering is the experience of love, or desire (Pali, taṇhā; T. 'Dod-chags), and hate (P. dosa; T. Zhe-sdang). Both states of consciousness are subject to time in the world of the transitory, and we suffer from their arising and disappearing. Suffering is also the cycle of birth, life, and death in a world rich in frustration and ephemeral joy (S. saṃsāra; T. 'Khor-ba). As long as man suffers in the world and from the circumstances of the world and his behavior, he is not liberated and finds himself in ignorance (S. avidyā; T. gTi-mug). Ignorance arises through desire, through lasting attachment to worldly things and events, and through attachments to one's own falsely understood personality, which through identification with the transitory world of existence remains bound to the then inevitable cycle of becoming and passing away. Everything that arises and passes away is of only relative value, the object of our illusions which can never be fulfilled. Attachment is the opposite of liberation. All activity that deepens the immersion in saṃsāra will detract from the goal of liberation and lead to suffering and to actions that are bad or negative according to the law of karma. There is no moral evaluation connected with this.

All actions that loosen the attachments to the transitory world of existence are directed towards liberation and lead to good or positive deeds, which lead out of the circle of saṃsāra. Karma as law signifies the conditionality of our actions and the absolute effect of these actions upon the present and future path of our existence. The law of karma places man in a position of unconditioned responsibility for his actions, for every deed and even every resolution to act has an inevitable visible or invisible consequence. According to the Buddhist view, man remains in the cycle of birth and death until perfected knowledge puts an end to it. Rebirth is a consequence of not having attained liberation in the previous life. Each life is the result of the working out of karma that has been formed by actions attached to the world.

Rebirth is not a personal event in which the same "I" re-emerges that has existed before. Buddhism denies the notion of a soul as an enduring I-personality. The pre-determinations of karma, the energetic impulses in a particular direction, are the basis and cause for a further life in the cycle of existence from one life to another. The development can take place on a lower or on a higher plane, in better or worse circumstances with respect to salvation, depending on the karmic facts. And so the unavoidable and incorruptible law of life is the path that man can build, given that he recognizes the significance of his actions and thereby the meaning of the life that can lead to freedom. The Tibetan yogi and mystic Mi-la ras-pa (1040–1123) says in his "Hundred Thousand Songs" of the effect of karma: "Do you not know that all suffering and the lower worlds are the result of bad deeds? You surely know that if you now practice virtue, you will have peace of mind and no worries in the face of approaching death."

The Buddhist teachings attempt to bring about the insight that evil is not the objective world in itself, but rather the constant identification with it through desire. Compared with the goal of nirvāṇa without suffering, which is absolute liberation in timeless eternity, everything earthly of the world of becoming must of course be characterized as unreal. What appears to us as reality is only seemingly so, since it is transitory and always changing in form. If the human spirit remains attached to the changeable and reveres this as the real, it will have to undergo its experience of suffering in precisely this changeability. Mi-la ras-pa describes it thus: If our usual thinking becomes deeply attached, it leads to good and bad deeds and thereby creates the bardo of the world of suffering, in which one is forced to experience pleasure and pain.

Life itself is an intermediate state, namely, between earthly birth and death. In this way one bardo succeeds another in this earthly world as well as in the world beyond. Just as the material world is subject to transitoriness, so also is man in his physical form. The Tibetan Book of the Dead follows the ancient Buddhist notion of the five-fold make-up of the human personality, and its meditations on this constitute a systematic psychology that has become the basic structure of all maṇḍalas of Mahāyāna Buddhism. The five groups, or skandhas (S. upādānaskandha; T. Phung-po lnga) of the personality are the body as a physical form (S. rūpa), sensation (S. vedanā), perception (S. saṃjñā), motivation (S. saṃskāra), and awareness (S. vijñāna). These five groups mutually interact and form what we call the human personality, or the presence of the individual in the world. All this is transitory and not absolute, for everything that arises passes away. The whole process of life, including thinking as the constant movement of consciousness, is characterized as constant flux. Nothing has real duration; everything is at every moment passing away or else is assigned to a new becoming. Life is not static, but dynamic, and all moments of existence are intermediate states, even between two different kinds of state in the process of transformation. To recognize the changeable nature of the whole empirical world means to see its deceptive insubstantiality. Thus, there opens up the path to the unchangeable, the reality of the deathless, which is identical with the knowledge of the perfected and liberated. Mahāyāna Buddhism, the basis of bardo teachings, introduced quite early the terminology to facilitate comprehension of the arising of images and visionary buddhas to be experienced through concentration of the mind. The question of transformation after death in particular lent itself to a better formulation when supported by the idea of a permanent ground of awareness.

The first important concept is "emptiness" (S. śūnyatā; T. sTong-pa-nyid) as the primordial ground underlying and connecting saṃsāra and nirvāṇa. The empirical world is ultimately empty, since nothing is permanent or has essential being; nirvāṇa is empty, since its all-pervading quality cannot be described or suitably characterized. So the concept of emptiness has with respect to the world a negative, and to transcendence a positive, value. The Vijñānavāda or Yogācāra School of Indian Mahāyāna[35] posited as the absolute foundation of the world and of nirvāṇa a "ground-consciousness" or universal awareness (S. ālayavijñāna; T. Kun-gzhi rnam-shes). We find this idea already in the Udāna: Everything is contained in awareness.

All suffering and experience of the seemingly real world comes about through perception in awareness. But nirvāna too, complete salvation, is a condition in awareness, namely, emptiness and freedom from suffering, without the fluctuating processes of thought. When all contents of thought and activities of the intellect cease, which normally come to awareness from the empirical world through perception, then the stillness and absolute depth and infinity of ground-consciousness begin. To attain this is one of the important goals of all meditative practices. Nirvāṇa is absolute freedom from the world and from the manifestations (saṃskāras) from the ālayavijñāna; saṃsāra is every step out from ground-consciousness into the world of appearances, and so also into the world of thoughts, which wells up from ground-consciousness in waves of thought.

Whatever karma is accumulated during life falls back down as a karmically or energetically charged seed (S. bīja) into ground-consciousness, into that all-pervading essence of awareness out of whose primordial ground beings are reincarnated when the maturation of karma presses towards a new manifestation. It is not the previously existing person as a constellation of the five skandhas who appears in a new incarnation, but his karma, the consequence of actions begun and not yet worked through. In a somewhat more concrete form this idea now becomes the basis of the doctrines of the Tibetan Book of the Dead; there, whatever survives physical death is called the awareness-principle (T. Yid; S. citta or manas), and this has through its karma the power to form itself into a subtle awareness-body (T. Yid-kyi lus; S. manomaya kāyā). It is this subtle body which stands in the intermediate state of the bardo at the central point of the process of transformation, and with whose guidance the monks who recite the ritual of the Books of the Dead concern themselves. As we shall see, this precise and uninterrupted directing of the awareness-principle of the dead person is so clear and real that it seems as if a person-to-person conversation is going on between the lamas and the dead person.

Only this phenomenological evidence allows us to fall into Western terminology and to speak of "guidance of the soul" after death. We mention this concept here only in order to show the possible relationship in technique with practices in other religions.

Let us consider a few further thoughts about life and death and possible perfection within this span. Life presupposes death, and after death there again comes life. But only in that individual span of existence between life and death can the law of individuation be consummated, in that life becomes fulfilled with meaning. In Buddhism this consummation consists in the liberation from suffering by perfection of the possibilities of human existence and virtues, through which the world can gradually be mastered in this existence. The Buddhist path (and, of course, with another orientation also many other genuinely philosophically or religiously grounded paths of salvation) thereby totally conforms with the development of the soul and the physical maturation of the person. Once the step into this world has been taken, there must also be a way to come back out of it. Whoever from ignorance has not come to know himself and the world to its depths must despair of it and is unable to recognize the final step that goes beyond death. In the Aṅguttara Nikāya we find the following statement:[36]

> Master, is it possible to travel far enough to come to the end of the world, to recognize and behold the place where there is no birth, no old age, no death, no passing away and no coming into being? . . .
>
> No traveling will bring one to the end of the world, and yet if one has not reached the end of the world, there is no liberation from suffering.

Indeed this end of the world is to be found; the beginning and end of all things, of all decisions in thinking and acting lie in us ourselves. To overcome suffering and to attain freedom from the world in the world, means precisely "to reach the end of the world." How many possibilities are contained in those words! Life in human form is the great opportunity to be and perfect oneself in it. Thereby a host of problems can be overcome without those passions that are precisely the cause of further suffering. Another very salutary meditation towards the understanding of the problem of death is brought to us by Buddhaghosa.[37] Whoever wishes to develop reflection on death should go into solitude, and in seclusion should ponder the following consideration: "Death will come at some time, the life force will be exhausted." One should by means of this reflection stimulate attention, emotion, and insight, for only so can one remove the blocks against ideas of death, and so "the notion of transitoriness becomes familiar, and as one pursues it further, the idea of suffering and lack-of-an-I will come."

Therefore, whoever has not been prepared by such exercises will be assailed in his last hour by "anxiety and terror," the threat arising from ignorance of himself, blocking his access to clear and liberated awareness. This is the same situation as in the Tibetan Book of the Dead. Anxiety and terror lead in the bardo to the experience of the wrathful deities as images of the opposing karmic forces which were in control of the unredeemed life—even at the moment before death with its engendered great fear of the unknown. With thoughts of transitoriness, suffering, and death, in life one should also arrive at the opposite recognition, namely, knowledge of the absolute and the transcendent. This is a totally positive attitude towards life, which values and directs what is essential. Thus Buddhaghosa affirms that one who "cannot attain the deathless in the course of his life" but has at least striven to attain it will achieve "with the disintegration of the body a more fortunate path of existence." That is to say, his rebirth will take place under better circumstances on a higher plane.

As this ancient text makes clear, the question of future transformation after death is of great importance. The Tibetan Book of the Dead instructs the dead person in finding the path through the bardo, and therefore proceeds from the well-known assumption in

Tibet that the awareness-principle will be reborn. The conditions of awareness set by previous karma fashion the awareness or spirit-body (T. Yid-kyi lus) which undergoes all the experiences of the after-death worlds, and these experiences in the realm beyond correspond to his karma (see also chapter II, 6).

It is of particular importance to the Tibetans that a person should appropriate during his earthly and fully conscious life all the knowledge which he will have to keep before his spiritual eye to guide him through the bardo. According to an important text from the "sNying-thig" tradition[38] the knowledge required for the path through the intermediate realm of the bardo is six-fold:

1. The knowledge of his former place of birth or realm of existence (T. sNgon-gyi skye-gnas shes-pa).
2. The knowledge of dying, of the crossing over of awareness, and of new rebirth (T. 'Chi-'pho dang skye-ba).
3. The knowledge of transcending spirit (T. pha-rol-gyi sems).
4. The knowledge of all hidden (occurring in the realm of the non-visible) appearances (T. sKang-ba lkog-tu-gyur-ba).
5. The knowledge of the six realms of existence, i.e., of rebirths (T. Rigs-drug-gi gnas mthong-zhing).
6. The perfect knowledge of all liberating (purifying) capabilities (T. dBang-po rnams).

Here we have a series of very subtle pieces of knowledge which all relate to how the path through the dangers of the bardo can be traversed with awareness. They are supposed to enable the spirit-body of the dead person to orient and guide itself in the realm beyond, recalling the teachings from this life. These things are therefore to be learned during life, so that they can be helpful in the life after death. Therefore the monk reciting the Book of the Dead admonishes the awareness-principle wandering through the bardo to remember these capabilities. In order to attain a basic understanding of the nature of incarnation and the three levels of existence of human beings and buddhas, we must briefly consider the doctrine of the "three bodies" (S. trikāya; T. sKu-gsum). Without this doctrine, fundamental to Mahāyāna Buddhism, the initiations into the maṇḍalas of the deities of the Tibetan Book of the Dead cannot be properly understood.

2. The Trikāya Doctrine as the Basis of the Initiations

Life is a category of possibility.
HEBBEL, *Journals*

THE DOCTRINE of the "three bodies" (S. trikāya; T. sKu-gsum) belongs to the indispensable foundations of Mahāyāna Buddhism. It constitutes at the same time an important background to understanding the structure of the teachings of the Tibetan Book of the Dead, in which all the deities are ordered according to this principle. The three bodies together ecompass the possibilities of Being, between the highest Being in the spiritual sense and objective existence in the world of form. They constitute a spiritual order in the self-understanding of Mahāyāna Buddhism as the possibility of the emanation of the spiritual as well as the spiritualization of the material.

It is not a simple matter to convey the true meaning of the three bodies by means of Western concepts, but we can perhaps grasp the essential core of the doctrine by a series of paraphrases. The highest spiritual principle as cosmic order, as law or reality, interpenetrates the whole empirical world of being; it manifests on the plane of the transitory as nirmāṇakāya in physical form; it reveals itself in a higher sense in supernatural, transcending, and radiating form as sambhogakāya; and through timeless self-positing, it manifests as the highest reality (S. dharmatā) and Buddha-nature in the form of dharmakāya.

Kaya in Sanskrit means body, not so much body as a visible form, but rather as a form of being, a plane of the working of dharma (law) between transcendence and immanence. Yogācāra philosophy divides this realm of the reflecting human spirit in the frame of absolute reality into three bodies, or categories of being.

We shall find again and again in the texts of the Tibetan Book of the Dead that these terms can be used in quite different ways, for they ultimately represent divisions of a spiritual principle. In the reality of life, in the ordering of spiritual hierarchies, in the portrayals of the visionary deities as reflections of awareness, and in the rites of initiation as the image and primordial pattern of psychic transformation, the trikāya system constitutes an indispensable foundation. With the help of some definitions, let us acquaint ourselves further with the nature and working of the three bodies.

The dharmakāya (T. Chos-kyi-sku) is the essence of doctrine and reality, it is highest Being as truth in itself, it has no form and is not visible. Its nature is the primordial ground of all appearances, emptiness (S. śūnyatā) as the condition of plurality, and from the psychological standpoint of the Tibetan Book of the Dead, it is the all-containing and all-embracing ground consciousness (S. ālayavijñāna; T. Kun-gzhi rnam-shes). As foundation, the dharmakāya is the principle of absolute totality, and in relation to pure matter it is spiritual Being. In their true essence the Buddha and all buddhas are identical with the nature of pure dharmakāya. Since the dharmakāya is absolute reality, beyond all ideas and concepts, there is also no image or form of it. It is not even possible to form an adequate conception of its absoluteness. Yet there are symbolic representations of the dharmakāya, which are supposed to convey a certain idea. In art, there are the representations of the Ādibuddha as Vajradhara (T. rDo-rje-'chang) or Samantabhadra (T. Kun-tu bzang-po), which are taken as embodiments of the dharmakāya. We shall come back to these later.

The dharmakāya in Mahāyāna Buddhism signifies an absoluteness in every aspect: in religion it is the Sacred; in philosophy it is Law, but also the highest being and perfection; as a *Gestalt* it is the perfect Buddha or the primordial image of all buddhas, the primordial or Ādibuddha (T. Thog-ma'i sangs-rgyas). We thereby understand dharmakāya as reality and also as embodiment in its purest form. The Tibetan sage sGam-po-pa (also called Dvags-po lha-rje), a pupil of the great Yogi Mi-la ras-pa in the 12th century, names a few qualities of the dharmakāya: it remains always the same, is profound, enduring, unified, harmonious, pure, radiant, and blessed.[39] The dharmakāya is the foundation of all appearances or emanations of the Law; it is the highest Idea and at the same time the possibility of its embodiment.

In the sphere of spiritual experience beyond sensory images and perceptions, reality can appear before the spiritual eye of bodhisattvas and the perfected or spiritually advanced person in the form of the "body of bliss," the sambhogakāya (T. Longs-spyod rdzogs-pa'i sku). The meaning of this concept is difficult to convey in our language and is yet of great importance for the understanding of the deities of the bardo visions. The sambhogakāya is also called the "body of heavenly delight," of other-worldly bliss. We could characterize it as the knowable manifestation of the spiritual pervasiveness of the absolute or of buddha-nature. In the sambhogakāya, reality manifests in radiant beings like the bodhisattvas and the meditation-buddhas (S. Tathāgatas; T. De-bzhin-gshegs-pa). The bodhisattvas (T. Byang-chub sems-dpa') are "enlightened beings" who have passed through the earthly worlds on the path towards perfection of buddha-nature and are now living on the ten planes[40] of perfected spirituality in transcendent spaces, where they participate in the bliss of the pure buddha-lands. The bodhisattvas have in their earthly existence made the great vow of active compassion for all beings (S. mahākaruṇā; T. sNying-rje chen-po), so that they may save all beings and lead them to the salvation of nirvāṇa.

In the heavenly buddha-spheres, it is supposed, they work further towards this lofty goal, until all living beings are saved. But what belongs above all to the spiritual realm of the sambhogakāya are those transcendent buddhas seen in visions or in flashes of enlightenment, that we know as Tathāgatas or meditation-buddhas. They are seen as the emanations from the absoluteness of the dharmakāya and represent certain basic forms of wisdom, of psychological and cosmological relationships, which are represented in Buddhist maṇḍalas, where they constitute the greater part of the mystical meditation teachings of the Mahāyāna. The supernatural reality of the sambhogakāya, as the spiritual realm of emanations of higher intellectual sight, forms the most important background for the visionary nature of the deities of the Tibetan Book of the Dead.

In the third phase of emanation the essence of reality manifests on the earthly plane in the form of buddhas, who from compassion appear in the transitory world of existence. They arise in a visible incarnated body (S. nirmāṇakāya; T. sPrul-pa'i-sku) and are subject like all beings to the earthly cycle of birth, life, and death. The historical Gautama Buddha is considered such a concrete manifestation of the Law. The nirmāṇakāya has as its foundation the dharmakāya; the cause of its existence on the earthly plane is the compassion of the transcendent buddhas and bodhisattvas. But it is also said that earthly buddhas, as the propagators of the doctrine of salvation, are particular personalities who are distinguished from ordinary people by the 32 bodily marks and by certain supernatural powers (heavenly sight and hearing, for example).

With the three bodies we have acquainted ourselves with the most important foundation for the understanding of the entire Tibetan Book of the Dead and its initiations. They are not only the basis of the initiations, which we shall soon discuss, but they also form the three planes of the death-experience, i.e., the transformation in the worlds beyond, which come between two forms of existence in earthly life. The Tibetan Book of the Dead shows us the dramatic events between the highest experience of the light and the deepest abysses as transformation between the absolute and its most empirical opposite. As we shall see later, the visions of the Tibetan Book of the Dead show us the emanation of the Sacred in its threefold aspect of the trikāya doctrine. The essence of buddha-nature is to be seen in Mahāyāna Buddhism as a symbol of the Sacred in itself (in opposition to the profane). The first emanation is the appearance, from out of the primordial Buddha, of the Sacred in the transcendent buddhas and bodhisattvas on the heavenly and visionary plane of the sambhogakāya. The second appears in earthly form as the Buddha preaching salvation in the nirmāṇakāya. Among the deities of the Tibetan Book of the Dead, it is only the six Buddhas from the six realms of incarnation who appear in the form of incarnated saviors.

The Buddhist doctrines of the Mahāyāna and particularly of tantric Vajrayāna Buddhism, which were privileged to incorporate the ancient experience of Indian Yoga in a mystical synthesis, developed a schema from the trikāya doctrine that was soon supplemented by a "fourth body." This "fourth body" is the indivisible trinity of the trikāya as unity in the great experience of their simultaneity (S. sahaja; T. Lhan-skyes) or the "great bliss" (S. mahāsukha; T. bDe-ba chen-po). This experience of the unity of all things after the perfection of the "three bodies" is characterized as the "fourth body" or as the fourth stage of the mahāsukhakāya (T. bDe-chen-gyi-sku), the spontaneously self-generating inner body (S. svabhāvikakāya; T. Ngo-bo-nyid-ki sku) or as sahajakāya (T. Lhan-gcig skyes-pa'i sku) of the "simultaneously originated body." It is the body of the authentic inner essence (T. Ngo-bo-nyid) and will be designated only as svabhāvikakāya in the following chapters. The trinity and the one body as the fourth experience of indivisible (T. dByer-med) unity were identified, as forms of spiritual experience, with certain centers in the human body, which in Yoga is seen as an image of the macrocosm in a psychophysical and microcosmic order. Man himself then becomes the plane of activity of the subtle emanations of the Sacred or of buddha-nature.

We shall again and again encounter these emanations of the Sacred from the mysterium of the diamond-nature of the Buddha, the suchness, the most perfect wisdom of the transcendent Tathāgatas, when we consider the exoteric and esoteric statements of the Tibetan Book of the Dead, which always present us with a wealth of symbols and symbolic relationships. Because of the variety of traditions and schools from which we have received the teachings of the Tibetan Books of the Dead, it is difficult to provide an overview that does justice to the various systems. The language of the Buddhist texts of Tibet is usually an aggregation of symbols and notions which are often capable of several meanings. Especially in the case of the initiations we must try to hold to one schema among the many that will prove to be of general validity.

The introductory verse of the Bar-do thos-grol chen-mo (the Great Book of Liberation through Hearing in the Bardo) begins by dividing up the cycle of deities into emanations according to the trikāya doctrines. From the dharmakāya comes the Buddha of the immeasurable shining light, the radiant Buddha Amitābha; in the light of the sambhogakāya shine the peaceful and wrathful deities; and as the incarnate disseminator of these teachings there appears in the nirmāṇakāya the Indian tantric and guru, Padmasambhava, who in the texts of the ancient Red Hat sect of Tibet is also referred to as a "second Buddha."[41]

According to the Indian Buddhist Yoga school's categorization of man's inner cosmology, there are various psycho-energetically concentrated centers called lotus cakras, situated on the axis of the vertebral column. We shall first consider the four most important of these centers, which we shall characterize as the planes of activity of the trikāya doctrine. Many Tibetan texts agree that a lotus center (S. cakra; T. 'Khor-lo) with a varying number of petals is situated in the region of the navel, the region of the heart, the larynx, and the top of the forehead. All four cakras are connected to each other by "subtle" nerve-channels. In the center of the navel region (solar plexus) is a 64-petalled lotus, the focus of the emanation of the nirmāṇakāya (T. sPrul-pa'i 'khor-lo). This is the physical plane of the development of action and karmic activity. Above this, in the region of the heart, is the eight-petalled lotus, the jñānacakra (T. Ye-shes-kyi 'khor-lo, or Thugs-kyi 'khor-lo). This is the plane of spiritual actualization in the dharmakāya. The heart-center is the place of highest experience. Above this, in the region of the throat, is a 16-petalled lotus, the center of the activity of the sambhogakāya (T. Longs-spyod-kyi 'khor-lo). This is the verbal plane of mantras and invocations to the transcendent buddhas. The topmost lotus center has 32 petals and is the plane of intellectual experience and of discriminating thought and is characterized as the focus of the great bliss of the svabhāvikakāya (T. bDe-chen-gyi 'khor-lo). This system will have to be supplemented later by another cakra, but this four-fold division will afford us a solid foundation for the initiation-schema of Vajrayāna Buddhism, which is also applied in detail in the Tibetan Books of the Dead. We must also remark, however, that the order of the four centers can be reversed in the initiations.

Fig. 3. Guru Padmasambhava (top), the Tibetan king Khri-srong lde-btsan (left), and the sage Śāntaraksita (right). From an old block print from Western Tibet.

There belongs to every ritual in Vajrayāna the initiation with consecrated water, which forms the central point of a symbolic purification of the adept. This rite is called abhiṣeka (T. dBang-bskur) and is performed together with initiations into a higher esoteric wisdom or system of teachings. Connected with this is the "dispensing" or "transmission of power" (T. dBang-lung) which empowers the pupil or adept to practice and perform certain esoteric doctrines and ritual activities. Only after such an initiation can the pupil himself transmit the teachings to a successor. With the abhiṣeka consecration the pupil is released and directed into self-responsibility for his further activity on the spiritual path.

Every transmission of Tibetan secret teachings of the Tantras and the higher doctrines of Vajrayāna is accompanied by such initiations with abhiṣeka. They are the ritual medium of the particular circumstances for the transmission of the secret mantras, texts, and such complex doctrines as are contained in the Tibetan Books of the Dead.

The whole person is included in the ritual initiations and is presented with the secret wisdom that will make comprehensible to him the path of emanations of the absolute buddha-nature. The person himself then becomes the place of the mystery, into which the planes of the trikāya will unfold. In our case the consecrations with water and other sanctified ritual objects serve to allow the meaning of the teachings of the Tibetan Book of the Dead to be grasped as a happening within the soul. Or, expressed in purely Buddhist terminology: all appearances and experiences of the deities of the Tibetan Book of the Dead are conditions of human awareness relative to the highest reality, which manifests itself in various ways.

To this end we have the schema of the four initiations (T. dBang-bzhi), which pertain to man's psychic transformation. They symbolize the four shapes of the realization of pure buddha-nature, which can be much better grasped and actualized if the four psychic centers, or lotus cakras, are purified of the stains of ignorance, delusion, hate, greed, and false ideas. The attainment of purity of mind and spirit on the path of liberation is the symbolic task of the four kinds of abhiṣeka-consecration. Each of the four initiations corresponds to a lotus center, and they are given either in the natural sequence or else in reverse order as a complement to the consecration. If we follow the course of the four abhiṣekas as presented already, we will recognize the manifestation of the Sacred in a sequence of emanations with four shapes, which through the consecration become an inner transformation.[42] We will learn a similar sequence of consecrations through the six sacred syllables when we come to consider the six Buddhas of the bhavacakra.

With the kumbhābhiṣeka (T. Bum-dbang) all hindrances and contaminations on the psychic plane are removed and purified. One must thereby meditate upon the mantric syllable OṂ, which emanates from the forehead of the Buddha as a radiant white syllable. Then the profane human body (T. Lus) is transformed into a higher sanctified body (T. sKu) of a purer form of being. With the guhyābhiṣeka (T. gSang-dbang) profane speech of error and hatred is purified, while the red syllable ĀḤ shines forth from the throat of the Buddha and descends into the lotus of the sambhogacakra. Ordinary speech thereby becomes the sacred Word, the mantra as the expression of the sambhogakāya. During the prajñābhiseka (T. Ye-shes-kyi dbang) one meditates upon the blue syllable HŪṂ, which radiates from the heart cakra of the Buddha. This purifies with its light the level of the heart as the place of pure spirit and feeling, and the pupil attains the true center of pure spirit in the heart (T. Thugs) as the origin of the dharmakāya. The fourth consecration is the sahajābhiseka, performed in the light of the red mantric syllable HRĪḤ (emanating from the navel of the Buddha), which goes to the nirmāṇacakra and purifies the whole trinity of body, speech, and spirit (thought), and thereby leads to the actualization of the indivisible svabhāvikakāya.[43]

With these four most important initiations of the Vajrayāna the profane person is transposed into the higher state of the diamond body (S. vajrakāya; T. rDo-rje'i sku), after his worldly existence has been transformed into higher spiritual being by the emanations of the diamond-nature or vajra-essence of the transcendent tathāgatas. The whole ritual of this four-fold consecration is naturally much more complex, but this paraphrase should suffice to convey the essence of the abhiṣeka-consecration with respect to the bardo.

The transmission of the initiations or the abhiṣeka consecration involves not only the ritual purification of the unenlightened awareness as described above, but each initiation is associated

Lotus					
32	Mahāsukhacakra (or Sahajācakra)	Svabhāvikakaya Intellect	Oṃ	Kumbha-Abhiṣeka	Kāyavajra
16	Sambhogacakra	Sambhogakāya Verbal Plane	Āḥ	Guhya-Abhiṣeka	Vāgvajra
8	Jñānacakra	Dharmakāya Spiritual Plane	Hūṃ	Prajñā Abhiṣeka	Cittavajra
64	Nirmāṇacakra	Nirmāṇakāya Physical Plane	Hrīḥ	Sahajā-Abhiṣeka	Jñānavajra

TABLE 1

with a particular piece of wisdom which is given to the adept for his further spiritual path. Thus, a concrete doctrinal content is connected with the initiation, one which relates to particular aspects of the Buddhist religion or to whole texts, such as a Tantra.

In the Tibetan Book of the Dead we find a series of initiations which always relate to certain groups of aspects. Throughout the whole ritual, the recitation of which lasts several hours, a series of systematically structured initiations is performed which have as their content the separate stages of knowledge from the visions of the Book of the Dead. These consecrations relate to, among others, the five errors and hindrances (T. Nyon-mongs-lnga), the five groups of the human personality (T. Phung-po-lnga), and the five elements (T. 'Byung-ba-lnga), and they explain the meaning of the five Buddhas, the eight Bodhisattvas, and the peaceful and wrathful emanations. With the help of the ritual they also explain in detail the deeper meaning of the famous six-syllable mantra, oṃ ma ṇi pad me hūṃ, and the associated six Buddhas (T. Thub-pa-drug).

This wisdom is taught on the various planes of the trikāya, i.e., for each of the three or four stages these contents can be expressed in a different form, in the form appropriate to the stage. There arises from this an abundance of initiatory symbolism, which for the same content can use quite different symbols, images, signs, mudrās, colors, elements, or mantras. The meanings of the most important groups of symbols, of the most significant religious, philosophical, and psychological contents, will be discussed in section II, 4.

3. The Six Kinds of Bardo and Other "Intermediate States"

> The essence of eternity is duration, the essence of the world is order, the essence of time is transformation, and the essence of birth is life and death.
>
> HERMES TRISMEGISTUS

THE KEY WORD for the understanding of life and death and their meaning in a constantly changing world is bardo (S. antarābhava), which means "intermediate state." From the Tibetan we have "bar," meaning "between," and "do," a numbering concept which designates the equality or equilibrium between two things or between two weights, values, numbers, or contents. In the Tibetan Book of the Dead "bardo" designates a state between two similar states or conditions, namely, the state "between two lines" or kinds of existence in bodily or earthly form. Thus we see that the word "bardo" names a third thing, namely, the state of existence of a person after his death and before his rebirth.

The concept of the bardo must be construed in a broader way in order to grasp its dynamics. For we are here touching upon a way of thinking common to Asia in general and particularly characteristic of Buddhism, namely, the idea of the continuity of being or of life. It is therefore quite natural that bardo, the intermediate state, has many more meanings than just the state of existence after death. We shall see in what follows that there are a number of defined intermediate states, and this leads us to the Buddhist recognition that there is ultimately in life, in knowledge, in every kind of existence and form or matter, nothing but intermediate states, and no definitive or final and immutable forms.

The absolute withdraws from definitions, it is above all conditions and changes, and outside it there is only the relative, the becoming, the existent, and the not yet become (future form).

We recognize all this through consciousness, which knows the empirical world or believes that it has grasped existence and is also conscious of something higher and imperishable, timeless and deathless. In the space between the manifold evolution of the transitory forms of existence and the continuity of Being itself is situated the great polarity of human consciousness.

Mahāyāna Buddhism and especially the Buddhist Tantras formed a further basic notion from this knowledge, which has the same importance to us as that of the bardo, namely, the paired concepts of saṃsāra and nirvāṇa (T. 'Khor-'das). Saṃsāra is the cycle of existences, of every kind of being in the world resulting from attachment to every kind of material existence. It is also the connection of the spiritual with matter. All persons and materials including the living bodies of humans, animals, and plants are transitory, subject to suffering through transformation and the perishability of their temporal form. Beyond all this lies the deathless realm of salvation, the totally Other, the immeasurable place of the Absolute, which is in all religions and philosophies characterized by the highest concepts of which language is capable.

In Buddhism this is nirvāṇa, the goal of the teachings of the Tibetan Book of the Dead. Yet it is not anything beyond, in a spatial sense, but it is, as the highest liberation, a possibility of Being. The more a fulfilled person comes to inner freedom from the transitory world, the nearer he approaches the goal of enlightenment and fully conscious presence and the more he diminishes the intermediate state between the highest transcendence and the greatest attachment to the world. Saṃsāra, the world of changes, and nirvāṇa, the condition of highest liberation and salvation from the perishable, are two inseparable poles of Being (T. 'Khor-'das). This specifically tantric insight of the Indian siddhas and gurus of the Vajrayāna is of considerable importance for the understanding of the bardo as a concept of dynamic *Weltanschauung*. Bardo unites two states, as a continuity of forms of existence, which only our discriminating consciousness tends to separate.

Only a few of the many kinds of bardo states mentioned in the Tibetan texts will be described here. They show that bardo is a central concept for continuity, a dynamic concept, which in the metaphorical sense stands for "intermediate states" in every moment of life. Every form of bardo is the recognition of an intermediate state in the course of continuously transforming existence, for there is no eternal state in the world of existence. Every instant, every minute, and second is a moment of the state in which a thing is situated between its past and its future. Although there are many kinds of bardo, the bardo of the world beyond between two possible earthly existences is the most important. It is the great opportunity for transformation by one's own power.

Every moment is different from the previous one, but each moment is also the point of departure for the direction of future conditions of existence. A river seems always to flow in the same way, and yet at every moment the water in the same place is different. Life, too, is a state, and so is death; both are conditions of unitary Being. If we recognize the intermediate state as a moment of change, each one is then a starting point of transformation, from which we can set about forming future becoming. All the more so when we recognize that the intermediate state binds together both ends of past and future. In relation to the bardo in the Tibetan Book of the Dead, this means the possibility of the unfolding of life and activity without temporal restriction in the sphere of being after death. For death for the Tibetans is only a form of life without the earthly veil. We shall now confirm this from the numerous definitions in Tibetan writings about the bardo.

The doctrines of the bardo emphasize that, from the Buddhist point of view, man himself can participate in the three planes of existence of the trikāya. If the buddhas and bodhisattvas have risen through earthly life to the highest form of being of the dharmakāya, this way must also be a possible spiritual path for man, on which he can experience in various forms the three kinds of absolute or dharma (law). From the "Six Doctrines" of the Indian siddha Nāropa (T. Nā-ro-chos-drug) and, for example, from the Tibetan Book of the Dead,[44] we are acquainted with six kinds of intermediate states, which we can tabulate as follows:

1. sKye-gnas bar-do	the bardo of the realm of life (place of birth)
2. rMi-lam bar-do	the bardo of the dream state
3. bSam-gtan bar-do	the bardo of meditation
4. 'Chi-kha'i bar-do	the bardo of the experience of death
5. Chos-nyid bar-do	the bardo of the experience of reality
6. Srid-pa'i bar-do	the bardo of seeking rebirth

A. THE FIRST GROUP OF THREE BARDOS AS INTERMEDIATE STATES FOR THE TRANSFORMATION OF AWARENESS IN THIS LIFE

The first intermediate state, the sKye-gnas bardo, designates birth in the sphere of existence and means that the whole span from birth to death is to be seen as an intermediate state. We can designate it as such because it is only one in a long chain of successive forms of existence of life. Life appears as a state between two death-experiences, one before birth and one at the end of life, and the state of death in the beyond always repeats itself between two forms of life on this side. Therefore Nāropa in the "Khrid-yig"[45] characterizes the first intermediate state as the bardo between life and death with the following definition: "If life is, and not death, between these two is the sKye-'chi bar-do." The great Tibetan yogi Mi-la ras-pa recommends that in the bardo between life and death, within the span of earthly existence, one should meditate upon the two kinds of yoga (T. bsKyed-rdzogs-rim), the yoga of meditative unfolding of images (S. utpattikrama; T. bsKyed-rim) and the yoga of the great unification (S. sampannakrama; T. rDzogs-rim).[46] These two yoga techniques develop the knowledge that all things arise from the ground of consciousness and that all images and ideas are to be dissolved again into the great emptiness. As we shall soon see, this practice for the after-death state is the only right way to escape the dangers of the bardo. If the path of earthly life is illuminated by such practices, then the bardo of the path (of life) is fulfilled (T. Lam-gyi bar-do). According to Mi-la ras-pa this means that the intermediate state on the earthly plane as a human being is fulfilled with meaning. In the "root verses of the six bardos" (T. Bar-do'i rtsa-tshig)[47] it is pointed out that one should dedicate oneself in the bardo of the realm of life (T. sKye-gnas bar-do) to the three basic forms of appropriating knowledge through hearing the teaching, contemplation, and meditation (T. Thos bsam sgom gsum).

The second bardo relates to the intermediate state in the dream state (T. rMi-lam-gyi bar-do). According to Nāropa in the "Khrid-yig,"[48] a person is in the bardo of the dream state "when sleep has come and sleep has not yet gone." In the Tibetan teachings about the dream state (T. rMi-lam) particularly important psychological directions are given as to how the continuity of waking consciousness can be influenced and controlled during sleep and dreaming, in such a way that the person even during the dream can be clear about deceptive dream-imagery. Identification with those images of the dream world would lead to the obfuscation of awareness and thereby to increasing ignorance and attachment. Just as by means of concentrated practice a person can as an impartial onlooker guide his own awareness through the intermediate state of the dream without being affected by delusions, so he is able, later, in the Chos-nyid bar-do of the experience of reality in the beyond, to recognize and follow the path of his awareness-principle. Mi-la ras-pa said that in the rMi-lam bar-do one should meditate upon the appearance of the clear light (T. 'Od-gsal) and the deceptive body. Thereby the hindrances of ignorance are overcome even in the dream, and they are therefore also no longer effectual in waking consciousness.[49] And so, with the help of certain yoga practices, dream visions change into forms of knowledge, and the intermediate state of dream and sleep becomes filled with meaning. It is interesting that the exercises from the teachings about dream consciousness work with an applied technique of opposed symbols, a polar and dynamic technique of knowledge, which as a psychological attitude also underlies the Tibetan Book of the Dead.

The third bardo is the intermediate state during meditation (S. dhyāna; T. bSam-gtan) and samādhi (T. Ting-nge-'dzin), the two states of concentrated awareness and ecstatic vision, in which all images and false ideas are dissolved. Here too, the yoga of meditative unfolding and of perfectly unified vision (T. bsKyed-rdzogs) should be practiced, in order to direct awareness towards the pure and imageless form of the dharmakāya. In samādhi, the high point of meditation, the clear light of the radiant dharmakāya is actualized. All deceptive images (T. 'Khrul-pa'i tshogs) are thereby dissolved and the pure nature of unmuddied and liberated awareness is attained. Only this yoga leads to the liberation of consciousness from the power of desire and passion, and from the attachments to the transitory world of illusion and thus constitutes the presupposition of salvation in the bardo after death. We can therefore characterize the three kinds of bardo state already discussed as those planes on which a progressive self-actualization and overcoming of the world can take place. They are therefore the most important preliminary stages of educating awareness for the great experience of the dramatic visions and events of a world beyond, and thus they constitute access to the renewal of life in the next existence.

B. THE SECOND GROUP OF THREE BARDOS AS INTERMEDIATE STATES FOR THE GUIDANCE OF AWARENESS IN THE WORLD BEYOND

With these three intermediate states we come to the experiences of awareness in the bardo of the world beyond or the after-death state, which the mystery of the trikāya doctrine will make transparent.

In the "Khrid-yig" of Nāropa[50] the three intermediate states of the bardo after death are identified with the great experience of the trikāya: "In the clear light (T. 'Od-gsal) of the highest (first) bardo (the 'Chi-kha'i bar-do) appears the dharmakāya. In the middle one (the second, or Chos-nyid bar-do) appears the sambhogakāya, and the last (the Srid-pa'i bar-do) is the not yet concretized nirmāṇakāya."

The first or 'Chi-kha'i bardo as the intermediate state at the moment of death brings before the spiritual eye the vision of the "clear light" which arises from the depths of awareness. The clear and radiant white light is the highest experience of the reality of the dharmakāya (see also chapter II, 6). Thereafter consciousness begins slowly to perceive the rays of the five elements, which develop into lights and visionary images of the peaceful and wrathful deities of the maṇḍalas of the Tibetan Book of the Dead. This is the radiant, "heavenly" realm of the sambhogakāya, the descent of the Chos-nyid bar-do as experience of reality.

In the third intermediate state after death, the Srid-pa'i bardo, awareness begins the descent into the concretions of the material realm, whose powers are concentrated into the potential of the nirmāṇakāya before rebirth. The relationship of awareness with the muddy emanations from the worlds of incarnation are taken up, and there appear the six Buddhas of the realms of existence as incarnate guides through the existences in one of the six worlds, or lokas (for a detailed account, see chapter III, 1). Nāropa has the following to say about these processes (Khrid-yig, Fol 46 6): "When the wisdom of the pure clear light in the awareness-principle of the dead person has been transformed into the clear light of bliss and emptiness (T. bDe-stong), then the first bardo has been entered. That is the dharmakāya in the experience of death. After this has arisen and become a certainty for the dead person in the bardo, there then appear in him as if in a dream the divine images (or forms, T. sKu), and then the radiance shines forth from the clear light. Thus the clear light emerging from itself is recognized. And if it has been recognized at the right time, bliss and emptiness and the fields of divine forms (namely, the transcendent buddhas) then endure without interruption."

"In the second, the middle (Chos-nyid) bardo, there appear the victorious forms of the sambhogakāya."[51] The text elucidates further that in this state of confronting the visionary deities all desires of thought are overcome and the awareness is totally purified. At this point one should contemplate the hindrances and sufferings of the beings in the six worlds of rebirth and use this last chance in this bardo of experience of reality in order to reach the state of sambhogakāya. Thereby the liberated awareness-principle remains in the fields of bliss on the plane of the bodhisattvas in view of the radiant Buddha Amitābha, who illuminates those realms as the Buddha of immeasurable shining light.

In the last intermediate state, the awareness of the dead person experiences, in the beyond, the Srid-pa'i bar-do as the search for a new existence and there experiences the pre-formations of the arising nirmāṇakāya. Here, there appear from the rays of the dim lights of the six worlds all the Herukas in male and female demonic form, and as guides through these worlds the six Buddhas of the bhavacakra come before the spiritual eye of the dead person.

In his "Hundred Thousand Songs" Mi-la ras-pa says that the dharmakāya can be reached by practicing a developing and unifying yoga (T. bsKyed-rdzogs) as well as the teachings of the Mahāmudrā.[52] The latter centers around the doctrine of the great experience of the "clear light." The sambhogakāya as the body of bliss fulfills itself in the bardo of the experience of reality through recognition of the peaceful and wrathful deities (T. Zhi-khro), while the nirmāṇakāya characterizes the Srid-pa'i bar-do before the beginning of the next incarnation. In the recognition of the possibility of determining in the Srid-pa'i bar-do the way and type of the next incarnation, lies the third great opportunity for transformation after death.

The awareness-principle recognizes the forms of the nirmāṇakāya and future conditions of being by way of particular signs, which are described in detail in the "Six Doctrines" of Nāropa and in the Tibetan Book of the Dead.[53] Thereby the conditions of rebirth can, even in the actual descent into incarnation, be determined by the dead person wandering through the bardo, in which the forces of his karma point the direction. Mi-la ras-pa affirms that all three bodies are immanent in every human being as possibilities of spiritual transformation, but that most people through ignorance do not realize it. "The clear light at the moment of death is the dharmakāya, the pure bardo of reality-experience is the sambhogakāya, the manifold births are the nirmāṇakāya, and the indivisible unity of the trikāya is the svabhāvikakāya (T. Ngo-bo-nyid sku) as the fourth; these are all in us even though we are not aware of them."[54]

In a song of the great yogi Mi-la ras-pa, the five "sisters of long life"[55] prayed for instructions about the doctrine of the bardo:

> Please teach us about the dharmakāya,
> explain the dharmakāya as the clear light of death.
> Please teach us about the sambhogakāya
> by explaining the deceptive forms of the pure bardo.
> Please teach us about the nirmāṇakāya,
> so that we may incarnate by our own powers.[56]

The Srid-pa'i bar-do as the intermediate state determinative for the kind of rebirth is the most important point in the journey through the beyond, without which the dharmakāya and the heavenly fields of the sambhogakāya cannot be reached. For only very few people thoroughly schooled in yoga may reach the goal of the perfect liberation of the dharmakāya in the immediacy of the great "clear light." In the last bardo the awareness-principle is furnished with a perceiving awareness-body (T. Yid-kyi lus), it experiences the working out of its previous karmic deeds as peaceful and terrifying visions, and it comes before the judge of death, Dharmarāja, where its actions are weighed in the balance (see the further descriptions in chapter III, 5). Therefore this intermediate state is also called the bardo of karmically conditioned finding of rebirth (T. Srid-pa'i las-kyi bar-do).

We have now established that the Buddhist doctrine of the three bodies is of great importance for continuing existence and the transformations of awareness in the three-fold bardo of the world after death. The significance of the bardo is thereby extended to conscious life, and the world beyond becomes a karmically corresponding image of earthly life. If a person in his earthly existence has not sufficiently loosened his craving attachments to the transitory world and thereby achieved a technique or practice of freedom of awareness, he will not be able to undertake the dangerous path through the bardo.

In one of the great Tibetan Books of the Dead[57] it is written that the soteriological meaning of the bardo experience is "the meaning of all beings, to recognize in the clear light of death the radiant dharmakāya," and "it's significance for all beings is to attain the highest perfection of the precious Mahāmudrā (the doctrine of the great symbol)." And "even if this has not been attained, let one be aware, in the bardo, of the bardo state," in order to perfect the body of the unity of the bardo and Mahāmudrā. The opportunity is thereby given to reach the sambhogakāya, a transcendent space.

We spoke earlier of the emanation of the Sacred, in connection with the absoluteness of the dharma, which emanates in the three or four bodies in various grades of knowledge. The teachings about the bardo show us that it is a dual process with one form of manifestation on the side of life and another on the side of death. Ordinary life is the intermediate state of the sKye-gnas bar-do and is incarnate existence (S. nirmāṇa; T. sPrul-sku) in the material world. There, everything is subject to suffering (P. dukkha; T. sDug-bsngal). In the dream state one is no longer aware of the body and experiences the illusory bodies of the ambiguous dream-visions. To master these by means of yoga leads to knowledge of the visionary sambhogakāya. Whoever goes further and in clear waking awareness dedicates himself to meditation upon the great emptiness (S. mahāśūnyatā) and the unity of awareness, will recognize the pure, imageless dharmakāya as the radiance of the clear light of enlightenment.

The experience of the transformations beyond in the threefold bardo are the reverse of the process towards renewed incarnation. The disembodied spirit slowly finds its way through the subtle forms of the clear light back into the world of visions and manifest forms. Just as, at the hour of death, the greatest concentration and attention is necessary for an awareness free of suffering to find the best and most lucid crossing into the critical part of the bardo, so there then appears the dharmakāya as the first light. Thus the greatest spiritual experience in the life of man takes place with the highest intensity on entering death. During earthly life man tries to raise himself from the lower plane of profane ignorance to the level of the highest wisdom, the dharmakāya. We are able fully to describe this significant process with words from our Western terminology. Life on earth is a process of constant spiritualization, of the actualization of the spiritual principle in man. If we now presuppose a bardo, then the transformation in the world of the dead is from the highest beginning a constant materialization of the spiritual, until a new earthly form is fashioned as the strong shell of the spirit. There then begins in the child, slowly at first, a continuous becoming-conscious until maturity, the mastery of awareness over the bodily principle.

We can schematize the Tibetan path through life into death and again to a new life as shown in table 2, where each bardo stage of life has a corresponding stage in death and also a corresponding level in the three bodies.

Earthly Life	Form of the Trikaya	The Life Beyond	Earthly Life
Bardo of the Place of Birth (sKye-gnas bar-do) →	Nirmāṇakāya	↑ Bardo of Rebirth (Srid-pa'i bar-do) →	Bardo of the Place of Birth
Bardo of the Dream State (rMi-lam bar-do)	Sambhogakāya	Bardo of Reality (Chos-nyid bar-do)	Bardo of the Dream State
Bardo of Meditation (bSam-gtan bar-do) ↓	Dharmakāya →	Bardo of the Death Experience ('Chi-kha'i bar-do) ↓	Bardo of Meditation —and so forth →

TABLE 2

C. BARDO AS THE INDIVISIBLE UNION OF THE ESSENTIAL

We have now, through particular consideration of the three intermediate states of the Tibetan Book of the Dead, become acquainted with those kinds of bardo relating to the continued existence of the dead person in other-worldly spheres, as is generally assumed in Tibet. They are of such great importance and treated in such detail in the scriptures because the conditions through which the awareness wanders in the bardo are considerably more difficult than those in this life. Considered psychologically, it can be foreseen what it means for man to immerse himself, without relation to embodiment or world, in the depths of the conscious and unconscious. We shall return to this question in chapter VII.

Here in the manifest world of existence it is possible consciously to direct one's life by coming to terms with the objective world, although only a few take advantage of these possibilities. Therefore, the Tibetan Book of the Dead continually instructs the awareness-body wandering through the bardo to recall the teachings it received during earthly life, which are said to be of considerable assistance for the path beyond. Conscious recall of wisdom previously learned and experienced in life is the best means of finding one's way through the bardo. It is believed that the practice of yoga gives awareness the ability to find its way, even in the difficult conditions of the bardo.

As in all teachings of Buddhist philosophy, it is a question of man's learning not to get caught in dualistic definitions in his seeking to grasp the Absolute. World and transcendence, conceived in static concepts and taken in themselves, lead only to man's striving to attach himself to one or the other. But the truth lies in between. Thereby even the highest concepts are relativized to such an extent that they are no longer alone capable of describing the totality. We are acquainted with the characterization of the Absolute as "neither-nor" from the philosophical dialectic of Taoism and from the Indian Tantras.

Also, the great emptiness as a central concept of Mahāyāna Buddhism does not allow any evaluation, as is clear from the comprehensive Prajñāpāramitā literature. Emptiness (S. śūnyatā) can neither be described in words nor signified in concepts. If one attains the highest experience of indescribable emptiness, this cannot even be adequately described by the emotional meaning of bliss (T. bDe-ba). Such occurrences remain, for the mind, an inexpressible phenomenon. The intermediate state between the polar opposites remains, for experience, a mystery of the ineffable. Here also there is a bardo, as Mi-la ras-pa says in his Songs:[58]

> In the bardo of all-embracing appearing and emptiness there is no place for the play of the transitory and the eternal.

In the bardo of bliss and emptiness there is no place for the appearance of a conditional object.

In the bardo between the word and its meaning there is no room for practicing scholarship.

The intermediate state of inseparable communities and conditioned polar opposites clearly points to the indivisibility of the whole. Intermediate states of manifest form and emptiness (T. sNang-stong gnyis-kyi bar-do), of bliss and emptiness (T. bDe-stong gnyis-kyi bar-do), and of word and meaning (T. Tshig-don gnyis-kyi bar-do) point to inner duality and show the unconditioned equivalence of two essential forms of expression, which symbolically embrace both the rational and the non-rational elements. Life and the life to come form an indivisible unity, since they are bound by the bardo as an inevitable condition. From these Tibetan experiences we recognize an unconditioned conviction, self-evident to the Asiatics, about the continued existence of life, and in addition we obtain valuable insights for the linguistic philosophy of symbolic forms, which have so far remained vital there with uninterrupted power. The bardo is then the inevitable connecting link between two rationally graspable states of opposite kind. Therefore, the other-worldly state of the inexplicable is a bardo.

Of the various other intermediate states characterized as bardos we shall mention a few more that Mi-la ras-pa describes.[59] In the symbolic and imaginal visions during developing yoga (bsKyed-rim), there is in the transition between various contents the intermediate state of the vision of both (T. lTa-ba'i bar-do); the practice of meditation knows a bardo of meditation (T. sGom-pa'i bar-do) as a state of neither perception nor non-perception; between the beginning and the end of religious practices is the intermediate state of sacred meditative action (T. sPyod-pa'i bar-do); the path from the unfolding of awareness through to the unifying vision of the spirit is the intermediate state of utpattikrama and sampannakrama (T. Lam bskyed-rdzogs-kyi bar-do); dwelling upon the quintessence of spiritual teachings one finds oneself in the gNad-kyi bar-do; if the vital and dynamic relation between the physical, verbal, and spiritual planes is attained, one is in the trikāya bardo; and if one finally achieves the fruits or results of the spiritual path in enlightenment, the liberated awareness then dwells in the state of perfection, that is, the bardo of the teleological goal (T. 'Bras-bu'i bar-do).

We should mention peripherally the psychic techniques of transmission of consciousness (S. saṃkrānti; T. 'Pho-ba) and the re-animation of a dead person (S. parakāyapraveśana; T. Grong-'jug). The purpose of the yoga practice of transmission of consciousness is to prepare the topmost point of the skull (the fontanelle) by psychophysical exercises in such a way that at death it is possible for consciousness to exit unhindered. This technique is not without its dangers and is practiced under the direction of a guru. Using meditation on the breath and on syllables, it lasts at least fourteen days, but once it has been practiced successfully it need not be repeated in life. The exercise is associated with meditation on the syllable HIG and the radiant light of the Buddha Amitābha. When blood or lymph appears at the fontanelle, the path for awareness has been opened and the yoga can be discontinued. It is characteristic of the significance of the bardo for the Tibetans that these preparatory exercises are not performed towards the end of life, but usually at a much younger age. Then one can face the future with a clear spirit. A brief overview of the esoteric doctrine of the transmission of consciousness can be found in Evans-Wentz.[60]

Even more secret was the ancient Indian tradition of the Tantric Nāropa (or Nāḍapāda), which was said to lead to the re-animation of a dead person (S. parakāyapraveśana). The technique was brought from India to Tibet by the Tibetan sage and translator, Mar-pa chos-kyi blo-gros of Lho-brag in southern Tibet, who is known as the guru of Mi-la ras-pa. The latter gave it to his son, Dharma mdo-sde, who, however, met with an unfortunate sudden death. Since he had not transmitted the doctrine further, the authentic secret wisdom of this technique was lost. We find that a few directions have been preserved in certain texts, in the "sNying-thig" literature, for example. Ancient shamanistic practices must have persisted in this kind of yoga, which is based on the assumption that one can breathe life back into a dead person. If we think of mouth-to-mouth resuscitation techniques practiced in contemporary emergency medicine, it seems as if the ancient Indians already had sound knowledge of how to reactivate the functioning of the heart. Yoga is without doubt one of the most effective methods of psychical and physical regulation of man.

We shall close our discussion of the bardo by emphasizing that in Tibet the intermediate state has had a central significance that goes beyond the Book of the Dead. It was the moment not only of uniting past and present but also of consciously forming the future. From the bardo leads the path towards improving the conditions of one's own future being; bardo is the plane of karmic transformation. Whoever does not understand this experiences the bardo as the plane of suffering, of progress through the terrifying visions of the world after death with its eighteen different forms of hellish torment. For one who has not attained liberation during life, the intermediate state becomes the suffering of the torments of death (T. 'Chi-kha'i bsdug-sngal-gyi bar-do).

4. On The Symbolism of Tantric Polarity, the Trinity, the Quaternity and the Fivefold, and of Colors and Elements

> Now appear the lights of the five orders, which constitute the unity of the four wisdoms: Take care to recognize them.
>
> TIBETAN BOOK OF THE DEAD

IF WE wish to attain a clear overview in our further descriptions of the teachings and deities of the Tibetan Book of the Dead, it will be necessary beforehand to acquaint ourselves with the schemata of its symbolism. Mahāyāna Buddhism and, to an even greater extent, Vajrayāna, which is more influenced by the Tantras, contain a wealth of symbolism which needs to be known in order to understand ritual and meditative practice. The Tibetan Book of the Dead, too, contains many of these symbols. There we find symbolic language (mantras, for example), colors, and deities, as cosmologically and psychologically conditioned symbols, as well as the many attributes of the deities which all have a definite signification. If, before discussing the individual visions of the deities, we present the foundations of this symbolism, we will find that the various parts of the Tibetan texts dealing with bardo visions are structured according to a quite clear and systematic principle of symbolic forms which stand in manifold consistent relationships with each other. Moreover, we shall establish that this symbolism evolves in definite stages towards the complex pantheon of all the bardo deities, who appear together on the fourteenth day in a great cosmic maṇḍala.

It should be remarked that we cannot discuss here the entire symbolism either of Vajrayāna in general or of the Tibetan Book of the Dead in particular. We shall only refer to the characteristic structure of an initiatory doctrine such as that of the Tibetan Book of the Dead, in order to facilitate understanding of the whole work. Later, in chapter III, we shall make a closer study of the symbolism of the deities, since we shall then be setting out on the path through the bardo visions in discrete symbolic steps.

It is already remarkable that the teachings of the Tibetan Book of the Dead proceed from the premise that the duration of the transformations in the bardo between two earthly forms of existence is forty-nine days. In this space of time of seven times seven days, beginning from the moment of the first vision, all the apparitions through to the moment of re-entry into earthly life (the moment of conception) occur in a way that corresponds to a progression of symbolic numbers and multiple values. The more the awareness-principle in the bardo state becomes conscious of its capabilities, the more the visionary forms and images appear, which are described in the Tibetan Book of the Dead as images from one's own awareness.

The symbols which are of interest to us here are not so much the individual numbers, colors, or forms, but rather the number and aspects of the divine worlds that appear in the visions. The Tibetans have always had a predilection for gathering together important concepts or groups of teachings into number-values. As a simple example we could mention "the three deities of long life," or the "four blisses" of yoga, the "five poisons," or the "six doctrines," or the "eight signs of good fortune." The language of the religious texts and especially of the great treatises of Tibet is extremely rich in such group-concepts. It is understandable that as definite verses they could be more easily remembered. We continually come across the same things in the texts of the Books of the Dead, which thereby afford us an important classification and overview.

We generally find in the writings of the Tibetan Book of the Dead a progression from the number one to the number two (as the most important tantric polarity), the number three (as trinity), the number four as quaternity (or as unity from out of the trinity), and the number five as the centering of the quaternity and the tantric uniting of the cosmological and psychological opposites. This leads in its double aspect to the number ten. There then follow the equally significant symbolic groupings under the number six, under seven unities, and finally various kinds of symbolic groupings of eight, of which many have a purely psychological background. It is clear, just from an overview of these symbolic groups, that the Tibetan Book of the Dead presents a masterfully developed work of applied psychology drawn from the ancient experiences of Yoga and Tantra, and that it has synthesized this knowledge about the direction of awareness into a harmonious unity as a guide through the bardo.

We can of course only explain the individual symbolic groups in their connection with the corresponding general concepts, in order to retain the character of an overview. For the relevant details see the explanations and descriptions of the individual visions in chapter III.

A. FROM UNITY TO MULTIPLICITY

The founder of Buddhism is known as the Buddha Gautama, or Śākyamuni. Although this historical figure laid the whole foundation of the teachings, he plays no role in the visions of the Book of the Dead. There we experience an exclusively tantric pantheon of deities from spiritual visions, in which the role of the bodhisattvas is of central importance. We are acquainted with the ideal figure of the bodhisattva from Mahāyāna Buddhism, the essence of which ultimately is represented by the activity of the bodhisattva. The enlightened beings, or bodhisattvas, participate in both earthly existence and the higher spheres of the way towards enlightenment. Vajrayāna Buddhism, which is also called Tantrayāna because of its use of the texts of the Tantras coming from Yoga practice, knows the Ādibuddha or primordial Buddha. He is a transcendent symbol of the dharma as primordial principle under the image not of a historical but of a hypothetical Buddha. From this single, all-embracing, and universal Buddha unfolds the whole schema of deities, in correspondence with the polarity symbolism so essential to and characteristic of Vajrayāna, so that all further buddhas and deities fundamentally always appear in a double aspect. A schematic representation (fig. 4) will make this clear. The teachings of the Tibetan Book of the Dead are a portrayal of a polar dynamism which discloses a high level of psychological relationships. We know not only the historical Buddha but we also find mentioned his predecessors (Dīpaṃkara-Buddha, for example) and the Buddha of the coming age, Maitreya (T. Byams-pa), and we become well acquainted in the Tibetan Book of the Dead with the transcendent buddhas or tathāgatas, who are the basis of the whole psychic transformation in the bardo. There are also many bodhisattvas, of whom eight are of particular importance to us.

B. DUALITY AS AN EXPRESSION OF POLARITY

In the symbolism of transcendent buddhas in mystical union with a female partner, we again find in the teachings of the Tibetan Book of the Dead a basic idea that is common to the whole of the Buddhist tantric tradition. Tantrism involves an integration of the feminine and is a doctrine concerned with embracing the opposites. In Tantra, the Buddha was raised to the level of an ideal spiritual image from meditative experience; his essence as the embodiment of the doctrine was portrayed in various forms and images, in order to show various aspects of awareness and psychic attachments. Or, to put it another way, certain virtues, meditative qualities, levels of awareness, and basic psychological truths were expressed by means of different kinds of images of the Buddha. These became primordial images of the psychic cosmos, which unfolded in front of the mirror of reflective thought. Thus the meditation-buddhas (S. tathāgata; T. De-bzhin gshegs-pa) were formed from intuitive vision as partial aspects of forms of appearance of the dharma and were assigned to quite definite realms of human existence on the spiritual plane. This ordering took place in the maṇḍala, or sacred circle, the total structure of which indicates the psychological laws of individuation.

After the follower of Vajrayāna has understood the whole of life, the human spirit, the physical realm, and the cosmos, as a common plane or a single space in which alone self-actualization and liberation from the suffering of impermanence can take place, then those buddhas were developed into figures of inner vision. Their image should be realized during meditation in the utmost detail. Therefore, from the psychological point of view, it is remarkable that precisely these five transcendent Buddhas are, in all representations, grouped into a maṇḍala as a square within a circle.

The emanation of the spiritual is a comprehensive manifestation of Being, which consists of the two opposites of purely static potentiality and of dynamic creation, or of masculine and feminine energy. Both are foundations of the creation process on the material and spiritual planes, and only from the union of both can evolution take place. The images of the buddhas in the double aspect of union with the feminine counterpart, or prajñā, show the totality of experience, its starting and ending points, which are shown to be totally inseparable in themselves (T. dByer-med). The path towards knowledge and enlightenment is represented in the image of the buddha, the goal of perfected wisdom in the prajñā, and both together are the totality in unbroken unity, or the continuity of integration.

At the beginning of the maṇḍalas of the Tibetan Book of the Dead is the Ādibuddha; in the developing yoga (T. bsKyed-rim) the visualized circling of the center begins with the vision of the tantric double aspect. Thus the Ādibuddha appears in tantric union with his female counterpart, and in this form he is the origin of all lights and deities which arise from the first unity.

The buddha (as path) and the female partner (as goal) are the two concepts (T. Thabs-shes) which serve to describe the process of meditation and ultimately also every activity. Every conscious act has a teleological purpose; it is goal-directed towards a physical or psychic accomplishment. In the Tantras the Buddha is the path or the method (S. upāya; T. Thabs) by means of which one can attain the goal of enlightenment. In our context the path means practicing the Buddhist teachings in such a way that they can become a means to liberation in the bardo. The highest wisdom is liberation as seen in the "clear primordial light" of the death experience. The goal is gnosis, the inseparable unity of path and goal, characterized by the union of the opposites of buddha and prajñā. The polarity of the tantric mystical union of the buddhas has two meanings. Firstly, it is the primordial image of the origination of all Being from inseparable totality, and secondly, it becomes the spiritual guiding image for a renewed integration of awareness which, on the path of disciminating knowledge in the "unifying yoga" (T. rDzogs-rim), overcomes and integrates all opposites. Tantra teaches the complete synthesis of all duality, since dualistic thinking is the cause of suffering from these opposites. Polarity is, however, the condition of Being.

All the deities of the Tibetan Book of the Dead, and in fact most deities in the Buddhist-Tantric systems of India, can be represented as a unity of polarities. In the lower stages of Buddhist Yoga the deities are considered in their single aspect, in the directions for meditating upon buddhas and bodhisattvas. The middle stages teach alternating realization of either the masculine or the feminine aspects of the buddhas and initiation deities. In the higher and highest Tantras the student experiences teachings connected with the simultaneously appearing double aspects of deity and female deity in tantric embrace (S. yuganaddha; T. Yab-yum). The way the deities are portrayed in the maṇḍalas therefore corresponds to the level of knowledge which is being communicated by the associated doctrine.

We meet yet another tantric polarity in the visions of the Tibetan Book of the Dead, since not only the buddhas but also the bodhisattvas appear with a female counterpart. Even more extensive is the next double aspect, in which both buddhas and bodhisattvas can assume a peaceful or a wrathful form of emanation. These are two ways of appearing of the same deity, also in the unity of male and female, which play an important role in the Book of the Dead during transformation in the bardo. They are related to two ways that human awareness manifests, namely, as pure knowledge, wisdom, and enlightenment on the one hand, and intellectual wisdom, discriminating thought, and rationality on the other.

The center of the heart is the place of perfect, self-contained wisdom. It is the heart lotus (T. sNying-ga'i 'khor-lo) as the center of man, from which the visions of the peaceful (S. śānti; T. Zhi-ba) deities and buddhas appear. In the schema of initiations we called the heart lotus the plane of the dharmakāya. In the uppermost cakra which is the physical location of the mental faculties or the mahāsukhacakra (T. bDe-chen-gyi 'khor-lo) as the center of intellectual awareness, there appear the visions of the wrathful (S. krodha; T. khro-bo) buddhas and other bardo deities, and these constitute the great opposition to the poise of the peaceful buddhas. The terrifying deities are seen as forms of the intellect which appear as long as it is involved in the dualistic struggle within itself of 'for and against.' As long as the opposition between heart and mind has not been overcome, there appear, through pure mental capability without primordial relationship, the countless thought forms which attach themselves to the impermanent material world of desire. This is the great inclination and attachment to earthly form (T. sKu), or, if we may so express it, the incarnation of spirit in matter. On the other hand, from the heart, the spiritual center of man, the path towards transcendence and the unification of awareness begins, represented by the five lights and wisdoms of the transcendent buddhas.

We shall return to these topics again in chapter III, since there are several relationships in the symbolism of polarity which we must first clarify. Figure 4 presents the emanation sequence of the polar relationships of the tantric deities.

C. THREEFOLD ARTICULATIONS

The best known symbolism of threefold articulation must for us be the doctrine of the "three bodies," which we have discussed in

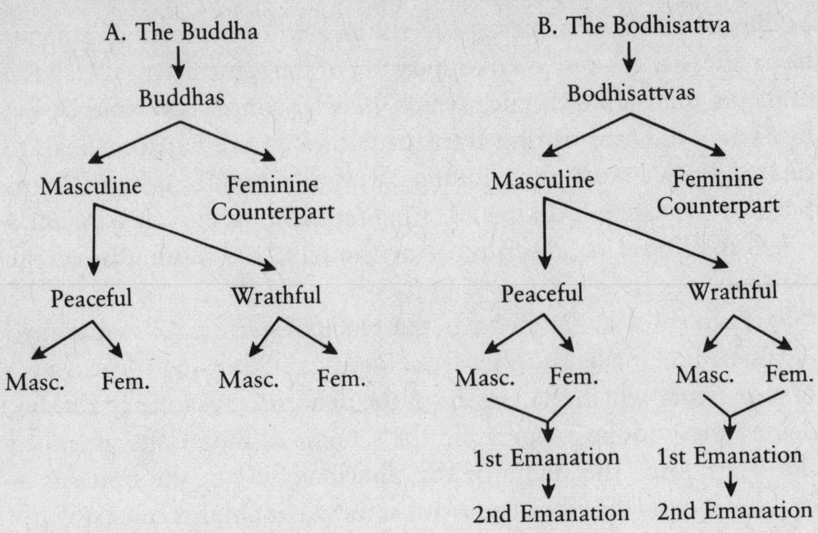

Fig. 4. Diagram of the emanation of polarities.

detail. In the Tibetan Book of the Dead the trikāya symbolism is closely related to the three bardo experiences which we saw to be planes of transformation in the world beyond. In the bardo of death experience (T. 'Chi-kha'i bar-do), achieving the vision of the "clear light" (T. 'Od-gsal) is the pure experience of the dharmakāya. The span of fourteen days with the dawning of the peaceful and wrathful deities in the bardo of reality-experience (T. Chos-nyid bar-do) is the actualization of manifestations of awareness in the sambhogakāya. Finally, with the descent into the Srid-pa'i bar-do, the new orientation of the awareness-body begins, which then enters into a new mortal shell, the nirmāṇakāya.

In Tibetan texts we often find mention of the "three jewels" (T. dKon-mchog gsum), which are supported by many layers of meaning. In the classical symbolism of Hīnayāna Buddhism, the oldest doctrine, the "three jewels" (S. triratna) are the Buddha, the teachings (S. dharma), and the community of disciples (S. saṅgha). Tibetan Vajrayāna Buddhism formulated a new version of this triad, which assumed even greater significance in connection with the transmission of tantric secret doctrines, and today it plays an important role in Tibetan religion. This is the trinity of lama, yi-dam, and ḍākinī. These three are also manifestations of a simple buddha-nature, even if they have a quite different effect on us from the original teachings of Buddhism. The secret doctrine is transmitted to the succeeding pupil by a guru or lama with specific instructions and an appropriate rite of initiation. The secret doctrine, the doctrine of the "great symbol" (T. Phyag-rgya chen-po) for example, is placed under the protection of a personal protective deity (S. iṣṭadevatā; T. Yi-dam), which the pupil chooses or which is already contained in the teaching.[61] The ḍākinī can be understood as a mystical female partner, somewhat like the prajñā, or feminine counterpart, of the buddhas. She is the "wise one" (S. vidyā), and the transmitter of secret teachings through listening to the inner voice.[62]

We thereby come to the third well known triad, which is a complex expression of three different processes of awareness. The religious teachings are to be learned by listening (T. Thos), deepened by contemplation (T. bSam), and actualized by meditation (T. sGom). This triad of apperception and inner elaboration of outer impressions is also an important aid for the awareness-principle in the bardo, which, precisely through these three reactions, can come into the position of liberating itself from the depths of the bardo. The threefold practice is one of the foundations of Buddhist teachings.

The introductory verse of the Bar-do thos-grol (the Tibetan Book of the Dead) shows us the trikāya aspect beginning with Buddha Amitābha. The threefold division of the emanations can happen under quite different preliminary signs. Their condition is the theory of the Buddhist maṇḍalas, which form the basis of all the assertions of the Tibetan Book of the Dead. In the tradition of our texts, Padmasambhava, the Indian Tantric and guru of the Vajrayāna, is held to be the founder of the Tibetan Book of the Dead. He is characterized as an emanation from the Buddha Amitābha, whose supernatural form in the sambhogakāya is identical with the Bodhisattva Avalokiteśvara. As a tantric trinity, Padmasambhava himself forms a threefold phenomenal aspect of lama, yi-dam, and ḍākinī, as table 3 will show. In it we have various relationships from the trikāya symbolism, which will make clear the manifold of appearances. The individual groups come from the ancient Buddhist trinity, composed of the "three jewels," Buddha, dharma, and saṅgha.

Triratna Three Jewels	Tantric Trinity	Example of this Tantric Trinity for Guru Padmasambhava
Buddha	Lama or Guru	Padmasambhava
Dharma, The Teachings	Yi-dam, Protective Deity	Guru drag-po, the Wrathful Guru
Saṅgha, The Community of Disciples	Ḍākinī, Mystical Female Partner	Siṃhavaktrā, the Lion-headed Ḍākinī as a Form of Appearing of Guru Padmasambhava

TABLE 3

There are several more threefold articulations of interest to us, most of which are related to the trikāya schema, since all visible form can appear on three planes of manifestation. One might be tempted here to think of Plato's theory of Ideas. There we have the eternal and pure and changeless Ideas, then the ideas and images of our will which have been formed from the Ideas by the Logos, and finally the forms and works created from the concrete ideas.

From the present threefold schema we can now project the structure of the bardo visions, which will have to be further elaborated in our discussion of fivefold orderings (chapter II, 4, E). The most important mantric triad in all the holy scriptures and ritual texts of Vajrayāna Buddhism is the three seed-syllables, Oṃ Āḥ Hūṃ. They are used in almost all mantric recitations and are also mystical syllables which denote the unity of the trikāya. They occupy a central place in initiations and are the point of departure for many meditations upon the buddhas and Buddhist virtues and wisdom. They are much used in ritual practice, in the visualization of deities and in Yoga, and they also occur in most mantras. They are used at the consecration of Tibetan paintings: it is customary to inscribe in red characters on the back of portrayals of the Buddha the three centers of body, speech, and mind. Oṃ then stands for the sacred body of the Buddha, Āḥ stands for pure speech, and Hūṃ for the spirit of the enlightened one. This is the prescribed trikāya consecration of religious pictures.

The white mantric seed-syllable Oṃ appears at the center of

Trikāya	Padmasambhava in his Trikaya Aspect	The Trikāya According to the Introductory Verse of the Tibetan Book of the Dead	The Trikāya Ordering of the Visions of the Tibetan Book of the Dead	The Three Corresponding levels of the Bardo
Dharmakāya	Buddha Amitābha as the Dharmakāya Form of Guru Padmasambhava	The Immeasurable Radiant Buddha Amitābha	The Ādibuddha Samantabhadra as a Symbol of the Dharma in itself	'Chi-kha'i Bardo, in the Death Experience
Sambhogakāya	The Bodhisattva Avalokiteśvara as the Sambhogakāya Form of Guru Padmasambhava	The Manifestations of the Peaceful and Wrathful Deities of the Bardo State	The Peaceful and Wrathful Deities of the Bardo State	Chos-nyid Bardo of the Experience of Reality
Nirmāṇakāya	The Earthly Incarnation of Guru Padmasambhava	Guru Padmasambhava as the Teacher of the Tibetan Book of the Dead	The six Buddhas of the Bhavacakra as Emanations of the Bodhisattva Avalokitesvara	Srid-pa'i Bardo, on the path towards Rebirth

TABLE 4

the skull as the light of the Buddha Vairocana and stands opposite the nirmāṇakāya. The center of the brow is the location of the active intellect and at the same time of desire (S. kāma; T. 'Dod-chags), which proceeds from the mind and attaches itself to impermanent things. The first attachment, and thereby actualization, begins with a decision process of the intellect. Desire belongs to the three basic faults of human behavior (T. Dug-gsum), which become the causes of all other failings and thereby of all suffering. The other two are hatred (S. krodha; T. Zhe-sdang) and ignorance (S. moha; T. gTi-mug). Hatred expresses itself in the speech center and is therefore assigned the red radiant syllable Āḥ, so that through its light the symbolic purification of this center can be achieved. The throat center as the place of language is ruled by the red Buddha Amitābha. However, the cause of all false attitudes is basic ignorance and unconsciousness of one's own actions, for all kinds of mistakes and burdens leading to attachment and suffering arise from behavior that is removed from knowledge and in spiritual darkness. In the threefold consecration (T. dBang-gsum), the heart lotus is assigned the radiant blue mantric syllable Hūṃ as the light of the Buddha Akṣobhya from the dharmakāya. The three cardinal errors are also called in Buddhism the three poisons, and are the vices of body, speech, and mind, which determine the karma of life and rebirth.

In the bardo the 110 deities of the maṇḍalas appear as emanations from the three centers of intellect, speech, and heart. We must conceive the three ranks of deities as complementary images whose purpose, according to the teachings of the Tibetan Book of the Dead, is to raise the totality of human awareness out of the realm of ignorance towards the light of knowledge, in order to attain the stage of imageless enlightenment as experienced in the "clear light" of the death experience. Certain Tibetan paintings, meditation pictures on the walls of monasteries or on scrolls, which give us a total portrayal of the visionary deities, also provide a schema of meditation in which a threefold ordering is evident. This corresponds to the path of initiation during recitations of the Tibetan Book of the Dead. It consists of three maṇḍalas which relate to the psychic centers of man as is known from yoga. Then the 58 wrathful deities appear in the center of the brow as emanations of the intellect; in the throat center is the maṇḍala of the five wisdom deities (S. vidyādhara; T. Rig-'dzin); and in the heart lotus appear the 42 peaceful deities, the buddhas and bodhisattvas in the fivefold radiance of the elements. All the deities together are images of states of awareness, from the most extreme intellectual antagonism and self-destructiveness in wrathful form (S. krodha), to the peaceful and detached form (S. śānti) of pure vision. Let us finish by tabulating (table 5) the threefold ordering according to the three mantric syllables and the psychic centers assigned to them.

D. SOME GROUPS OF FOUR

With the ordering of our symbols or concepts we come to the spatial images of the maṇḍalas. However, we should also remember here the four mystical bodies, which we saw were the triad of the trikāya and the sahajakāya arising from it. Associated

Three Syllables	Color	Lotus-center	The Three Basic Failings	The Three Maṇḍalas	The Deities of the Tibetan Book of the Dead
Oṃ	White	Brow	Desire	Kāyamaṇḍala	58 Wrathful Deities
Āḥ	Red	Throat	Hatred	Vāgmaṇḍala	5 Vidyādharas (with Prajñā)
Hūṃ	Blue	Heart	Ignorance	Cittamaṇḍala	42 Peaceful Deities

TABLE 5

with these four mystical bodies or realms of mind and action are the four initiations (T. dBang-bzhi), which we meet frequently as the tantric rituals of Tibetan Buddhism. Even though this fourfold consecration may be the most important kind of Tibetan initiation in the Vajrayāna teachings, we find among the followers of the ancient and non-reformed rNying-ma-pa sect, which goes back to Guru Padmasambhava, a system with five consecrations for five psychic planes of human being which play an important role in the tradition of the Tibetan Book of the Dead in particular. We shall return to this in the following chapter.

Another fourfold symbolism is the viśvavajra or crossed vajra (see figure 8, upper right). The vajra, or diamond scepter (T. rDo-rje), is the most important Tibetan ritual object and is central to the "diamond" or "diamond-clear" doctrine of the Vajrayāna (T. rDo-rje theg-pa), included in which are the texts of the Tibetan Books of the Dead. They constitute a synoptic essence of these Vajrayāna teachings which form a rounded inner structure of the Buddhist religion, of Yoga, and of psychology, which were synthesized in the Tibetan Book of the Dead into a beautiful and harmonious cosmic-visionary world of all aspects of human awareness. The viśvavajra (T. rDo-rje rgya-gram), with its ends that point to the four directions of heaven, forms the basis of the symbolism of Tibetan Buddhist cosmology and of the maṇḍalas. In the cosmology there are the four continents (S. catvāri dvīpāni; T. gLing-bzhi) which arise from a gold viśvavajra as the foundation of the cosmos, and they thereby form the orientation of a mythical-cosmological world. In a similar schema, the four triangular fields in the square of the maṇḍala are formed, which are assigned to the four directions and elements. Because of the necessary addition of the fifth we shall return to the maṇḍalas below.

An interesting iconographic and psychological phenomenon in the Tibetan Book of the Dead are the deities known as the four Guardians. These guardians of the four gates (T. sGo-ba bzhi) of the maṇḍala have a wrathful appearance and are assigned various cosmic colors (see the description in chapter III). Like all deities of the Tibetan Book of the Dead the four Guardians appear as masculine-feminine pairs, i.e., in the initiation ritual the guardians are introduced separately from their female partners, in groups of four. As a rule, the four male Guardians point towards the "four limitless ultimate questions" (T. rTag-chad mu-bzhi), if we may use this collective concept in a somewhat free translation. On the other side, the four female Guardians usually stand for the "four divine boundless states" (S. catur-apramāṇāni; T. Tshad-med bzhi).

Both groups together constitute the most important elements of a meditational practice that in every respect transcends the individual personality and which is said to lead to correct insight into the right kind of awareness and of corresponding human behavior. The "four limitless ultimate questions" concern the meaning of birth and death, of immortality and extinction (of life), of Being and Not-Being, and of the phenomenal world and emptiness. These are, in relation to the maṇḍala of the demonic deities, the questions that determines one's fate, since they are put at the beginning of the visions of the wrathful deities. They are associated in their meaning with the well known "four infinities" (P. cakkhu-āyatana), which are practiced as a meditation upon the expansiveness of awareness.[63]

The other group of four is usually associated with the four female Guardians (T. sGo-ma bzhi) and is called the "four divine boundless states" (S. brahma-vihāra, or apramāṇāni). These are the most important qualities or ways of acting for leading a spiritual life in the sense of Buddhist teachings. The "four divine boundless states" are the conscious development of kindness (S. maitrī), compassion (S. karuṇā), sympathy (S. muditā), and equanimity (S. upekṣā). These four developments of the divine virtues (T. Tshad-med bzhi) are ancient Buddhist ethical demands for leading a life of virtue, which had already been established by Hīnayāna Buddhism. They now appear in connection with certain iconographic images from the Tibetan Book of the Dead which point towards this task. A further fact worth noting is the fourfold arrangement in the sequence of the visions of the 110 deities of the bardo. The 49 days of the after-death state until the next incarnation include four groups of seven days in which the peaceful deities appear (7 days), the wrathful deities (7 days), and all the deities together (14 days). Behind this remarkable arrangement lie symbolic and psychological realities of various aspects.

We shall again and again be returning to the issue of the process of symbolic and ritual purification and consecration in tantric initiations; for again in the fourfold articulation of symbolic actions we come across a complete initiation system (T. dBang-bskur) which corresponds to psychophysical planes of man. The "four consecrations" (T. dBang-bzhi) briefly mentioned above constitute for us the most important foundation for an understanding of the "four bodies," which we localized in four different lotus centers as planes of psychic development of spiritual powers (cf. p. 59). We must accustom ourselves, in dealing with this difficult material which comes from various traditions, to the fact that in the realm of the initiations there is a huge and often confusing multiplicity. There are several hundred consecrations in various Tantras and secret systems, in which the transmission of initiations from school to school can be different.

Let us now follow the initiation schema of the four consecrations in the maṇḍalas of the bardo deities according to the Nges-don snying-po,[64] an important Book of the Dead from the rNying-ma-pa tradition of Tibet. Here we have the four consecrations in descending order, i.e., the highest consecration belongs to the svabhāvikakāya above the navel center. The ascending and descending progress of the initiation, symbolizing the cycle of enlightenment and the dissolution of opposites, is something we shall meet again later when we come to describe the six Buddhas and the path from the six lokas. In the fourfold (and thereby for tantric ritual complete) initiation, the kumbhābhiṣeka (T. Bum-dbang) is given, in order to transform the profane body into the nirmāṇakāya of the Buddha. With the guhyābhiṣeka (T. gSang-dbang) profane language becomes the pure word, with the prajñābhiṣeka one attains the purity of the dharmakāya in one's heart, and with the sahajābhiṣeka (T. dByer-med lhan-skyes dbang) the center of the person fulfills itself as the sahajakāya, or body of indivisible totality of the four planes of a religiously and spiritually effective wholeness. This is shown in table 6.

Seed-Syllable	Color	Initiation	Profane Existence	Consecrated Existence	Psychic Center
OṂ	White	Kumbhābhiṣeka	Profane Body (T. Lus)	Consecrated Body (T. sKu)	Skull
ĀḤ	Red	Guhyābhiṣeka	Verbal Plane (T. Ngag)	Pure Word (T. gSung)	Throat
HŪṂ	Blue	Prajñābhiṣeka	Heart (T. sNying)	Spiritual Center (T. Thugs)	Heart Region
HRĪḤ	Red	Sahajābhiṣeka	Earthly Man	Universal Man	Navel

TABLE 6

In order to show once again the inseparability or the functional interdependence of the four emanations of the deities of the bardo maṇḍala, we represent in figure 5 the male peaceful deities by A, their female counterparts by B, and the wrathful emanations of both by A_1 and B_1. All deities are considered to be emanations from emptiness, in which the Ādibuddha appears as primordial image. There then follows the polarity of the Ādibuddha in unity with the prajñā (represented in figure 6 as YY), and from the primordial couple the 110 deities of the bardo, who fill out the circle of the visions in the center of the pyramid. Ultimately, however, all deities are yab-yum, indivisible unity, and dissolve again as visionary images from one's own awareness into the great emptiness.

E. THE FIVEFOLD ARRANGEMENT OF THE MAṆḌALA

In the Buddhist mysticism of the Vajrayāna the most important part of esoteric symbolism is concentrated in the fivefold arrange-

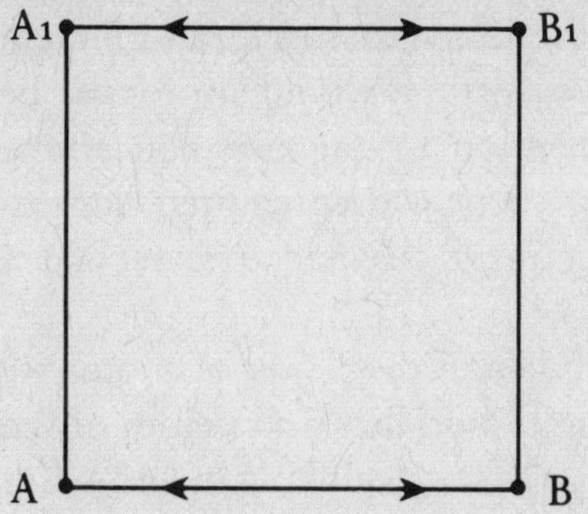

Fig. 5. Correspondences between the four kinds of emanation.

ment of symbols, images, or values, grouped in a square with the middle point as the *quinta essentia.* This pentad in which the elements are interrelated is enclosed by the sacred circle of the maṇḍala. This circle, too, is constructed from an articulated symbolism which points towards the path of awareness and its stages of actualization. In the center of the maṇḍala, which consists of a lotus blossom, is the central or fifth point, which constitutes a key to knowledge of the contents of the maṇḍala. Maṇḍalas in Buddhism are quite specific religious and philosophical symbols, the meaning of which is unconditionally determined, and there is no random interchanging of symbols. Without this stable inner logic

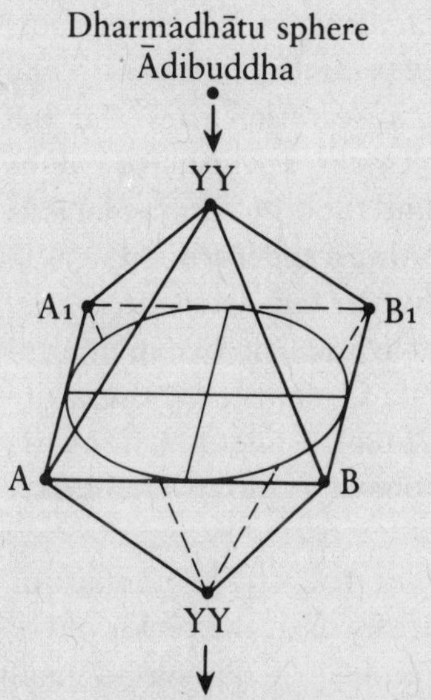

Fig. 6. Double pyramid representing the visions (double quaternity).

of maṇḍala construction, the secret teachings associated with them could no longer be transmitted, since they would no longer be meaningful. We call particular attention to the rules concerning the maṇḍala here, because of the current widespread tendency to call every conceivable kind of square or circular arrangement a maṇḍala.

In the central point of the maṇḍala as the center of a lotus we have the identity with the origin of all buddhas and deities of the Tibetan Book of the Dead; the center is the beginning or end-point of contemplation, according to the way the meditation process is set up. In the course of our portrayal of the visions we shall describe all the arrangements of the deities and their symbolism as they occur in the maṇḍala. For the detailed theory of the maṇḍala and the meanings of its elements, the reader is referred to the appropriate literature.[65]

The first part of the visions of the Bar-do thos-grol consists of the appearance of the five Tathāgatas and the eight Bodhisattvas, together with their female counterparts, or Ḍākinīs. All these manifestations of the peaceful deities are represented in the fivefold grouping of the maṇḍala, which also reveals a significant psychological structure in the formation and synthesis of symbols. The same schema is used for the second part of the bardo visions and is applied with certain changes and supplements to the emanations of the wrathful deities. To this complex arrangement with the same basic structure correspond the consecration rites and the initiations, which now relate to a supplemented schema of five or of seven psychic lotus centers. The foundation of all maṇḍalas is the schema of the five Tathāgatas or transcendent Buddhas (T. rGyal-ba rigs-lnga), who, together with their female counterparts, the Buddha-Ḍākinīs, open up a realm of symbolism rich in interrelationships. In the center of the maṇḍala is Vairocana, the white Buddha, and from him radiate in the four cosmic directions the Buddhas Akṣobhya (blue), Ratnasambhava (yellow), Amitābha (red), and Amoghasiddhi (green).

The five Tathāgatas correspond to the five skandhas or groups of the human personality, which stands at the center of the Buddhist analysis of Being. The five skandhas (T. Phung-po lnga) are causally connected with the five hindrances (S. kleśa; T. Dug-lnga) which must be overcome if man wishes to tread the path of enlightenment and liberation. This path is symbolized as a clarification by the five elements, which are represented by the five female counterparts of the Buddhas (T. Yum-chen lnga). The five elements (T. Byung-ba lnga) form the five rays or lights out of which the Buddhas coming from the realm of emptiness unfold in the vision. The five elemental lights at the same time become the basic colors of the directions of the maṇḍala and of the elements. Moreover, the five lights are the rays of the five transcendent wisdoms, the buddha-wisdoms (T. Ye-shes lnga), which are to be actualized if one wishes to overcome the five great hindrances or failings of human behavior.

We can recognize here what a comprehensive and systematic symbolism was developed in Buddhist teachings to be able to portray subtle psychic and spiritual as well as cosmological processes. These are all connected with the symbolism of the maṇḍala and appear there in a fourfold polarity, namely of the peaceful and the wrathful and the male and the female aspects. The colors of the five transcendent Buddhas, which are experienced on the plane of the sambhogakāya in the bardo, are also symbolic and relate to the cosmology and psychology of the maṇḍala. That is to say, the maṇḍala is a microcosmic image of the universe and at the same time the image of an intrapsychic and spiritual world, in which divine forms are reflected in determinate symbolic images of awareness.

Figure 7 shows the basic schema of the five Tathāgatas, which can be taken as a model of all maṇḍalas and symbolic relationships in the Tibetan Book of the Dead. All other representations are derived from this basic form. In the center appears the Buddha Vairocana (A), he is followed by the Buddha Akṣobhya (B) in the east, the Buddha Ratnasambhava (C) in the south, the Buddha Amitābha (D) in the west, and the Buddha Amoghasiddhi (E) in the north.

The five Tathāgatas as emanations of the five transcendent wisdoms are each assigned to a specific psychic center, in order to eliminate in it, by means of certain meditative practices, one of the

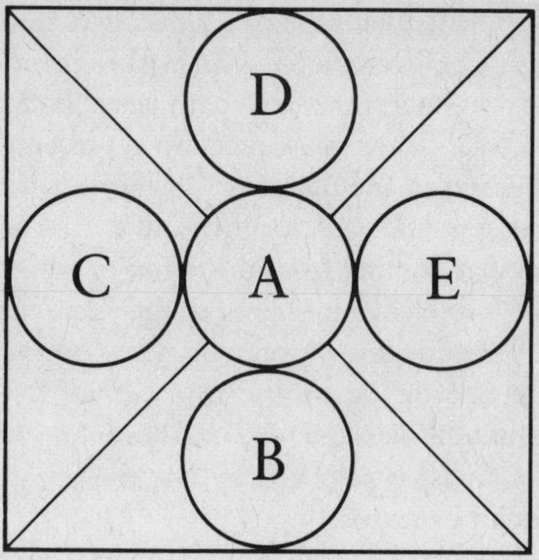

Fig. 7. Basic schema of the five Tathāgatas.

five poisons, or hindrances, which obstruct the path towards enlightenment and liberation. For psychospiritual purification and the loosening of the attachments of the five skandhas are prerequisites for the recognition of the "clear light" in the bardo. The five wisdoms of the Buddhas become the great guides on the illuminated path of the five Tathāgatas through the terrifying realms of the bardo.

In one of the most important Tibetan Books of the Dead[66] from the rNying-ma-pa sect we find a fivefold arrangement of the psychic centers which is associated with the five Tathāgatas. In the lotus centers in the skull, the throat, the heart, the navel, and the perineum are situated the spiritual forces, in the form of the five Tathāgatas, that oppose the five hindrances. They correspond to a descending arrangement of tantric psychophysical symbols for the transformation of the five planes of human activity by means of body, speech, mind, deserving action, and karma. As a fifth center we find in the perineum the sukhapālacakra (corresponding to the mūlādhāracakra in Yoga), which signifies that only by sublimation and constant conscious overcoming of earthly desires can transcendence and progressive knowledge be attained. This is where action (karma) takes root and becomes the cause of all further

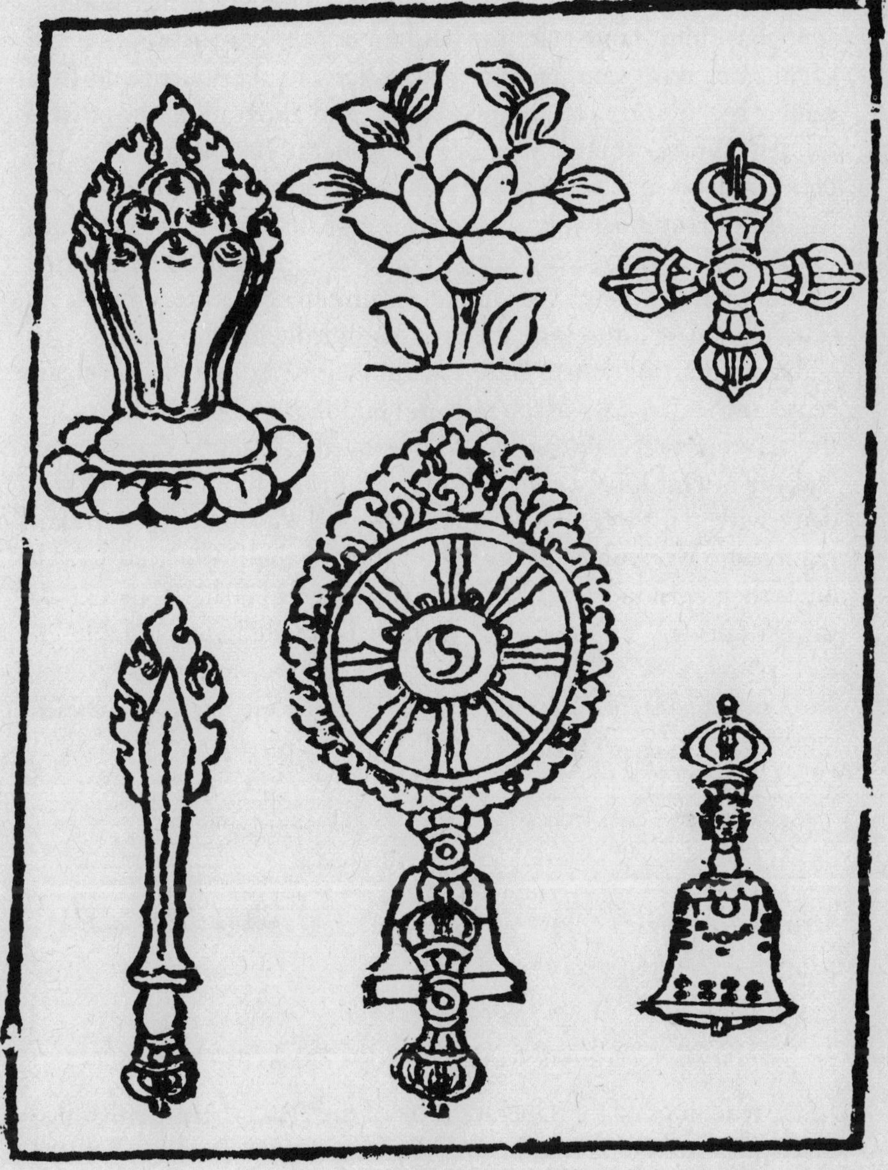

Fig. 8. The attributes of the five Tathāgatas. Block print of an initiation card for a death ritual. The symbols show vajra and ghaṇṭā, dharmacakra, sword, cintāmaṇi, lotus, and viśvavajra.

conditions of later life; karma decides the nature of the path through the bardo to a new rebirth. Therefore the Buddha Amoghasiddhi stands with the wisdom of perfected action over the sukhapālacakra. Our Tibetan text assigns to the fourth and fifth centers the appearance of more ḍākinīs and above all of the powerful deity Vajrakumāra, who are not generally to be found in the better known maṇḍalas of the Bar-do thos-grol.

In the topmost cakra as the place of the intellect, the visions of the 58 terrifying deities appear; these blood-drinking deities rule the four directions of the human brain. In the center of speech, standing on a lotus, are the five knowledge-holding deities, or Vidyādharas, in tantric union with their Ḍākinīs. In the heart center is the maṇḍala of the peaceful buddhas and bodhisattvas. In the navel center appear five forms of the Ḍākinī Vajravārāhī, and the lowest lotus center is the place of the wrathful protective deity with the three-bladed magic dagger, Vajrakīla or Vajrakumāra, who overcomes the three poisons of the instinctual world. Since the lower-most cakras are not assigned in all Tibetan texts to the Ḍākinīs and Vajrakumāra, we have bracketed them in table 7.

LOCATION	CENTER	PLANE OF ACTUALIZATION	ACTIVITY	TATHAGATA	EMNANATION IN THE BARDO
1. Skull	Mahāsukha-cakra	Svabhāvika-kāya	Body Kāya	Vairocana	Wrathful Deities
2. Throat	Sambhoga-cakra	Sambhoga-kāya	Speech Vāc	Amitābha	Wisdom-possessing Deities
3. Heart	Dharma-cakra	Dharma-kāya	Mind Citta	Aksobhya	Peaceful Deities
4. Navel	Nirmāṇa-cakra	Nirmāṇa-kāya	Merit Guṇa	Ratnasambhava	Ḍākinīs
5. Perineum	Sukhapāla-cakra	Abhisambodhi-kāya	Deed Karma	Amoghasiddhi	Vajrakumāra

TABLE 7

F. THE SIX REALMS OF INCARNATION

In the teachings of the Tibetan Book of the Dead there is a detailed description of the six realms of incarnation which are called the wheel of life (S. bhavacakra; T. Srid-pa'i 'khor-lo). This sixfold world opens up to the wandering awareness-principle on its descent into the Srid-pa'i bar-do, where it seeks a place for rebirth. We find a detailed portrayal of the Srid-pa'i bar-do in Evans-

Wentz's translation of the Tibetan Book of the Dead, that well-known work to which we must continually refer.

On the path leading down to the Srid-pa'i bar-do the six dim lights appear, which flicker up from the sixfold world of existence below. Already in the first days of the bardo visions these six lights are perceived close to the clear cosmic radiance of the five Tathāgatas, and they are considered to be elemental lights from the six worlds of existence, which are to be overcome by knowledge. The six dim lights are associated with the appearing of the six Buddhas of the bhavacakra.

The most important directions in the texts of the Tibetan Book of the Dead for the guidance of awareness in the bardo emphasize that the dead person should strive for liberation through his own knowledge. At all stages of the bardo it is stressed that clear knowledge and consciousness is the best path, and that rebirth in any form of existence involves suffering and impermanence and the difficulties of attaining liberation. If all the temptations of deceptive visionary images, which are continually referred to in the texts as hostile forms of the intellect, can be recognized as empty creations of one's own mind and can be immediately penetrated, one will attain liberation. These images dissolve away and the awareness reaches the peaceful and imageless release of nirvāṇa. Every fleeing from these fearsome and terrifying bardo images and every feeling of being seduced by certain colors and visionary apparitions is a step into the ambivalence of the feelings of hatred and desire and is attachment to the opposites of divisive consciousness. It is therefore a step back into ignorance, for the antagonistic forces of desire and aversion prevent salvation and unity of awareness in the state of liberation. The awareness-body (T. Yid-kyi lus) transforming into salvation of the spirit in the bardo knows no neither-nor and endures detached from all apparitions.

If this state on the various planes and stages of awareness described in the Tibetan Book of the Dead cannot be maintained, rebirth is unavoidable. The path through the bardo is either the great liberation (T. Grol-lam) or the great suffering and rebirth. Karma that has not been worked off drives the wandering awareness-body towards the six worlds; it is attracted by them, and its wishes and desires lead it to a new impermanent form. We can describe the six realms of existence as symbols of the working out of human vices.

They are those realms of existence which are described in various Tibetan scriptures by means of a rich treasury of mythological and psychological symbolism. The six forms of existence appear as one-sided exaggerations of human ways of behaving and can be derived from the six failings or hindrances. They are represented pictorially as the worlds of gods, titans, human beings, animals, hungry ghosts, and denizens of hell. Thus the six realms of incarnation communicate in a primordial imaginal typology of the human character the realms of experience ranging from divine joy to the most hellish torments, all of which result from human behavior. In a characteristic psychological and tantric symbolism of opposites, the vices are portrayed along with the corresponding ways of overcoming them.

The six worlds of incarnation are the realm in which the great Bodhisattva of active compassion, Avalokiteśvara ("the merciful onlooker"), manifests. He is the strongest symbolic figure of Mahāyāna Buddhism and the embodiment of the doctrine of salvation on the path from suffering to liberation. In the Tibetan Book of the Dead Avalokiteśvara appears as the bringer of salvation who shows the path of release to the beings in the six worlds. We find him described there in his four-armed form or more often in his eleven-headed and eight-armed form as Avalokiteśvara of great compassion (S. mahākāruṇika-avalokiteśvara; T. sPyan-gzigs thugs-rje chen-po). The various texts explain his various aspects and say that he appears in the six worlds of incarnation in the form of six different Buddhas (Thub-pa drug). These are Buddhas from the famous six holy syllables of the great mantra, Oṃ ma ṇi pad me hūṃ, who have assumed visible bodily form in the nirmāṇakāya. This six-syllable mantra is for every Tibetan the most holy invocation of Avalokiteśvara who is directly associated with the six worlds (see chapter III). In the Maṇi bka'-'bum, an ancient Tibetan text attributed to the first Buddhist king Srong-btsan sgam-po (617–650), we find many clarifications of the meaning of the six-syllable mantra of Avalokiteśvara.[67] This work is indispensable for an understanding of the six worlds of the Srid-pa'i bar-do. There too it says that the five Tathāgatas are to be understood as emanations from the six syllables of the great mantra.

In the elucidations from the Maṇi bka'-'bum we recognize the great soteriological significance of the Bodhisattva "Yi-ge drug-pa," of the "six-syllable" Bodhisattva Avalokiteśvara. Beyond the forms of the six Buddhas of the bhavacakra, the Bodhisattva becomes the proclaimer of the "six perfections" (T. Pha-rol-phyin drug), of those "six pāramitās" necessary to overcome basic human failings and to attain liberation. We shall offer one further overview of the many relationships of the sixfold symbolism of the great mantra Oṃ ma ṇi pad me hūṃ to the six Buddhas of the realms of existence. Further details of this important symbolism will be explained in chapter III. Table 8 shows the relationships between the six worlds, the Buddhas as incarnations of Avalokiteśvara, the six dim lights, and the assignment of the great mantra to the Tathāgatas (Fol. 32 a-b from part Vaṃ).

Six Worlds	Six Buddhas	Six Lights	Six-Syllable Mantra	Avalokiteśvara and the Five Tathāgatas
Gods	brGya-byin	White	Oṃ	Avalokiteśvara
Titans	Thags-bzang-ris	Green	Ma	Vairocana
Human beings	Śākya thub-pa	Yellow	Ṇi	Vajrasattva-Akṣobhya
Animals	Seng-ge rab-brtan	Blue	Pad	Ratnasambhava
Pretas (Hungry Ghosts)	Kha-'bar-ma	Red	Me	Amitābha
Denizens of Hell	Chos-rgyal Dharmarāja	Black	Hūṃ	Amoghasiddhi

TABLE 8

G. OTHER SYMBOLIC GROUPINGS

From the rich symbolism of tantric Buddhism in Tibet we should mention the remarkable sevenfold temporal division of the bardo.

The time from the beginning of the experience of death in the 'Chi-kha'i bar-do until the next incarnation, which is said to take place 49 days later, is an interval of seven times seven days. The visions of the bardo deities last fourteen days, the first half bringing in six days the 42 peaceful deities and on the seventh day the Vidyādharas, and in the second half the 58 terrifying deities appear as the tantric counter-image of the previous visions. Among these are also the 28 powerful animal-headed ḍākinīs (T. rNal-'byor nyer-brgyad), who appear in groups of seven. These groups thereby correspond to the fourfold orientation of lamaistic cosmology and to the arrangements of the maṇḍala as the foundation of all divine emanations of the Buddhas.

The four continents of Buddhist cosmology (S. catvāri dvīpāni) have eight smaller sub-continents (T. gLing-'phran brgyad) and thus constitute as a cosmological foundation an important mythological aspect of the description of the Srid-pa'i bar-do, in which the dead person seeking a place of rebirth (T. sKye-gnas) experiences the nature of these world-regions.

A final eightfold grouping is that of the Bodhisattvas and the sixteen Ḍākinīs who appear as visions in the bardo. The eight Bodhisattvas rule over the eight kinds of awareness (S. aṣṭavijñāna) and their Ḍākinīs over the eight realms covered by these kinds of awareness. Their counter-images are the eight Keurima and the eight Phra-men-ma deities, who together form a group of sixteen wrathful Ḍākinīs. And so we can recognize from these few examples that the teachings of the Tibetan Book of the Dead possess a well ordered and primordially imaginal structure which results from the use of the Buddhist maṇḍalas as the fundamental images of all visionary phenomena and divine emanations.

It would be possible to say much more about the details of the symbolism; however, to consider a larger number of Tibetan texts beyond the Books of the Dead would necessitate taking so many variations and differences into account as to overstep the bounds of comprehension. Yet to look at Tibetan paintings and the iconographic portrayal of the bardo deities would bring to light a large number of things about which one must have exact knowledge if one wishes to penetrate further into the essence of the teachings. Even though we should explain as much as possible in describing the pictures, we shall give here a general arrangement of the cosmologically relevant symbolism of the maṇḍalas of the bardo deities. In this we take account only of the cosmic directions, the colors, and the elements:

Center	East	South	West	North
white	blue	yellow	red	green
ether	water	earth	fire	air

All other visible signs, colors and symbols have likewise a more or less fixed meaning. The colors of the Buddhas and Bodhisattvas as well as of all other deities are related to their cosmic position in the maṇḍala or to their kind of emanation in the hierarchy of the Buddhas. In contrast, the five Tathāgatas are pictured riding various kinds of animals. The deities are equipped with the trappings of the sambhogakāya-state, which is in turn used in the tantric symbolism of opposites. The Buddhas wear the heavenly buddha-crowns, whereas the wrathful deities have skull crowns and are adorned with bones, which indicate the impermanence of all earthly existence. The peaceful Buddhas appear seated on lotus thrones in front of a radiant aureole, the color schemes of which can vary. In absolute contrast we see the wrathful deities appear in aggressive postures with threatening gestures, on the lotus in front of an aureole of flames and smoke; they display extreme power and inspire great terror. All the deities show various gestures of the hand, which are related to quite definite spiritual attitudes or activities. These will be described when we discuss the individual deities in chapter III.

Apart from the hand gestures, the deities' attributes are the most important. We find the peaceful deities holding the lotus, the wheel of the teachings (S. cakra), the ritual bell (S. ghaṇṭā), the vajra, the precious stone (S. cintāmaṇi), or the pātra (begging bowl). Among the most important tantric symbols of the wrathful deities are the sling (S. pāśa), the sword, the club, the spear, the arrow, the axe, and above all the tantric skull vessel, or kapāla, in contrast to the pātra. The Indian Guru Padmasambhava, for example, is portrayed in various forms of emanation. One shows him as the second Buddha portrayed in the same way as the Buddha, carrying the pātra in his left hand and with the name Śākyasiṃha. As the tantric master of the Tibetan tradition we see the same guru with flowing garments, a vajra in his right hand and the white kapāla in his left. The attributes or hand gestures are also important symbols in denoting the various states or forms of emanation of the gurus and deities of the Buddhist tantric tradition.

We should mention here in particular the trikāya doctrine of the three different states of being of the buddhas and deities of the Mahāyāna. On each of the three planes they assume different symbols or colors and forms of representation. By means of the representation of mystical seed-syllables, the bījas (T. Sa-bon), or by the transcription of a sequence of mantras, the deities of the Tibetan Book of the Dead can be concentrated into an extremely small space in the so-called speech maṇḍala (S. vāgmaṇḍala; T. gSung-gi dkhyil-'khor). We also know Tibetan paintings with maṇḍalas to the bardo deities, in which the deities' presence is portrayed only by colors and small groupings of dots of color. Thus the Tibetan Book of the Dead with its visionary deities constitutes an individual, self-contained, and complete symbolic world within the tradition of Tibetan Buddhism, of which the images discussed and shown here are only a small and incomplete part.

5. The Death Ritual as Guidance through the Bardo

THE AUTHENTIC Tibetan death ritual consists of a whole series of ceremonies and recitations as well as various consecrations, which dramatically and vitally supplement the contents of the Tibetan Book of the Dead. The dead person, together with those present at the rites, is summoned to attentive participation in the ritual event. Here we shall concentrate on the most important consecrations during the recitation of the death ritual, as given in two particular books in the great collective work "Peaceful and Wrathful Deities according to the Tradition of Karma gling-pa."[68] The order of the initiations can be quite different in the various Books of the Dead, and the following one has been chosen as representative. We shall arrange all further descriptions and also the pictorial material according to this order, so that, in spite of the variations, some of which will be explained in the appendix, we can maintain a direct line of progression. In chapter III we shall follow exactly in text and picture the ritual instructions of the above-mentioned sources, from which we can bring an explanatory overview of the symbolism to the descriptions.

We should mention once again that the various texts of the death ritual consist of several books. Some communicate knowledge about the process of dying and about the kinds of visions that occur in the bardo, as well as speculations about the best technique for seeking a place of rebirth. Other texts consist of ritual instructions for symbolic sacrifices to the buddhas and deities, for the exorcism of vicious demons, and for the initiations and magical-ritual guidance of the dead person.

To the authentic ritual texts intended only for the lamas practicing the rite belong also the wide-ranging mantric texts. The ritual books with exact directions for the necessary ritual objects and their use during the ceremonies provide for the most part religious and psychological knowledge and also symbolism associated with the ritual activity. Many symbolic contents and teachings appear within the ritual in abbreviated form and in all possible variations. Thus the Tibetan death ritual has come to communicate esoteric and practical wisdom to the participants in the dramatic course of the ritual activities. A part of the death ritual books is quite comprehensible to anyone hearing or reading it. The religious, ethico-philosophical, and above all psychological content is presented in a theoretical and comprehensive manner. Another large portion of the various books within the Tibetan Book of the Dead has a purely ritual or mantric character and is not in this form comprehensible to the layperson.

The vehicle of the "way of the mantra" (S. mantrayāna; T. sNgags-kyi theg-pa) is of a highly esoteric nature, since in it all the wisdom is communicated solely by means of syllables and mantras, which have to be learned with great precision. Mantras and invocations open and conclude the Tibetan Book of the Dead, and they often start and finish each sentence. In many cases only a few syllables of a mantra will suggest to the initiated what encoded subject matter is being dealt with or to what the mantra is to be applied.

We can gauge approximately the size of a Tibetan Book of the Dead, the Bar-do thos-grol chen-mo for example, a few of whose seventeen volumes were published by Evans-Wentz, by considering that a translation of the entire work together with a commentary would be at least three times as large as Evans-Wentz' work. We could get the clearest idea of this by attending the readings and the death ceremonies themselves. For example, the relevant passages from the collective work "Kar-gling zhi-khro" take at least 14 days to recite, and can last up to 49 days. In the first 14 days, which are dedicated to the epiphany of the peaceful and wrathful bardo deities, the ritual recitations begin about six or seven o'clock in the morning and last about four hours, and they usually take the same amount of time again in the afternoon. The guidance of the dead person's awareness through the bardo is continuous for the first fourteen days, and the following fourteen days are given to explanations of the Srid-pa'i bar-do, the world of hell, and the bhavacakra.

Many preparations, which we shall now briefly describe, must be made for the setting up of the death ritual, the placing of the offerings on the shrine, and for the recitation of the rites.

The shrine or house altar, which is found in every Tibetan household, is furnished with the pictures and objects necessary for the bardo ritual. In addition to the usual images of the Buddha and other sacred figures or deities of Buddhism, one or two scroll paintings (T. Thang-ka) are hung up, depicting the peaceful and wrathful deities. Some pictures show the 42 peaceful deities, others the 58 wrathful ones, and yet others show all the deities together. If such pictures are not already in the house, they are brought by the monks from the monastery who have been invited to the recitation. Ceremonies for monks who have died are even more elaborate, and for the death rituals of important abbots and saints certain Mahākāla dances are performed by monks in black robes and accompanied by special death music on drums. In these dances certain emanations of the terrible black tantric protective deity Mahākāla or of the god of death, Yama, are invoked so that they may accompany the dead person on his way through the bardo.

Let us turn again to the normal death ritual in which the recitations are for a lay person who has died. The house altar is decorated with flowers, and bowls of water, sacrificial cakes (T. gTor-ma), incense, and fruit are arranged in front of the ritual pictures. Then sometimes in addition to the usual candles, a set of 108 sacrificial lamps is used, made of brass, copper, or silver, or else made out of dough and filled with butter. Another possible addition to the symbolic arrangement of the altar is the placing of various groups of Buddhist signs, made out of wood or brass (or silver), in rows in front of the sacrificial bowls. Included among these might be the offerings of the five senses (T. 'Dod-yon sna-lnga),[69] the eight Buddhist auspicious signs (S. aṣṭamaṅgala; T. bKra-shis rtags brgyad),[70] the eight sacrificial gifts that bring good fortune (S. aṣṭadravyaka; T. rDzas brgyad),[71] and the seven symbols of the royal rulers (S. saptaratnāni; T. Rin-chen sna bdun).[72] Also indispensable is the great rice maṇḍala as the symbolic offering of all precious gifts of this impermanent world to the buddhas.

First, the monks (at least two or more) arrange the ritual objects on the narrow tables in front of which they sit. In the tantric ritual for the bardo deities these are the vajra (T. rDo-rje), the ritual bell (T. Dril-bu), the small hand-drum (S. ḍamaru; T. cang-te'u) of wood or skull-bone with hide stretched on both sides, the pair of small cymbals (T. Ting-shags), the tanṭric kapāla (T. Thod-pa), a bowl of yellow sacrificial rice, and the ritual jug for consecrated water (T. Khrus-bum). This vessel of sacred water is of special symbolic significance for the introduction into the teachings concerning the visions of the deities of the Tibetan Book of the Dead. In the upper opening of the vessel rests a crown of peacock feathers on a stick, which is used as a sprinkler. For the death ritual a small picture of the blue Ādibuddha Samantabhadra (T. Kun-tu bzang-po) with his white counterpart, or prajñā, is attached to the front side of these feathers. This Buddha is the most important figure in the maṇḍala of the bardo deities, being the primordial image of all emanations from the dharmadhātu sphere of the pure dharmakāya. A final indispensable part of every bardo ritual is the small cards with pictures of the deities of the Book of the Dead, which the monk holds in his hand. With these cards he guides the dead person's awareness, and symbolically that of all the participants in the ritual, through the realm of the bardo. The cards (T. Tsa-ka-li) are usually only half the size of a postcard, have a red border, and portray in separate groups all the deities in an order corresponding to the Book of the Dead. According to the number of deities pictured together on one card and to the way they correspond to the structure of the appropriate Book of the Dead, there are various sets of these cards containing from 50 to 80 of them. The small cards are often true masterpieces of Tibetan painting, since often as many as 28 detailed icons of deities may be painted in a very small space, care being taken to include all the appropriate colors and attributes. We are also acquainted with similar cards for the death rituals of the ancient Tibetan and pre-Buddhist Bon religion. There too, they are used to guide the dead person through the realms of the bardo, the cards being shown and explained one at a time during the ritual. Connected with the showing of the cards, which the presiding lama holds up at certain points in the text, are the initiations for the dead person to be described below.

However, without the presence of the dead person the recitation of the Book of the Dead cannot begin. It is true that after his burial (or cremation) he is no longer physically present, but in his place is a picture of him, called his sByang-bu (also mTshan-sbyang, Byang-bu, or sByang-gzhi). This usually takes the form of a Tibetan woodblock print but can also be drawn by one of the monks on white paper. Figures 9–13 show five different kinds of Tibetan block prints, and two similar examples can be found in Evans-Wentz[73] and in Schlagintweit.[74] The prints are different for men and for women. We see first a dead man symbolically represented in a praying attitude kneeling on a lotus with a lotus blossom in his hand (fig. 10). He is sitting under a canopy of

Fig. 9. sByang-bu for a dead man. Block print from Bum-thang.

Fig. 10. sByang-bu for a dead man. Tibetan block print.

Fig. 11. sByang-bu for a dead woman. Tibetan block print.

honor, and on the altar to the side we see an altar lamp (T. Mar-me), a gTor-ma (sacrificial cake), and a bowl of rice. These three objects play a special role in the death ritual by representing the six lokas. The next picture shows a woman with folded hands under the canopy of honor kneeling on a lotus. She too holds a lotus blossom in her hand. The Tibetan inscription reads: "She who has left life." The other two pictures show a mantric syllable standing for the dead man from the ritual for the Srid-pa'i bar-do. The syllable is Nṛ, the mantra for the human world. It stands on the lotus throne under the canopy. In the case of a dead man one can see in the center of the Nṛ the mantric syllable Hūṃ, in the case of a woman, the syllable Vaṃ.

For the dead man the reverse side of the Byang-bu (see fig. 12) bears an inscription invoking the god of death, Yamāntaka, as a protective deity. The gap in the text is to be filled by the dead person's name. The text reads:

"May the deceased, (Name), through the assembled deities of the Śrī-Vajrabhairava (another name for Yamāntaka) be freed from all his failings and taken to the realm of the buddhas." The other Byang-du, for a dead woman, is quite similar, but on the reverse side the inscription invokes the tantric Ḍākinī Vajrayoginī (T. rDo-rje rnal-'byor-ma) as the protective deity and guide through the bardo. The text reads:

"May the deceased, (Name), through the venerable Ḍākinī Vajrayoginī, when freed from and purged of all failings, be taken to the heavenly realm" (fig. 13).

We see from these prints that various forms of representation are used in Byang-bus. These pictures are attached to a stick for the rite and placed on a lotus made from clay or dough. A small canopy of material of five colors is placed over the picture. The use of the Byang-bu in the ritual will be explained in chapter III in our discussion of the six Buddhas.

The most interesting and dramatic part of the whole death ritual is the initiation and conversation with the dead person through his image, the Byang-bu. In several verses the deceased is called upon by the lama and entreated to appear from the bardo beyond and to take his place in the picture that has been prepared

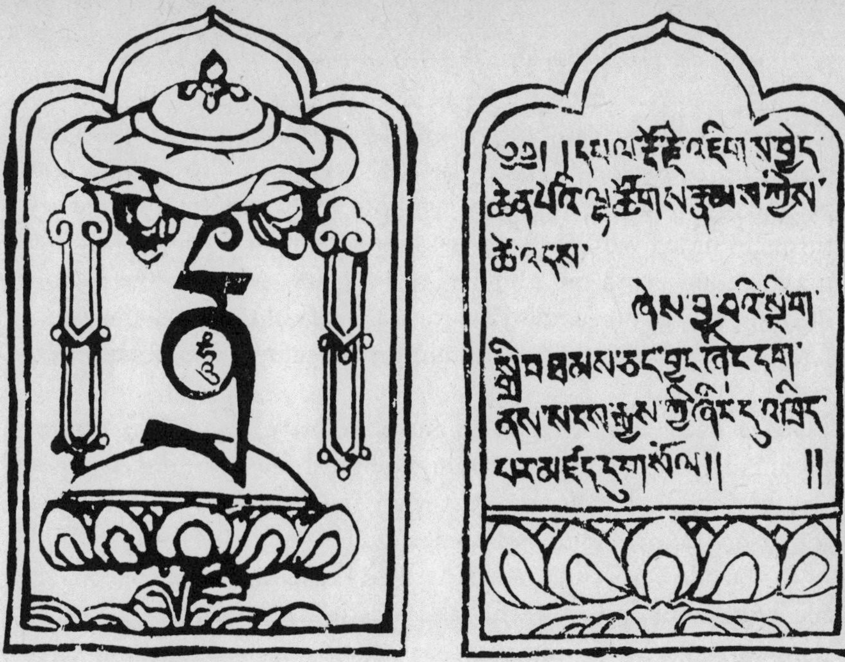

Fig. 12. sByang-bu for a dead man, front and back. Tibetan block print.

Fig. 13. sByang-bu for a dead woman, front and back. Tibetan block print.

for him, so that he can take part in the ceremony and its blessings. Thus the Byang-bu becomes the dead person who has become present again and who is now symbolically beginning the journey through the six worlds. At the end the picture is burned, symbolizing a second death on a higher, ritual plane, whereby the earthly death of physical decay is overcome. We shall return to this ritual later, since we must here maintain the character of a general overview.

Let us begin now with the introductory contemplation of the "maṇḍala of the most sublime magical-illusory peaceful and wrathful deities."[75] We shall determine the general sequence of the initiations according to a particular work[76] from the Tibetan Book of the Dead. The deities are also called "the most venerable assembly of the hundred peaceful and wrathful deities" (T. Zhi-khro dam-pa rigs brgya), and they are usually divided into two large groups. In the heart center (T. sNying-ga'i 'khor-lo) the 42 peaceful deities appear in the midst of a bundle of light rays, and in the "white couch" of the skull the 58 wrathful deities arise from flaming rays. In addition (although not according to all texts) the five Vidyādharas with their Ḍākinīs (ten deities altogether) appear in the throat center (T. Longs-spyod 'khor-lo), and according to the tradition of the bKa' rdzogs-pa chen-po scriptures[77] the five Jñānaḍākinīs (T. Ye-shes mkha-'gro lnga) appear in the navel center (T. lTe-ba'i 'khor-lo) and the wrathful blue Vajrakīla-Heruka appears with his Prajñā in the perineum (T. gSang-gnas 'khor-lo). From these, in the visions in the Chos nyid bardo (the bardo of reality experience), arise the three great maṇḍalas of the bardo deities:

1. The hundred peaceful and wrathful deities
2. The 110 deities including the Vidyādharas
3. The 117 deities of the supplemental bardo cycle

We encounter all three groupings in the scriptures as well as in the iconographic paintings for the Tibetan Book of the Dead. In agreement with our text[78] we shall now put the initiations of the first grouping together with the hundred deities of the bardo maṇḍala, and these should then serve, as the consecrations of the deities, or rather in the name of the deities (T. Lha-dbang), to transpose all the psycho-physical centers of the human body out of the state of profane ignorance into the condition of perfect knowledge.

In all initiations the Tibetan lamas use the jug of consecrated water with the peacock feathers and the picture of the blue Ādibuddha Samantabhadra (Yab-Yum). Firstly, the dead person is summoned to his Byang-bu by the lama performing the ceremony, who lifts up the jug (S. kalaśa) and says that, although the outer form is that of a jug, yet the great heavenly dwelling place of the deities is within it.[79] Then he addresses the dead person: "Hūṃ! In the kalaśa of the Buddha Samantabhadra (in unity) with his Prajñā dwells the divine assembly of the victorious peaceful and wrathful deities. In being blessed, O dead person, may you receive the deities' initiation."

Thus the Samantabhadra-abhiṣeka (T. Kun-bzang yab-yum dbang) leads into the series of the thirteen important initiations, during the course of which all knowledge about the visionary deities and the symbolic significance of their groupings is made manifest. There is a further series of consecrations which we cannot, for the sake of clarity, consider here. The first consecration concerns the representation of the immeasurable Ādibuddha Samantabhadra in the dharmakāya, whose illuminated vision belongs to the 'Chi-kha'i bar-do. Therefore the Ādibuddha, an in itself unrepresentable idea of the dharmakāya, is not counted among the visions of the Chos-nyid bar-do. He is the mystical father and medium of all the bardo deities. All the other consecrations except one have to do with the sambhogakāya, i.e., with the visions in the Chos-nyid bar-do of reality-experience. There then follow the initiations for the five Tathāgatas or transcendent Buddhas (T. Rigs lnga yab lnga'i dbang), in order to purify the realm of the five skandhas, and then the consecration for the knowledge of the five female counterparts of the Buddhas (T. bDe-gshegs yum lnga'i dbang), in order to clarify the five elemental realms. Then come the initiations of the eight Mahābodhisattvas and their Ḍākinis, for the purification of the eight functions of consciousness and their realms of activity. The next consecration, for knowledge of the six Buddhas as incarnations of Avalokiteśvara, is the only one carried out in the plane of the nirmāṇakāya (T. sPrul-sku thub-pa drug-gi dbang). With this consecration the six vices which cause people repeatedly to arrive at karmically conditioned rebirth are said to be overcome. At the end of the consecrations for knowledge of the peaceful deities stand the two for the four male and the four female Guardians of the maṇḍala, which help the dead person to attain the "four limitless ultimates" and the "four divine boundless states."

Then begin the initiations for the wrathful deities, starting with the one for the powerful Mahāśrī-Heruka (T. dPal chemchog), the lord of the "blood-drinking deities" (T. Khrag-'thung rab-'byams dbang). He is the extremely wrathful emanation of the peaceful Ādibuddha Samantabhadra. With a significance corresponding to those for the peaceful deities, except now in the powerful (T. Drag-po) form of the tantric deities, there follow the initiations for the five wrathful Buddha-Herukas, their five Ḍākinīs, for the eight Keurima and the eight Phra-men-ma deities, the four animal-headed female Guardians of the second maṇḍala, for the purification of the four places of birth, and finally for the 28 powerful theriomorphic Ḍākinīs, in order to overcome any remaining false ideas or chimeras of consciousness. We shall give an explanatory overview of this central part of the important initiations, in which the Ādibuddha Samantabhadra stands in the dharmakāya above all deities as the experience of the clear light in the bardo of the moment of death. Only the sequence has been altered in the list (see table 9) in order to make clear the correspondences with the psychic centers.

Cakra or Center	Karmic Plane	The Deities of the Bardo	Initiations of the Three Stages of the Trikāya	The Three Stages of the Bardo
Brain-Center	Kāya sKu	Mahāśrī-Heruka with Prajñā (Yab-yum)	Sambhogakāya	Chos-nyid Bar-do
–		the Five Wrathful Buddha-Herukas	–	–

Cakra or Center	Karmic Plane	The Deities of the Bardo	Initiations of the Three Stages of the Trikāya	The Three Stages of the Bardo
–		The Five Prajñās of the Buddha Herukas	–	–
–		The Eight Keurima	–	–
–		The Eight Phra-men-ma	–	–
–		The Four Animal-headed Female Guardians	–	–
–		the 28 Powerful Animal-headed Ḍākinīs	–	–
Throat-Center	Vāc gSung	The Five Vidyā-dharas with Prajñā (Yab-Yum)	–	–
Heart-Center	Citta Thugs	The Ādibuddha Samantabhadra (Yab-Yum)	Dharmakāya	'Chi-kha'i Bar-do
Heart-Center	Citta Thugs	The Five Tathā-gatas	Sambhogakāya	Chos-nyid Bar-do
		The Five Prajñās of the Tathāgatas		
		The Eight Bodhi-sattvas		
		The Eight Ḍākinīs of the Bodhisattvas		
		The Six Buddhas of the Bhavacakra	Nirmāṇakāya	
		The Four Guardians with Prajñā (Yab-Yum)	Sambhogakāya	
Navel-Center	Guṇa Yon-tan	The Five Jñānaḍākinīs	A Supplemented Bar-do Maṇḍala according to Certain Traditions (see note 77).	
Perineum	Karma 'Prin-las	The Magical Dagger-God Vajrakīla or Vajrakumāra (Yab-Yum)		

TABLE 9. Diagram of the initiations of the bardo deities. This arrangement corresponds to the psychic centers where the bardo visions appear.

Fig. 14. The supplemented great maṇḍala of the 117 deities of the Tibetan Book of the Dead. Tibetan block print. The peaceful deities appear in circles of light, the wrathful deities among flames.

6. Signs in the Transition between the Two Worlds and the Primordial Light at the Onset of Death

> A farness overtakes one when the sun sinks into the immeasurable, and the dear and welcome night arrives. At no moment, I believe, would one more easily die.
>
> W. V. HUMBOLDT

ACCORDING to the Buddhist teachings of the Tibetan Book of the Dead, man reaches the zenith of his life at its end, at the moment of death and a short time beyond it. This notion may well have justification if we take two things as essential to the end of life. These are the final and personal stage of psychic individuation, and the awaiting of the great unknown which we characterize by the concept of death. If we read the Tibetan Books of the Dead, we get the impression that in Asia they have almost looked beyond death; and although only speculative, this vision yet seems to have an uncanny reality. There is in any case something unbelievably convincing in the Tibetan's expectations about death and the beyond and in his recognition of the highly numinous and extremely ambivalent power that manifests itself in death. The events are described with such penetrating clarity, it is as if they could not possibly be otherwise. What is certain is that considerable empathetic powers are there as well as a precognitive kind of thinking that goes beyond the everyday.

If we choose to exercise our Western and seemingly modern way of thinking and brand the contents of the Tibetan Book of the Dead as merely the result of the magical-mythical world view of the Tibetans—a fine and scholarly kind of rationalization—the problem of death is thereby neither illuminated nor solved. We easily fall prey to the deceptive conclusions of pure thinking, by means of which we believe we can easily overlook simple reality. But the problem remains. Whatever kinds of apparitions and visions, transformations, torments and exaltations, terrors and salvation may or may not occur in the bardo—that remains to be seen. Nevertheless, the subtle knowledge to be found in the writings of the Tibetan Book of the Dead concerning dying and experiences in guiding souls still presents us with much that is concretely and psychologically valuable. The introductory quotation from von Humboldt shows (and it is by no means alone in this) the way in which premonitions and experiences of death concur in the oldest writings and the most recent contemporary testimonies. Myth, religion, history, and personal biography bring before our eyes presentiments of the realm of death in similar primordial images, and this correspondence indicates a psychic reality, though without proving it. Precisely for this reason, the ancient Tibetan sages, who were not merely scholars but were also men of experience, focused their strongest powers of imagination towards representing the events of death and of the period immediately after it. From careful observation of people dying, they were able to compile a sufficient amount of experience which, together with the Buddhist teachings, formed a handbook of living and dying which has an extraordinarily tight psychological structure.

We mentioned earlier that a person should maintain the clearest presence of mind at the moment of death, so that he may have all the power of his unified spirit at his disposal when the first step into the world of the unknown must be taken. There he needs all his powers in order gradually to re-attain awareness on the trans-physical plane of the bardo. The process of dying and of the entry into the sphere of the bardo is portrayed in the Book of the Dead in detail. The relevant passage was translated and commented upon by Evans-Wentz (pp. 89–97). We shall therefore not repeat all the descriptions but shall rather bring out those points that are of particular psychological interest. Among these are the decline of the physical organization with the allegory of the elements, and the "clear light."

According to the tradition of the "Six Doctrines" of the Indian siddha Nāropa, as well as the work Ye-shes bla-ma,[80] the process of dying is a kind of regression back through the elements, in which they, in their vital functions as composite physical organic entities, collapse step by step into themselves. Seen from the buddhological point of view, this is the dissolution and decline of the five skandhas (T. Phung-po lnga) through the disintegration of the five elements (T. 'Byung-ba lnga). With the dissolution of the outer functions in this world of existence there begins the dawning of an other-worldly sphere in the innermost center of human awareness through the experience of the "clear light." The process is quite similar to that of attaining samādhi in the highest, most unified state of meditation. The more the outer world sinks away as a result of concentration, and mind and spirit center in themselves, the more light and self-reflection of awareness occur. The highest awareness is therefore also enlightenment, the light of knowledge. This is why we said in agreement with the Tibetan Book of the Dead that the event of samādhi in life is comparable to the experience of the clear light in the bardo. If we accept the hypothesis of the clear light of the first bardo, then the psychological parallels of the two manifestations of awareness are striking.

We shall once again briefly outline the event of dying according to the doctrine of the bardo state from the traditions of Nāropa and the Kaṃ-tshang tradition of Tibet.[81]

> Firstly the light of the eye disappears and the forms become blurred, then the powers of hearing are extinguished and one hears sound no more. Next, the sense of smell fails, followed by the sense of taste. Then the sense of one's body disappears and one can no longer feel anything by touch. Earth (the element) sinks into water (the element), and the water of the body can no longer be maintained. Water sinks into fire and dries out speech; fire sinks into air, and the warmth of the body dissipates. Then the element of wind sinks into awareness, and the outer and inner breath consume one another. Signs which were perceived in life as external, appear in time precisely as inner signs; the outer signs appear like the moon, and with the passage of time the inner signs appear as sparks of fire. Then the outer signs appear as the sun, and the inner as candlelight. Then the outer signs have the effect of being in darkness. Then, when one suddenly reaches the fourth stage and sinks into the clear light, the outer signs appear dim and distant, and one recognizes the inner signs as a peaceful and cloudless sky. In the absence of thinking and mental activity the clear light now appears, boundless and without a center. May the immutable clear light in the dharmakāya be perfected.

If we consider these three processes which succeed each other in the dying, we have first of all the physical-functional dissolution of all the senses ending with the discontinuation of perceived embodiment, secondly the dissolution of the bound elements (corresponding to psychological dissolution), and thirdly the intrapsychic illumination of awareness beyond death. In the second phase, earth sinks into water, water into fire, fire into air, and air into the awareness-principle. This is a continuous process of dematerialization and a visible progression from the heaviest element (earth) to the most spiritual. There are therefore always two opposites dissolving into elementary fusion, to the point where pure awareness remains and is freed from all attachments to the material world. When the last elements and their interrelated effects are dissolved, the clear light is experienced boundlessly in an all pervading, or nondimensional space. The nature of this experience of illumination will be described in more detail below.

If we want to present a clear diagram of the second, or elementary phase, we must take the basic schema of the Buddhist maṇḍala, consisting of a square with the "five directions" as the locations of the elements (see fig. 15). In this form it is the basis of the cosmic world and of the elemental, microcosmic structure of man. Each triangle corresponds to an element. In the process of dying, two triangles (elements) always merge, until, at the end, the center, the location of ethereal awareness, is left.

At the end of the elemental dissolution, the state of infinite awareness begins; it becomes free and experiences boundless iden-

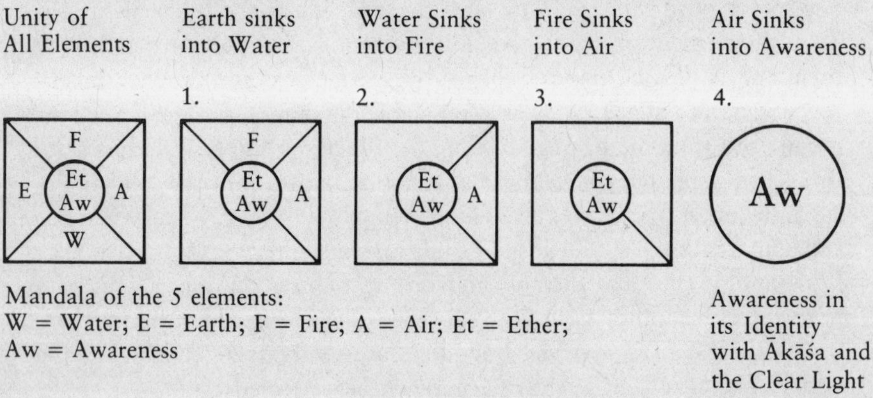

Fig. 15. The dissolution of the maṇḍalas of the elements in the process of death.

tity with the ether-element, which is like the blue autumn sky, and at the same time it experiences in the ether the boundless clear light. For this primary and most important stage three concepts are used synonymously: awareness, ether, and light. The last two are archetypal concepts or symbols for the spirit, not only in Asia, but also in the Western world.

The third phase of the outer and inner signs also has five stages and makes it clear that ultimately the inner space of awareness develops into the infinite, that it grows into a new dimension as the so-called external world ends. It is a self-representation of awareness (table 10).

	1	2	3	4	5
Outer World	Similarity of Signs	Moon	Sun	Darkness	Dissolution of Objects
Inner World	Similarity of Signs	Sparks	Candlelight	Light	Boundless Sky of Clear Light

TABLE 10

From this description we could say that for the Tibetans it was a certainty that after death, awareness enters into a state of boundlessness. It is described as an identity with the world-totality of transcendence; it is sky, light, and the great emptiness simultaneously. Salvation in the sense of the Mahāyāna scriptures is therefore the attainment of the condition of the great emptiness, the synonym of nirvāṇa for the Mahāyāna. This emptiness is not, however, a nihilistic form of nothingness but is a positive concept for something that transcends all possibility of description. To this extent the stage of emptiness (of all conceptual dimensions) is the realm of deathlessness, where there is neither coming nor going. From the writings about the problem of death in the pre-Buddhist Bon religion of Tibet,[82] whose bardo deities we shall describe later, we shall take the following very realistic text which portrays the desolate situation of death but does not forget to indicate the great perfection:

> Today the earthly sojourn is ended, and flesh and bones, hitherto inseparable, are parted.

Birth, old age, illness, and death are the origin of all suffering. After death everything decomposes back into the earth. Everything is devoured by birds, dogs, foxes, wolves, worms, and flies.

There, all religious worship is without purpose. Bones become like stone, flesh becomes earth, blood becomes water, and cavities become air; and the spirit is like the emptiness of the heavens.

What is said to happen after death may not seem much to us, since infinite emptiness is for us a negative concept. It takes the wisdom of a mystic to be able to intuit the positive aspect of emptiness, the ineffability of the infinite and the transcendent, that positive realm which lies beyond the range of words and concepts. This space without support or dimensions, the entry into death, is characterized by the all pervading radiant inner light, which from countless texts must be considered identical with the occurrence of perfect enlightenment and awareness. It is interesting to consider here the Egyptian Book of the Dead, since there too, death is immediately followed by entry into the "clear light of day," prior to the events associated with a renewed becoming-conscious.

In the first bardo, the 'Chi-kha'i bar-do, the person for the first time experiences briefly the state of "only awareness without a second," namely pure consciousness without embodiment. We are admittedly unable to prove this, which to our way of thinking is only a hypothesis, but we can theoretically think it through in order to appreciate its significance. The Tibetan Book of the Dead has already taken this step and has in some respects gone further. Looked at from the psychological point of view we have no concrete idea of how the two forms of conscious and unconscious might interact when dematerialized. We do not even know if they continue to interact, or even if they continue to exist at all. In short, we are unable to speculate about the unknown, for it transcends all scientifically provable occurrences.

Nevertheless, the Tibetan Book of the Dead demands that we go further. In the Western world we venture the astonishing and yet logical and justifiable hypothesis of a pre-natal psychology. That is to say that we concern ourselves with knowledge about conscious process before physical birth. We thereby begin to approach the well known question of the Zen Buddhist koan: What was your face before you were born? Buddhism developed a rich psychology (above all in the Abhidharma of Aśvaghoṣa) which described a great variety of states of awareness for which we in the West do not have the adequate conceptual apparatus, for we lack subtlety with regard to self-representations of awareness. However, the Tibetans believed that they could equally define forms of awareness that occur during the time after death. In the Tibetan Book of the Dead several traditions—Indian, Tibetan, and central Asian—flow together. Many of the forms of soul guidance are reminiscent of the practice of central Asian shamanistic rites and of other forms of deities and symbolic systems which appear to be related to the Bon religion of ancient Tibet. We must consider these forms of manifestation of awareness that go beyond our normal understanding of things. This is not intended as an evaluation of our performance and achievements in the humanistic sciences but is a necessary affirmation of different facts that have their validity in the East. We could also say that the East proceeds from a recognition of different psychic realities than does the Western world.

The scholar and sister of the great Indian yogi and siddha Nāropa was Niguma. In her version of the "Six Doctrines" (T. Zah-lam sukha chos drug)[83] she wrote: "The darkness of ignorance is illumined by the sun of the clear light." If the dead person has become wise in the bardo, he should prepare himself for attaining proper access to the knowledge of reality of the bardo visions. Therefore Niguma admonishes: "Strive zealously toward the hidden (secret) pathway to the great sphere beyond, where the visions of the bardo appear in the magnificent sambhogakāya." Therefore "one's body becomes like a rainbow of divine light and emptiness, outwardly a heavenly realm, and inwardly divine beings appear. Meditate upon a high mantra and the clear light of unborn reality."

The clear light plays an extraordinary role in the symbolism of the bardo experience: it is the "radiance from the seed of emptiness, the radiance in the realm of knowing, and the light of self-generating wisdom."[84] As the coming of light, it is an archetypal symbol of the many myths from the emergence of the conscious world; it is a presupposition of every kind of knowledge and extension of awareness and is a characteristic of spontaneous and natural processes of consciousness. According to the various texts of the Tibetan Books of the Dead, the experience of the clear light signifies full entry into the light of dharmakāya, which is itself entirely knowledge, and this becomes by means of light the pinnacle of experience. In Zen Buddhism one therefore talks of the lightning-like flash of satori.

The Tibetan texts say that complete and perfected awareness, a consciousness that is totally pervaded by light, is a precondition of the state of dharmakāya. If this perfect awareness is not attained, there will be parts that remain unconscious, which then as ignorance (S. avidyā) cause the descent into the bardo. Death is, therefore, before the person experiences it totally, a sinking of bodily phenomena into a state of nonfunctioning. This is of significance from the biological-medical point of view. The second phase of the elemental dissolution assumed in Tibet is of unknown duration. But true death is that highest experience of light that no longer has anything to do with this world of suffering. Thus, for the Tibetan Book of the Dead the entry into the death state is accompanied by an extremely positive event, which becomes all the more important if through it liberation can be attained simultaneously, without having to cross the bardo once again.

If the "primordial clear light" (T. gZhi'i 'od-gsal) coincides with a perfectly detached and karmically pure awareness, the "unborn dharmakāya" has been attained. One reaches the realm beyond all becoming, the deathless realm. This is an important meditation practice, which should be actualized under the aspect of the five Buddhas. The so-called fivefold path of light in the Book of the Dead is the path of the five radiant wisdoms of the Tathāgatas; the fivefold rainbow-like radiance forms, in its unity, the clear primordial light. Meditation on light is one of the most important exercises in the various schools of Tibetan Yoga. The more these psychic and spiritual powers can be achieved during life, the stronger is the ability to penetrate and overcome in the bardo.

"If the indivisible clear light of one's own spirit that appears in radiance and emptiness endures in the five skandhas, this is then the imperishable clear light of the unborn and immortal buddhas."[85] The manifestation of the clear light has been subdivided into five stages in the recognition of extremely subtle processes in experience. In a Tibetan work about the clarification of all meanings of the bardo the dawning of the clear light from the center of awareness is outlined in five stages:[86]

> In the first, one catches sight of it in its fivefold radiance like a visionary reflection; in the second it is like a moon; in the third like the sun; in the fourth it is like a dawning. These are the signs of the clear light, and then in the fifth stage it itself appears like the cloudless vault of heaven.

The first clear primordial light has great intensity and the power of transformation into liberation; the second primordial light (T. 'Od-gsal gnyis-pa) appears with lesser intensity and is of longer duration. Yet from this stage as well, the awareness-body of the dead person can find its way toward liberation, for the process is hindered only by slight karmic taints as the effects of the previous life. If during this period there is no breakthrough into the higher spheres of the dharmakāya, gradually the visions of the deities begin to dawn. Day by day in increasing fullness the great maṇḍala of the peaceful deities unfolds, until the second phase commences with the appearance of the maṇḍala of the terrifying deities who are to test and purify the awareness. "The awareness wanders through the bardo like a lost dog," and in this condition the deities can contribute in their ambivalent symbolism to guidance and refusal, to knowledge and reactions of flight, which bring the dead person back to an incarnation. But all reactions of awareness to the various appearances of the deities are processes that are determined by karma and by the spiritual capabilities the person has acquired during his previous life.

Before we come to consider the heroic peaceful and wrathful deities and their individual meanings, we should say something more about the duration of the bardo state as hypothesized in the various Tibetan texts. It is generally accepted that the total time of the intermediate state between two successive earthly incarnations is 49 days. The various cycles of emanation of the deities divide this time into a rhythm that is always determined by the number seven. After three to four days the awareness-body has newly formed itself again and completely left its body of earthly life. The Yid-kyi lus is absolutely capable of experiencing the events of the bardo, as if it were equipped with all the corresponding senses for earthly life. From the fourth until the eleventh day there is the successive emanation of the 42 peaceful bardo deities from out of the fivefold radiant light of the buddhas. From the twelfth until the nineteenth day the 58 terrifying deities take shape from out of the flames, and the journey through the Srid-pa'i bar-do lasts three times seven days, twenty-one days in all. The last seven days are dedicated to the search for the place of rebirth which is supposed to take place on the eighth day. From a state of the highest experience in the 'Chi-ka'i bar-do, the awareness slowly sinks down through the realms of visions back into a state of unconsciousness and ignorance, which leads to rebirth in the bhavacakra. But if the karmic pre-conditions are better than in the previous existence, the incarnation can take place under better omens for evolution.

1. 'Chi-ka'i Bar-do		The Experience of the Primordial (Clear Light)
2. 3 to 4 Days		Unconscious State and Formation of the Awareness-Body for the Path through the Bardo
3. 4th to 11th Day	Chos-nyid	Vision of the 42 Peaceful Deities
4. 12th to 19th Day	Bar-do	Vision of the 58 Wrathful Deities
5. 20th to 41st Day	Srid-pa'i Bar-do	Journey through the bardo and the Experience of the Worlds of Hell
6. 42nd to 49th Day	Srid-pa'i Bar-do	The Search for the Appropriate Place of Rebirth

TABLE 11

III

The Great Ritual of the Initiations into the Maṇḍalas of the Peaceful and Wrathful Deities

1. The Peaceful Deities

> The only place of becoming divine that is accessible to us is the human heart, as a true part of this transcendent process itself.
>
> G. R. HEYER

THE VISIONARY apparitions from the bardo with which awareness is confronted after death, are of a fascinating and terrifying, unattractive form. As numinous figures they contain within themselves the most extreme antinomies of meaning and seem to be unbridgeable manifestations of polarity itself. Yet in this extreme polar opposition they are only various manifestations of the same phenomenon, namely, of human awareness. They appear with such a forceful and convincing effect of psychic reality that it is impossible to overlook them or to rationalize them away.

However, we must always bear in mind the contention of the Tibetan Book of the Dead that in all phenomenological reality the bardo deities are not gods in the traditional sense. They are not to be relegated to any heavenly or under-worldly realms of spatial dimensions, nor are they mythological figures that are supposed to fulfill a mythological or soteriological purpose. Morever, the bardo visions are not to be understood as the forms of emanation of a god or of his hierarchical order. They are also not a theophany but a psychic reality, a primordial imaginal manifestation of numinous powers, which occur as images in the inner space of human awareness and also out from this (as projections). Therefore they are called "illusory images of one's own mind," or "illusory" figures, or even "visions." Even as such visionary deities of one's own mind, they yet have the character of a psychic reality. The deities of the afterdeath visions are an intra-psychic occurrence, represented by archetypal symbols of the Buddhist tradition, which were practically proven as spiritual realities in the great maṇḍalas. In particular, the five Tathāgatas are primordial images of the corresponding wisdoms, of Buddhist virtues, of cosmological and psychological relationships which were brought together in the five skandhas of the human personality.

However, the deities of the bardo also appear as a reply to karma, the self-perpetuated and personal fate of the individual, and so they become in the bardo an image of the personal situation of awareness on the path towards karmically conditioned rebirth. We shall have to come back to this foundational aspect of the bardo deities again. The function of the Tibetan Book of the Dead must be understood against the background of the answer to one of the most fateful of man's questions, as a profound answer to the question of death and the beyond, an answer which touches the transcendent. To make connections with mythology would from this point of view miss the true point of the Tibetan Book of the Dead. The deities of the bardo are not mythological and therefore occupy a special place in the pantheon of the deities of Buddhism, since they are attributed no reality for earthly existence. This is specifically true of the wrathful deities, who are hardly shown in representations of the pantheon.

All bardo deities are manifestations of a "combination of radiance and emptiness"; they come "from the realm of pure self-nature" and appear "in the sphere of the precious own mind,"[87] after in the bardo of the experience of death the clear primordial light has first been illuminated "in the boundless mind." We find many similar definitions of the nature of the deities in the Tibetan texts.

All visionary deities appear on a lotus in a posture (S. āsana) of sitting, standing, or moving. The lotus (S. padma) is a symbol of heavenly ecstasy, an unearthly throne, a symbol of unfolding from the cakras and from the center of awareness, and its purpose is to establish in the mind a heavenly throne for the deities. The lotus signifies that the deities have overcome the cycle of suffering in saṃsāra and are far from the world of suffering. The peaceful buddhas and bodhisattvas appear on a lotus-moon throne of the heart maṇḍala, and the wrathful deities appear on a lotus-sun throne of the forehead maṇḍala. The peaceful deities radiate in the five elemental colors, and the wrathful deities stand in a blazing aureole of flames. Two ancient symbolic relationships with Indian Yoga are evident in this, namely the cosmologically related sun-and-moon-significance of the deities and of the psychic powers in

Plate 1

Plate 2

a

b

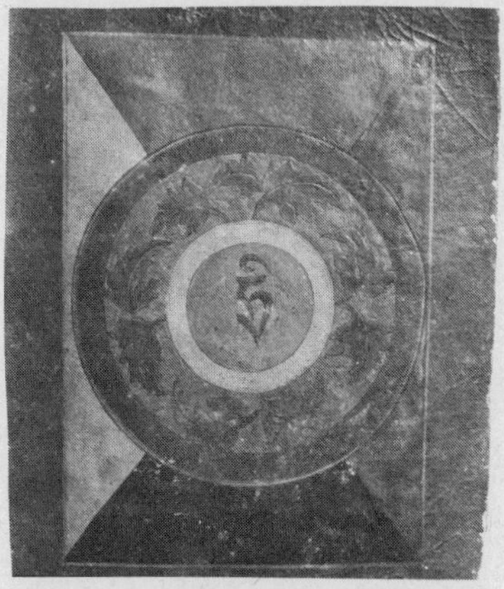

c

d

e

f

Plate 3
a–f

Plate 4

a

b

c

d

Plate 5 a–d

a

b

c

d

Plate 6 a–d

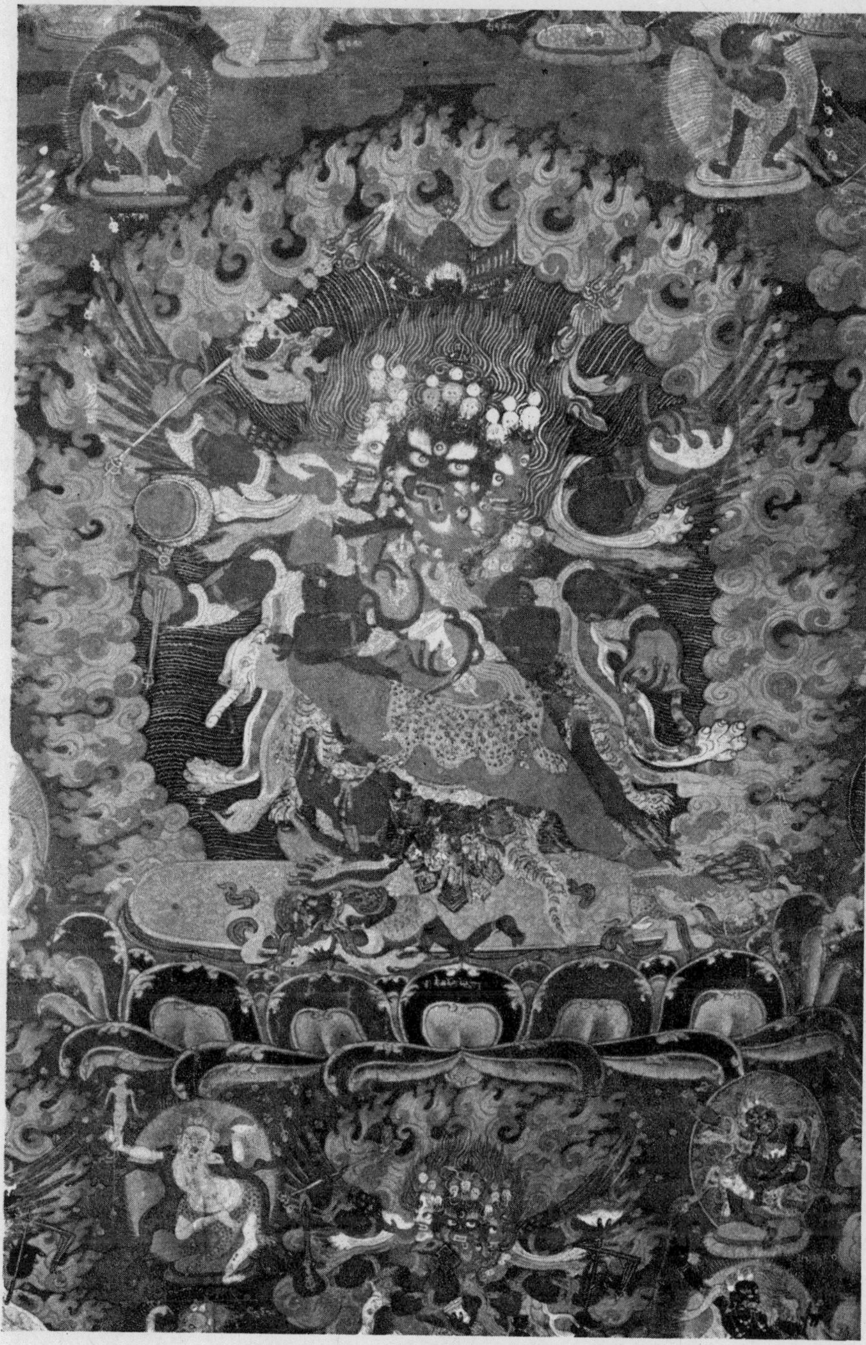

Plate 7

Plate 8

Plate 9

Plate 10

Plate 11

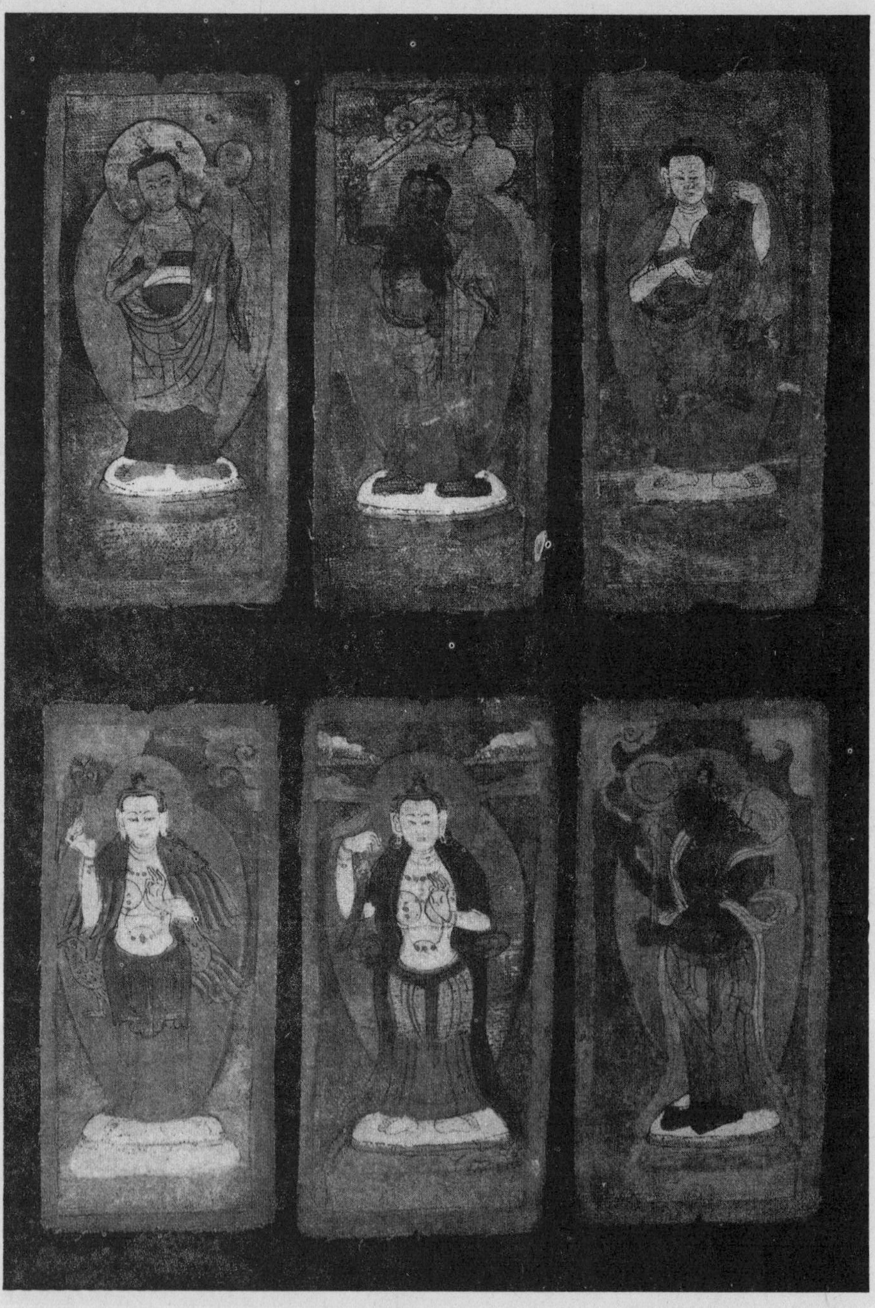

Plate 12

Plates

Plate 1. The assembly of the 42 peaceful deities of the bardo maṇḍala (T. Zhi-ba'i lha-tshogs). In the center is the Ādibuddha Samantabhadra in mystical union with his white prajñā. He sits on a lotus above the lion-throne and holds a golden vessel (T. Rin-chen bum-pa) for the initiation into the divine visions (T. lha-dbang) of the peaceful and wrathful deities. Above him are the five Vidyādhara and three of the six Buddhas of the bhavacakra; the other three Buddhas are standing at the bottom of the picture. In the four corners of the picture we find the four Guardians. Grouped around the Ādibuddha we recognize the five Tathāgatas with their accompanying Mahābodhisattvas and their Ḍākinīs.

Tibetan thanka in the Kun-bzang-brag monastery in Bum-thang at the birthplace of the treasure-discoverer gTer-ston Padma gling-pa.

Plate 2. Tibetan thanka portraying the 58 wrathful deities of the bardo maṇḍala (T. Khro-bo'i lha-tshogs). In addition we see the blue Ādi-buddha Samantabhadra (above center), and the great, red-brown Che-mchog Heruka as his terrifying emanation in the center of the visions. He is accompanied by the five Buddha-Herukas as wrathful emanations of the five Tathāgatas. The eight Keurima appear in radiant aureoles, as well as the eight Phra-men-ma and the 28 powerful, animal-headed Ḍākinīs.

Tibetan painting from Kun-bzang-brag in Bum-thang.

Plate 3. In the ceremonies of the ritual recitation of the Book of the Dead and the guiding of the dead person's awareness through the bardo, initiation cards (T. Tsa-ka-li) are used, and these are mostly painted in colors. To these belong also the maṇḍalas of the six realms of incarnation (T. Rigs-drug dkyil-'khor). In the center of each maṇḍala is the mantric seed-syllable of the "place of birth." The six worlds of incarnation are those of the gods, titans or demi-gods, human beings, animals, pretas, and denizens of hell.

Plate 4. This painting shows the white Buddha Vajrasattva (T. rDo-rje sems-dpa') as the mystical revealer of all visionary deities of the Tibetan Book of the Dead. In the heart-center the maṇḍala of the 42 peaceful deities appears with the blue Ādibuddha in the center. In the forehead-center the maṇḍala of the 58 wrathful deities unfolds as emanations of the intellect. Both are opposing aspects of the Numinous as reflections in the mind on the plane of human awareness, in which karma is originated and suffered. These visions are to be unified and penetrated as visionary manifestations of the great emptiness. The essence of liberation in pure transcendence is beyond all images and visions, which are themselves only a radiant imaginal expression of transcendence. The Buddha Vajrasattva carries the vajra and the ghaṇṭā, the ritual symbols and implements of Buddhism, as attributes, representing the way of the gnostic unity of method, or path (vajra = upāya), and goal, or wisdom (ghaṇṭā = prajñā). Gnosis is prajñopāya, in which the opposites of a self-conditioned polarity attain a higher unity.

Plate 5. Four initiation cards for the recitation of the death-ceremonies of the Kar-gling zhi-khor: (a) the Buddha Vajrasattva (Yab-Yum); (b) the Tathāgata Vairocana with the initiation symbols, vajra, ghaṇṭā, kalaśa, and buddha-crown (T. rDo-rje, Dril-bu, Zhi-khro lha-tshogs rin-chen bum-pa, and dBu-rgyan; (c) the five Tathāgatas or Meditation-Buddhas; (d) the four female guardians as Ḍākinīs of the male guardians of the maṇḍala conclude the peaceful visions of the bardo deities.

Plate 6. Four initiation cards for the death ritual. The first picture (a) shows the wrathful Che-mchog Heruka, with whose appearance the visions of the wrathful deities begin. In (b) we see the Ḍākinīs of the five wrathful Buddha-Herukas. Picture (c) shows the four theriomorphic Ḍākinīs as the guardians (T. sGo-ma bzhi); these are the snake-headed, lion-headed, horse-headed, and boar-headed Ḍākinīs. In (d) we see the eight Keurima as the wrathful counterparts to the eight Bodhisattvas from the maṇḍala of the peaceful deities.

Plate 7. The great and terrible Che-mchog Heruka as the emanation of the Ādi-buddha, who on the eight day of the bardo visions opens the maṇḍala of the wrathful deities. He appears in tantric union with his Ḍākinī Krodheśvarī upon a lotus in front of an aureole of flames. The red-brown Heruka with the garuḍa-wings has three heads, six arms, and four legs. As symbols he carries the khaṭvāṅga, ḍarmaru, kapāla, a sling made of innards, as well as a vajra and ghaṇṭā.

Detail from the painting in Plate 2, from Bum-thang.

Plate 8. The Great Maṇḍala of the hundred peaceful and wrathful deities of the Bar-do thos-grol. In the center is the blue Ādibuddha Samantabhadra with his white Prajñā. Below him we see against a background of hilly countryside the 40 peaceful deities (without the five Vidyādharas). The sky is filled with the 58 terrifying emanations of the bardo deities, led by the five Buddha-Herukas at top center. The middle Heruka is the dPal-chen Buddha-Heruka, who appears on the eighth day of the bardo visions (see Evans-Wentz, *Tibetan Book of the Dead,* p. 137). The wrathful Ḍākinīs and animal-headed deities appear amidst lambent flames in a vital and dynamic, but strictly measured, rhythm which is characteristic of the fine art of Tibetan tantric iconography, especially in the rNying-ma-pa tradition.

Plate 9. A high point in the death ritual is the symbolic guiding of the dead person through the six worlds of the bhavacakra, in which the six Buddhas appear as emanations of the Bodhisattva Avalokiteśvara. The Tibetan thanka shows in the center the four-armed Avalokiteśvara (T. sPyan-ras-gzigs), who as the Bodhisattva of great compassion lets the six Buddhas appear as emanations in the various realms of existence. On the left we recognize the three Buddhas of the worlds of human beings, titans, and gods, and on the right those of the worlds of animals, pretas, and denizens of hell. Avalokiteśvara too is an emanation, from the heavenly eye of the red Buddha Amitābha (immeasurable light), who is at the center of the upper part of the picture, while at his sides can be seen siddhas and lamas of the rNying-ma-pa sect. So we have in this picture the whole trikāya structure symbolized in the deities: Buddha Amitābha as the dharmakāya, Bodhisattva Avalokiteśvara as the sambhogakāya, and the six Buddhas as incarnations on the level of the nirmāṇakāya in the form of saviors in the six worlds.

Plate 10. A red-brown, demonic Mahākāla as the powerful and temporal aspects of the great wisdom holds the bhavacakra (T. Srid-pa'i 'khor-lo) with representations of the six worlds of incarnation and the twelve self-conditioning dependencies of the nidānas (T. rTen-'brel yan-lag bcu-gnyis), which are sketched on the outer ring. The "three poisons" or cardinal failings of human behavior are symbolized in the center by the cock, the snake, and the pig. They occasion the black path that leads down to the hells, or in the case of full enlightenment, the white path that leads up to the realm of the immeasurable light of Buddha Amitābha in sukhāvatī (above left), to which the Buddha (above right) is pointing. The six worlds of incarnation are those of the gods (above) with the cosmic Mount Sumeru; of the demigods or titans (left), who are striving to fell the tree of knowledge, the top of which is blooming with fruit in the realm of the gods; then the world of human beings (right); beneath this the world of the pretas; opposite this the world of animals; and at the bottom the world of hells. In this world we recognize a bridge crossing over the river of hell, the court of hell presided over by the judge Dharmarāja, the great rack of the fire-vessel, and the eight hot and eight cold hells.

Modern Tibetan painting from an earlier print, with very precise execution of the details.

Plate 11. We rarely find Tibetan portrayals of individual scenes of the happenings in the worlds of hell. Here in the greater part of the picture we see the judge of death Dharmarāja in his hellish palace presiding over the dead souls. The huge figure of Dharmarāja is red, and he is holding the sword in his right hand and the mirror of justice in his left. He is sitting on a throne and is resting his feet upon a lotus. In front of him are the white and black "simultaneously born geniuses," who are shaking out the white and black stones from their sacks onto separate piles. The scribe of the deeds is here an animal-headed deity. Before them are standing various people to be tried. To the right of the scribe the white stones are being weighed on the scale against an iron weight. At the bottom to the right and the left we see the various hellish tortures, from glowing fires to freezing cold, and also the sufferings in the woods of sword-leaf trees. In the center the animal-headed demons are stoking the fire under a huge kettle full of suffering souls. At top left we recognize the illuminated path of people who have attained release and are proceeding towards the western paradise of Buddha Amitābha.

Plate 12. As in the Buddhist death rituals, we also find an ordered pantheon of bardo deities in the ancient Bon religion. On the six initiation cards we see, in the upper row, dSang-ba ngang-ring, LCe-rgyal par-ti, and Lha'i thub-pa, who are the three Buddhas as gShen-rab-emanations for the worlds of hells, of titans, and of gods. Just as the Bon-po Books of the Dead talk of six Buddhas of the Srid-pa'i 'khor-lo, they similarly know a kind of "bodhisattva," here called Ye-gshen gyung-drung sems-dpa'. The lower pictures show three of these. The symbols and colors of these deities are different from the Buddhist ones, but otherwise the layperson could hardly distinguish them from Buddhist bardo deities.

Plates

Front Cover. The blue Ādibuddha Samantabhadra as the highest dharmakāya and pure awareness is the highest deity of the Tibetan Book of the Dead. Tibetan painting from dKor-rdzogs in Ladakh.

Back Cover. The initiations into the visions of the Tibetan Book of the Dead conclude with strongly abstract symbols. Among these are the sign of initiation into the highest knowledge (T. Sher-dbang), with the sword, the peacock feathers, and the five radiant lights of the Tathāgatas, which dissolve into pure elemental radiance. All visions are merely forms of one's own awareness, and their dissolution at the end is a precondition of perfect liberation on the imageless plane of pure knowledge. Initiation card for the ritual of the Bar-do thos-grol from Tibet.

ACKNOWLEDGEMENTS

All the drawings, reproductions, and photographs are by the author, with the exception of the following: Figures 1, 10, 11, 14, 16, and 25 are from block prints in the collection of Professor Spiegelberg, San Francisco. Figures 12 and 13 as well as plates 10 and 11 are from private collections in New York. Plates 4, 8, and 9 are from private collections in Stuttgart; Plate 12 is by kind permission of the Bavarian State Library in Munich, and Figure 26 is from a drawing of the Bon-po monastic center in Dolanji, India.

man himself. This doctrine plays an important role in the practice of Kuṇḍalinī Yoga and in the Tantras for the representation of esoteric polarity-symbolism.

Let us begin with the spectacle of the peaceful deities: "In the innermost center of the sphere of the spirit in one's own body there is a concentration of the radiance of the five lights, and from its center appears the assembly of the 42 peaceful deities."

These 42 peaceful deities begin with the group of the five Tathāgatas. Above this in the highest rank stands the blue Ādibuddha as pure dharmakāya and as the primordial image and the quintessence of all further emanations. We shall describe him first.

A. THE ĀDIBUDDHA AS THE MYSTICAL CREATOR OF THE MAṆḌALA

As the highest, only thinkable form of the primordial spectacle of the spirit, we find in the Tibetan Book of the Dead the dark blue Ādibuddha Samantabhadra (T. Kun-tu bzang-po), whose image is theoretically not portrayable. Therefore, the Tibetan texts which describe the nature of the Ādibuddha are full of symbolic concepts and transcendent ideas, the depth of which can hardly be adequately expressed in our language. As a first concretion of the envisioned transcendent body in the dharmakāya, the Ādibuddha Samantabhadra is portrayed sitting on a lotus without any kind of robes and in a pure deep blue color. An ancient Tibetan fragment from the writings of the Tibetan Book of the Dead[88] calls the Ādibuddha the "king of knowledge and wisdom," who "originated spontaneously from spirit," and who has his origin in the "pure and secret sphere of universal awareness" (S. ālayavijñāna; T. Kun-gzhi rnam-shes). The invocational text continues: "We invoke the (spiritual) father of all buddhas of the three ages, who brings about knowledge, who is pure and free from passions and sits without covering upon the lotus, and who possesses the mudrā of the omniscience that embraces all buddhas and creatures, the lord of all maṇḍalas, the exalted Śrī-Samantabhadra."

Another text from the Tibetan Books of the Dead describes the second vision of the Ādibuddha, the pure spectacle of the first tantric union of the great male-female polarity, in which the Ādibuddha appears with his white Prajñā Samantabhadrī (T. Kun-tu bzang-mo), the great mother and creator of all buddhas.[89]

> Glory to the Ādibuddha, the body of imperishable light, the lord of all buddhas of pure intellect and wisdom, whose color is like the sky's, and who sits on the lotus seat in composed concentration. We call upon the dharmakāya Samantabhadra. The Prajñā who produces all Buddhas of the three ages, who is as white as the crystal of all purest dharma-spheres, who is united in great bliss with the Buddha, we call upon the great mother Samantabhadrī.

This kind of invocation belongs to the sādhanas, the descriptive invocational texts about the buddhas and deities which accurately portray the imagery of the meditation. The Ādibuddha Samantabhadra in union with his white Prajñā is the most exalted figure in the visions of the Tibetan Book of the Dead; he is the highest dharmakāya principle in the tradition of the rNying-ma-pa sect, which goes back to its founder, Padmasambhava.

We encounter the blue Ādibuddha in almost all Tibetan paintings for the Tibetan Book of the Dead, either at the top or in the center of the picture. He often has an aura and five-colored bundles of rays radiating from his center out into the heavenly spheres. His white Prajñā also appears without clothing of any kind (T. ma-gos-pa) and in close tantric union with Samantabhadra; she is the "source of the origination of all maṇḍalas."

With the great symbol of the first tantric couple of the Ādibuddha, all subsequent deities begin to appear in a similar polarity-symbolism. The blue Ādibuddha in union with his Prajñā embodies the path of tantric gnosis (S. prajñopāya; T. thabs-shes), the synthesis of the polarity of path, or method (represented by the Buddha), and goal (prajñā). The path is the definite method for the attainment of knowledge, and the goal is wisdom, or the knowledge of appearance and emptiness. Since the Ādibuddha in his transcendent qualities is beyond all possibility of description, he is portrayed without clothing. His essential nature is pure knowledge, similar to the all-pervading universal- or ground-awareness (S. ālayavijñāna; T. Kun-gzhi rnam-shes); the pure nature of awareness is light, and therefore the Buddha is the color of the heavens—he is nondiscriminating universal-awareness. This color simile is reminiscent of the clear light of the first bardo. As the pure form of the highest dharmakāya state of transcendence, Samantabhadra wears neither robes nor heavenly adornment nor the buddha-crown of the sambhogakāya, which is found with all other deities of the bardo maṇḍala.

Before we come to the five Tathāgatas, we must describe Vajrasattva (T. rDo-rje sems-dpa'), the white Buddha called "Diamond nature," who is to be understood as the first emanation of the Ādibuddha in the sambhogakāya. He too may appear alone or in a tantric union with his Prajñā, Vajrasattvātmikā. Vajrasattva can be seen as one of the oldest symbolic figures of the "Diamond Teaching" of Vajrayāna Buddhism. He is the quintessence of diamond-nature or pure self-nature (S. svabhāva; T. Ngo-bo-nyid). Vajrasattva is also seen in his spiritual aspect in the transcendent realm of the dharmadhātu sphere. He appears in radiance and emptiness from the center of one's own spirit, white in color, and on a lotus throne. In his right hand he holds the vajra of wisdom and emptiness (T. Rig-stong rdo-rje) in front of his heart, and in his left hand he holds in his lap the ghaṇṭā (bell) of appearance and emptiness (T. sNang-stong dril-bu). Vajrasattva wears the heavenly ornaments of the magnificent sambhogakāya: he has the golden five-petalled buddha-crown (T. dBu-rgyan), white robes, and golden necklaces, arm- and ankle-bands. He sits upon a lotus in front of a radiant aureole. The aureole, or halo (S. prabhāmaṇḍala) indicates the transcendent and radiant nature of the meditation-Buddhas of the saṃbhogakāya. They are not to be understood as outmoded or mythical figures, but rather as symbolic primordial images of definite teachings, images placed in the elemental cosmic order of Buddhist wisdom. They are transcendent and come from the heavenly "inner sphere of one's own pure awareness" as projections of active imagination. They are projections of the immeasurable space of inner awareness into the cosmic spheres of a visionary heavenly space. These Buddhas are not then deities in the sense of gods but symbols of determinate levels of wisdom and awareness. The whole tantric richness of meaning of Vajrayāna Buddhism is embodied in Vajrasattva. For this reason the mystical presence of the Buddha Vajrasattva is invoked at the beginning of so many Tibetan initiations, from whose 108-syllable mantra the blessings of transcendental meditation for the four mystical bodies of the human microcosm unfold.

B. THE FIVE TATHĀGATAS (YAB-YUM)

At the center of all bardo visions stand the five Tathāgatas (T. rGyal-ba rigs lnga). They form a first pentad in the Buddhist maṇḍala, and in their comprehensive multiplicity of meaning they constitute a many-leveled background for the development of most of the esoteric teachings of Vajrayāna Buddhism. For the various

Fig. 16. Maṇḍala of the five Tathāgatas, with the other deities represented by inscriptions of their mantras in Sanskrit. Tibetan block print.

versions of the Tibetan Book of the Dead, which has its own tradition, they are the essence and the foundation for statements about the nature of man and his psychophysical structure, and they are at the same time primordial images for the spiritual path to transcendence and liberation. The doctrine of the five Tathāgatas concerns possibilities of clarification of awareness in this earthly life as well as the possibility of attaining the illuminated path of the wisdom of the Buddhas in the bardo. As a constant consequence of a five-fold symbolism, there continually appear in the maṇḍala of the five Tathāgatas other symbolic groupings related to that of the Buddhas. The square as the place of manifestation of all buddhas is enclosed by the flaming circle of the maṇḍala. It encloses the five points in the cosmic directions as the places of the buddhas and expresses the corresponding aspect of elemental (physicalistic), psychological, cosmological, philosophical, and meditative contents.

All maṇḍalas originate from the seed-syllables or bīja-mantras of the deities. During meditation upon these mantras, an elemental radiance of light develops, from which comes the image of the buddhas. In the mantric parts of the Tibetan Book of the Dead we find for all deities the corresponding seed-syllables and the mantras developed from these for the invocation of the Buddhas and the wrathful deities. In the following descriptions of the five Buddhas, which we shall present in an overview at the end of our discussion of the development of maṇḍala symbolism, we have taken our orientation from six different Books of the Dead,[90] although there are many other groupings. Our description draws heavily from texts handed down by the scholars Śrī Siṃha, Padmasambhava, Vimalamitra, and Karma gling-pa. For an in-depth study of the profound meaning of the five Tathāgatas, it is worthwhile to consult some of the secondary sources mentioned in the bibliography.[91]

C. THE BUDDHA VAIROCANA

The mantric syllable Oṃ radiates in a clear white light in the center of awareness, and from this arises the Buddha Vairocana (T. rNam-par snang-mdzad), the color of the white conch (T.

Dung-mdog). He sits on a lotus over a throne with a symbol of a white lion. He characteristically holds the wheel of the teachings in his right hand and the ritual bell (ghaṇṭā) in his left. The wheel of the teachings (S. dharmacakra) is a golden color and has eight spokes, which denote the eight-fold path of the Buddhist teachings (S. aṣṭamārga). Vairocana appears in inseparable tantric union with his female counterpart, or Prajñā, Ākāśadhātvīśvarī (T. Nam-mkha'i dbyings-phyug-ma). The Prajñā is the color of the moon and has the same hand symbols as the Buddha Vairocana. The Buddha rules over the realm of embodiment (S. rūpaskandha), the first of the five components of the human personality. Through meditation upon this Buddha the earthly and profane person is transformed into the universal body of the buddhas.[92] But as long as the total person is still attached to the world of impermanence, ignorance (S. avidyā; T. gTi-mug) prevents him from attaining knowledge. Wisdom, on the other hand, expands awareness into a space like the heavens, which consists of only the pure element of ether, over which Ākāśadhātvīśvarī, the Prajñā of the Buddha, rules. If the dead person in the bardo meditates upon the all-pervading wisdom of the dharma spheres of the Buddha Vairocana (S. dharmadhātujñāna; T. chos-dbyings ye-shes),[93] the hindrances of ignorance are thereby overcome. The awareness-body of the dead person attains union with Vairocana on the illuminated path of enlightenment. Vairocana[94] radiates in the blue light of ethereal awareness, with which in many texts he is identified.

D. THE BUDDHA AKṢOBHYA

From the deep blue rays of the mantric syllable Hūṃ, the blue Tathāgata Akṣobhya, the "Unshakeable" (T. Mi-bskyod-pa or Mi-'khrugs-pa), appears in the eastern quarter. In his left hand he holds the diamond scepter, or vajra, in his lap, or—according to other texts—in both hands, vajra and ghaṇṭā (bell). Usually two aspects are united in the Buddha Akṣobhya, namely, those of the white Buddha Vajrasattva and of the blue Akṣobhya as Vajrasattva-Akṣobhya (T. rDor-sems mi-bskyod-pa), which points to the unchangeability of the pure diamond-nature.

Akṣobhya appears in inseparable tantric union with the Prajñā Locanā (T. Sangs-rgyas spyan-ma), the ruler of the element water (T. Chu'i khams). She has the color of the vaiḍūrya-jewel and carries the same symbols as the Buddha. The Buddha Akṣobhya is associated with the plane of awareness (S. vijñānaskandha),[92] which manifests in the heart center in the dharmakāya. Man generates the greatest spiritual and mental contradiction through the vice of hatred (S. dveṣa; T. Zhe-sdang), which cuts him off from all possibility of union. From this arises base dualism and denial, which destroys the path towards peace of mind. In meditating upon Akṣobhya, the adept should attain "mirror-like wisdom" (T. Me-long lta-bu'i ye-shes),[95] in which all opposites are seen to be illusions. In the mirror of knowledge the opposites collapse into themselves, and all grounds for the duality of accepting and rejecting become brittle. The Buddha Akṣobhya radiates in the white, diamond-clear light of Vajrasattva.

E. THE BUDDHA RATNASAMBHAVA

The mantric seed-syllable Trāṃ radiates in beams of yellow light, and from this arises the yellow Buddha Ratnasambhava (T. Rin-chen 'byung-ldan) in the southern quarter. As symbols he holds the jewel (S. ratna) and the ghaṇṭā. He appears in tantric union with the yellow Prajñā Māmakī, who is associated with the element earth.

Of the five skandhas Ratnasambhava represents the function of feeling (S. vedanāskandha), and the meditation upon this Buddha serves to enlighten the third vice, pride, which arises from attachment to the I (S. ahaṃkāra; T. Nga-rgyal). Therefore this Buddha stands for the "wisdom of equality" (T. mNyam-nyid ye-shes),[96] for the law of the dharma is only of "one taste," in that all beings are seen as equal. The Buddha Ratnasambhava holds his right hand in the gesture of varadamudrā, the giving of the teachings, and his iconographic yellow color is the same as the Buddha of the human world, Śākyamuni. The precious jewel in his hand is often shown in its threefold form as the triratna. The triratna symbol unites the triad of Buddha, dharma, and saṅgha.

F. THE BUDDHA AMITĀBHA

From a beam of red light in the western quarter of the maṇḍala the mantric seed-syllable Hrīḥ appears, known as the invocational formula for the red Buddha Amitābha (T. 'Od-dpag-med or sNang-ba mtha'-yas). Amitābha is the Buddha of the "immeasurable shining light," and his color is red or copper-red. The symbols he holds are the eight-petalled lotus blossom and the ghaṇṭā. He sits in inseparable tantric union with his female counterpart, the Prajñā Pāṇḍarā (T. Gos dkar-mo) who is the color of a red-glowing crystal and wears a white robe. She too carries a lotus and ritual bell and rules over the element fire (T. Me'i-khams). The Buddha Amitābha is associated with the realm of discriminating perception (S. samjñāskandha) and holds both hands in the meditation gesture (S. dhyānamudrā) in his lap. His opposite is the human failing of desire (S. kāma, T. 'Dod-chags), which leads to constant attachment to and suffering in the world of impermanence. In order to overcome it, the "wisdom of clear sight" (T. Sor-rtogs ye-shes)[97] is necessary, by means of which the causes of karmic conditions can be recognized. The Buddha Amitābha is at the same time the ruler of the "Western Paradise," Sukhāvatī (T. bDe-ba can), which liberated souls hope to reach.

G. THE BUDDHA AMOGHASIDDHI

The last Buddha, Amoghasiddhi (T. Don-yod grub-ba), completes the maṇḍala. First the mantric syllable Āḥ appears from a green light in the northern quarter, and from this arises the figure of the Buddha Amoghasiddhi sitting on a lotus. His color is green and radiates like turquoise. As symbols he holds the crossed vajra (S. viśvavajra; T. rDo-rje rgya-gram) and the ghaṇṭā. His right hand is raised in a gesture of fearlessness and protection (S. abhayamudrā). Amoghasiddhi also appears in tantric union with his Prajñā Samayatārā (T. Dam-tshig sgrol-ma). Her color is also green, and she carries the same symbols; her realm is the element air (T. rLung-gi khams). The Buddha Amoghasiddhi is associated with the last of the five skandhas, the saṃskāras, which are the impulses of the will and intentions (T. 'Du-byed). As the last group in the maṇḍala they decide the person's fate, his future karma in the bardo and in the next incarnation. On the human side are greed and envy (S. īrṣya; T. Phrad-dog), which can be transformed by meditating upon the attributes of the Buddha Amoghasiddhi. This is the "wisdom of (karmic) perfection of deed," (T. Bya-grub ye-shes),[98] with the help of which all remaining karmic conditions can be loosened and finally overcome. Therefore Amoghasiddhi has the goddess of salvation, Tārā, as his Prajñā. In the Buddhist arrangement of psychic cakras she appears in the center of the perfection of all karmic activity (T. Phrin-las), which we called the sukhapālacakra.

Now the first great visionary maṇḍala of the Buddhas is completed and stands in its fivefold radiance before the spiritual eye of the spectating awareness, to which all the deities in the bardo will successively reveal themselves in such circles of light. We also know texts and representations in which the Buddhas carry only one symbol (i.e., they appear without the ghaṇṭā), and in which some of the arrangements are different; but in the interests of a clear overview we have omitted those variations.

We shall now present the meanings of the five Tathāgatas in separate stages as maṇḍalas (fig. 17). Consideration of the images always begins from the center and then proceeds to the east (always pictured at the bottom) and thence clockwise, ending at the north with the Buddha Amoghasiddhi.

1. The elemental maṇḍala shows the arrangements of the five elements and the four cosmic directions. It is an image of the cosmos as matter and also as man in his physical constitution. The elements are ether (Et), water (W), earth (E), fire (F), and air (A).

2. The second maṇḍala shows the arrangement of the colors for these elements and for the Buddhas. Blue and white can be used interchangeably. At the same time we have here the five lights of the Buddhas and their mantric seed-syllables.

3. The third maṇḍala is a picture of the profane man subjected to the passions. Ignorance and delusion are the causes of the "five poisons" (T. Dug-lnga), the counter-forces to the wisdom of the Buddhas.

4. In this maṇḍala we recognize the basic arrangement of the five Tathāgatas. The Ādibuddha Samantabhadra stands as the first vision above and outside the maṇḍala. Thus the maṇḍala is a first manifestation from the boundless universal-awareness of the Ādibuddha Samantabhadra in the dharmakāya.

5. If the person recognizes and actualizes the five wisdoms (T. Ye-shes lnga) of the five Tathāgatas, he then experiences the maṇḍala of wisdom (S. cittamaṇḍala). This is the maṇḍala of the enlightened and initiated person on a higher plane of knowledge. At this stage only concepts of the spiritual world appear as symbols.

6. In the maṇḍala of karmic activity (S. karmamaṇḍala) the wisdoms of the Buddhas are perfected in the five psychic centers which we called the five levels of the cakras or "bodies." This is therefore the maṇḍala of action as a prototype of activity proceeding from wisdom.

7. A comparison from Western alchemy shows cosmology and man in unity with it. The arrangement of the elements corresponds to the Tibetan. The drawing is from the Zainer Offizin in Augsburg from the year 1472.

With these six maṇḍalas we have learned a small portion of the symbolism of the five Tathāgatas. In such representations the symbols of the Buddhas, and their gestures, or mudrās, may also be shown, as well as the mantric seed-syllables or the corresponding points of color. In the concluding overview we shall present a table of symbols derived from the Tibetan secret teachings about the five Tathāgatas and the five Ḍākinīs (table 12). We shall place a small Tibetan drawing, which came to us from the will of a recently deceased Tibetan scholar, in the middle of our overview, and we shall be using it again later.

The drawing proceeds from the seven psychic centers, with the uppermost sphere lying in transphysical space above the skull. This is the maṇḍala of perfect wisdom in the Akaniṣṭha-Heaven (T. 'Og-min). The next five cakras which follow below contain the mantric syllables of the five Ḍākinīs, and at the sides are short descriptions of the locations of the cakras and the Buddha-

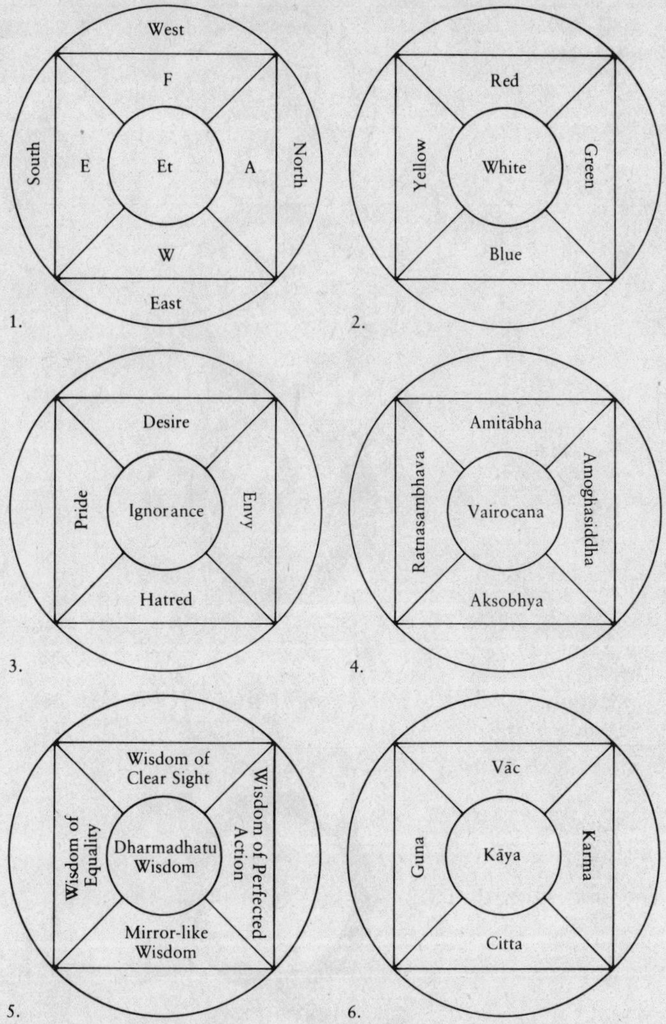

Alchemical diagram of the elements in relation to man, year, and world from a representation from the Zainer Cffizin in Angsburg 1472

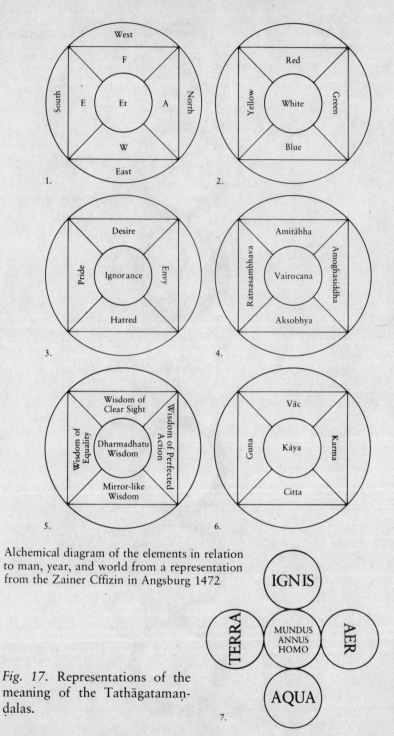

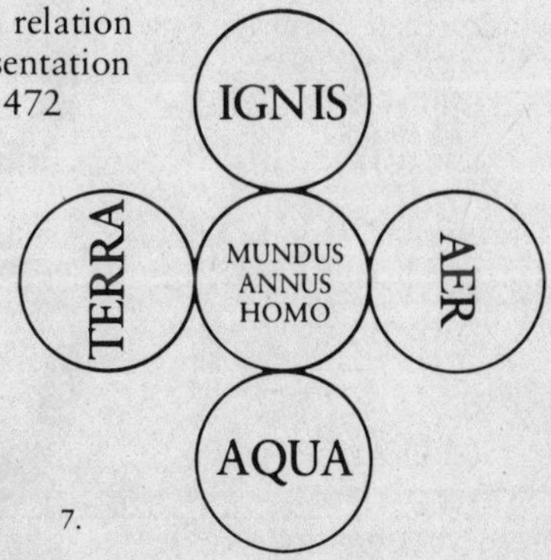

Fig. 17. Representations of the meaning of the Tathāgatamaṇḍalas.

Cakra or Level	Appearance of the Deities	The Mantras of the Buddhas and Ḍākinīs	
Body (Kāya) སྐུ	The 58 wrathful deities in the bardo	Oṃ	Laṃ
Speech (vāc) གསུང་	The 5 wisdom-possessing deities, vidyādhara, with Prajña	Hrīḥ	Paṃ
Heart (citta) ཐུགས་	The 42 peaceful deities in the bardo The Ādibuddha Samantabhadra	Hūṃ	Muṃ
Navel (guṇa) ཡོན་ཏན་	The 5 wisdom Ḍākinīs (T. Ye-shes mKha-'gro lnga)	Traṃ	Maṃ
Perineum (karma) འཕྲིན་ལས་	The magic dagger-deity Vajrākīla-Heruka in the form of Vajrakumāra with Prajñā	Āḥ	Taṃ

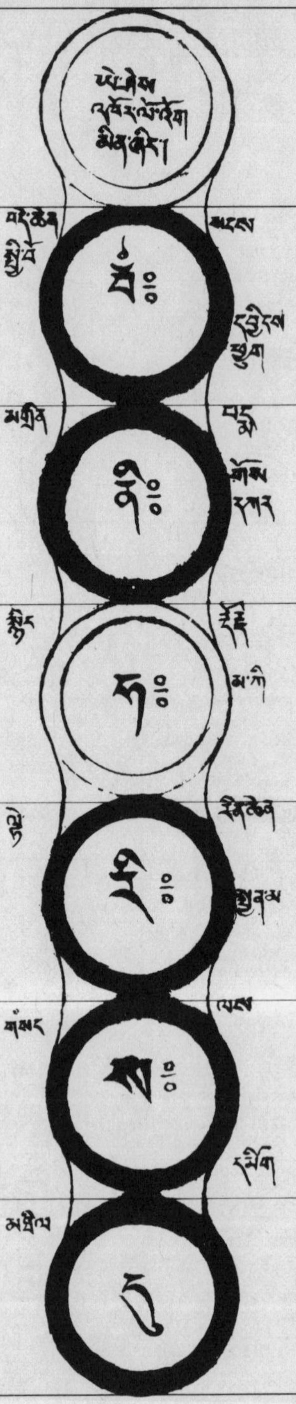

TABLE 12

The five Tathāgatas of the Psychic Centers	The five female Counterparts of the Buddhas	The Five regions of the Maṇḍala	The Five elements	The Five Skandhas	The Five Poisons or Failings	The Five Wisdoms of the Buddhas
Buddha Vairocana White	Prajñā Ākāśa Dhātvīśvarī	Center	Ether	Rūpa-skandha Body	Ignorance	Dharma-dhātu-Wisdom
Buddha Amitābha Red the Buddha of the Western Paradise (sukhāvatī)	Prajñā Pāṇḍarā	West	Fire	Samjñā-skandha Perception	Desire, Passions	Wisdom of Clear Sight
Buddha Akṣobhya Vajrasattva-Akṣobhya Blue	Prajñā Locanā	East	Water	Vijñāna-skandha Awareness	Hatred	Mirror-like Wisdom
Buddha Ratnasambhava Yellow	Prajñā-Māmaki	South	Earth	Vedanā-skandha Feeling	Pride	Wisdom of Equality
Buddha Amoghasiddhi Green	Prajñā Samayatārā	North	Air	Saṃskāra-skandha Will, Intention	Envy, Greed	Wisdom of Perfected Action

Ḍākinīs. For the Tibetans the most important symbols are contained in such drawings, after which further meditations can be developed.

H. THE EIGHT MAHĀBODHISATTVAS (YAB-YUM)

With the group of the eight great Bodhisattvas (S. mahābodhisattva, T. Byang-chub sems-dpa' chen-po) we enter a further phase of psychological and physiological aspects of the transformation in the bardo, which forms the functional components of the five skandhas. As in all symbolism of opposites in tantric Buddhism the eight mahābodhisattvas appear in the bardo as self-generating male-female pairs. The eight Bodhisattvas[99] and the eight Bodhisattva-Ḍākinīs together form a group of 16 deities, who generally appear in maṇḍalas together with the five Buddhas, for they symbolize the psychical and physical organs of perception and their realms of operation in the objective world. The Bodhisattvas rule over the eight kinds of awareness (T. rNam-shes brgyad), and the eight Ḍākinīs are associated with the eight realms of operation of these kinds of awareness (T. rNam-shes yul brgyad). Thereby the potential inner world of man is addressed, as well as his outer world with which he is connected by the eight functions of awareness. The synthesis of all these connections corresponds to complete detachment from the material world as a means toward liberation. In paintings of visions of the deities we usually find the eight Bodhisattvas closely associated with the four Buddhas of the cosmic directions of the maṇḍala. Therefore each of the four Buddhas is assigned to two Bodhisattvas and two Ḍākinīs. In figure 18 we have the complete maṇḍala of the five Tathāgatas (yab-yum) and the eight Bodhisattvas (yab-yum), in which Ḍākinīs and Bodhisattvas appear separately in the circles of light.

We shall now present an overview of the eight Bodhisattvas and their female counterparts. We should mention that the sequence given here can vary from text to text. We also find a similar irregularity (independent of the tradition of the gurus) in the assignment of the eight kinds of awareness to the individual

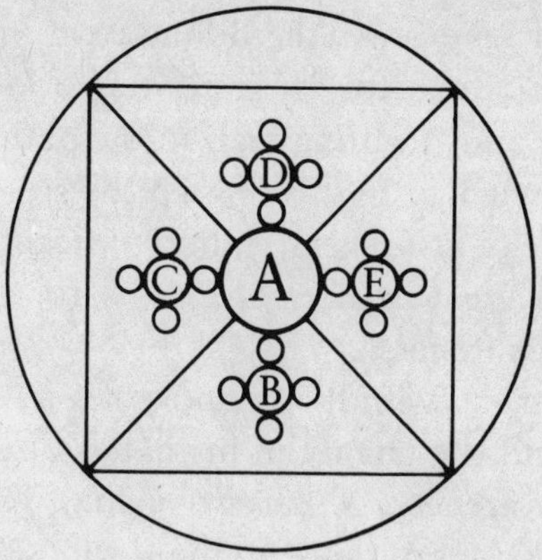

Fig. 18. Diagram of the maṇḍala of the five Buddhas and the eight Bodhisattvas.

Bodhisattvas. However, this is only of secondary importance with relation to the total meaning, and so we shall here consider only one single Tibetan text.[100]

The eight Mahābodhisattvas effect the transformation in the bardo of awareness in all its eight points and realms of communication. With the great ideal of enlightened thinking (S. bodhicitta),

Bodhisattva	Bījamantra Seed-Syllable	Bodhi-sattva-Dākinī	Seed-Syllable	Direction in Maṇḍala
Kṣitigarbha (T. Sa-yi snying-po)	Kṣiḥ	Lāsyā	Hūṃ	East
Maitreya (T. Byams-pa)	Meḥ	Puṣpā	Hūṃ	Southeast
Samantabhadra (T. Kun-tu bzang-po)	Hūṃ	Mālā	Traṃ	Northwest
Ākāśagarbha (T. Nam-mkha'i snying-po)	Triḥ	Dhūpā	Dza	South
Avalokiteśvara (T. sPyan-ras-gzigs)	Hrīḥ	Gītā	Hrīḥ	West
Mañjuśrī (T. 'Jam-dpal-dbyangs)	Muṃ	Ālokā	Vaṃ	Northeast
Nīvaraṇaviṣkambhin (T. sGrib-pa rnam-sel)	Thīḥ	Gandhā	Ho	Southwest
Vajrapāṇi (T. Phyag-na rdo-rje)	Dziḥ	Nṛtyā	A	North

TABLE 13

in order to banish the darkness of ignorance, the Bodhisattva in Mahāyāna Buddhism became a paradigm for the inner transformation of the human spirit, which aims to bring man to the path of enlightenment or increased knowledge. In dividing up the separate functions of the total structure of awareness, eight significant images have been chosen from the great number of Bodhisattvas and associated with the kinds of awareness.

The white Bodhisattva Kṣitagarbha with the symbols of a red branch from the tree of wishing and the ghaṇṭā in his hands appears in order to purify visual awareness (S. cakṣurvijñāna; T. Mig-gi rnam-shes) from false impressions of things in the world, so that the illusory aspect (S. māyā) of all impermanent things can be recognized. The Bodhisattva Kṣitigarbha has as his Ḍākinī the goddess Lāsyā whose color is clear as water. She carries the mirror and the ghaṇṭā, and her realm is the visual field and all objective things. The "cloud-colored" (whitish-yellow) Bodhisattva Maitreya (T. Byams-pa) carries the Nāgakeśara branch and the bell (ghaṇṭā). His aim is the enlightenment of hearing (S. śrotravijñāna; T. rNa-ba'i rnam-shes), in order that the ear may perceive the unchanging voice of the dharma. The Ḍākinī of Maitreya is the "mother of pearl" goddess Puṣpā, who carries the symbols of the white lotus and the bell. She clears awareness of all previous and karmically effective illusory thinking. The third Bodhisattva is the "topaz-colored" Samantabhadra, who carries the ear of corn and the bell. His realm is the sense of smell (S. ghrāṇavijñāna; T. sNa-ba'i rnam-shes). His Prajñā is the Ḍākinī Mālā, whose symbols are the garland of flowers and the bell; she leads awareness towards religious thinking.

The Bodhisattva Ākāśagarbha, whose color is yellow and whose symbols are the sword and the bell, is associated with the sense of taste (S. jihvāvijñāna; T. lCe'i rnam-shes). His Ḍākinī is the goddess Dhūpā, who carries a vessel filled with sweet-smelling essences and also the bell. The fifth Bodhisattva is Avalokiteśvara with an eight-petalled lotus and the bell. He is associated with the sense of the body (S. kāyavijñāna; T. Lus-kyi rnam-shes). His Ḍākinī is the coral-red goddess Gītā, who carries a lute. She appears in order to enlighten all perceptions of tone with the sound of the heavenly music of the Kinnaras, which permeates the spheres. The Bodhisattva Mañjuśrī has a saffron-yellow color, and he carries the blue utpala-blossom and the bell. He is familiar to us from the teachings of the Mahāyāna as the Bodhisattva of knowledge, and so he appears here to enlighten the faculty of thinking (S. manovijñāna; T. Yid-kyi rnam-shes). As long as normal thinking is ruled by the intellect and its deceptive reflections, a breakthrough to perfect knowledge is impossible. The female counterpart of Mañjuśrī is the red Ḍākinī Ālokā, who carries the all-illuminating light. She appears in order to enlighten thought-awareness, in that she protects it from all future intellectual activity with the clear radiance of her light.

The seventh Bodhisattva, the reddish-yellow Nīvaraṇaviṣkambhin, appears in the southwest of the maṇḍala with the book of wisdom and the bell. The book as the symbol of the highest wisdom and the bell with the tone of all-pervading emptiness indicate that this Bodhisattva is able to enlighten the universal- or ground-awareness (S. ālayavijñāna; T. Kun-gzhi rnam-shes). His Ḍākinī is the green Gandhā, who carries incense and the bell, and who overcomes all presently-occurring intellectual activities. The eighth Bodhisattva is the "turmaline-green" Vajrapāṇi (the vajra-bearer), who holds the diamond scepter (vajra) and the ghaṇṭā. He appears in order to enlighten all hindrances still remaining in collective awareness (S. ādānavijñāna; T. Nyon-yid rnam-shes). His blue-green Ḍākinī Nṛtyā carries a bowl of heavenly food as a foretaste of the bliss of liberation.

We have now completed the circle of the Bodhisattvas and their female counterparts. Of course, in the various writings of the Tibetan Book of the Dead, we find different sequences, color-symbolism, or divergent descriptions of the attributes or of the associations to the eight kinds of awareness. It would not, however, be worthwhile to go into these confusing differences here. We shall later encounter the Bodhisattvas again in their negative aspect in the form of the eight Keurimas and the eight Phra-menmas. They then constitute a demonic and wrathful intensification of the aspect of power manifesting on the level of the profane intellect.

1. THE SIX BUDDHAS

a. The Six Buddhas of the Bhavacakra and the Ritual of Guidance through the Six Realms of Existence

With the six Buddhas of the so-called wheel of life (S. bhavacakra; T. Srid-pa'i 'khor-lo), who appear on the sixth day of the bardo visions together with the five Tathāgatas and the eight Bodhisattvas, we come to the central ritual and symbolic portion of the Tibetan Book of the Dead. The six Buddhas are, among all the visionary figures of the bardo, the only ones to appear under the aspect of the nirmāṇakāya, that of the incarnated body. They are the six incarnated Buddhas (T. sPrul-sku thub-pa drug) as reincarnations of the great compassionate Bodhisattva Avalokiteśvara, and they appear in the Srid-pa'i bardo as figures of salvation in the six realms of existence of karmically conditioned rebirth.

There are figures quite similar to the six Buddhas in the bardo teachings of the pre-Buddhist Bon religion, who there bear the names gShen-rab, since they are held to be incarnations of the founder of the religion who had the same name (see also section 3A).

The six Buddhas are contemplated in detail in separate images during the death ritual, in order that the dead person in the bardo can realize early why these Buddhas appear as incarnations of the great Bodhisattva in the six realms of existence. To the ritual enactment of the six worlds belong also the various symbols of the Buddhas, which are displayed on individual initiation cards. The ritual sequence with the symbolic guidance of the image of the dead person (his sByang-bu) in connection with the six Buddhas will be described later. Seen symbolically, the six Buddhas represent the heroic descent of Avalokiteśvara into the cycle of saṃsāra. Thus the Buddhas are emanations of the Bodhisattva, so that in this form they may show the six kinds of beings the path out of the cycle of rebirth. To this end they make use of certain symbols and attributes; they appear in the six worlds as the heralds of a certain great virtue which leads to the overcoming of the corresponding world of existence. Together the Buddhas represent the six virtues of perfection, which belong to the ten moral principles of the Bodhisattvas.

In the important ancient Tibetan work Maṇi bka'-'bum[101] Avalokiteśvara is described in many verses as the eleven-headed and thousand-armed "noble king of heaven" (T. 'Phags-pa nam-mkha'i rgyal-po); in another part of the same work it is his four-armed manifestation as the Bodhisattva of compassion who appears in the center of the maṇḍala of the six Buddhas. According to the meditation texts one should first meditate upon the mantric seed-syllable Hrīḥ, which radiates in the middle of the heart center, standing on a sun lotus. Then the four-armed and pure white Bodhisattva Avalokiteśvara (T. sPyan-ras-gzigs) appears from it, sitting upon a moon-lotus throne. In his first pair of hands he holds a rosary of 108 pearls in his right hand and in his left the eight-petalled lotus. His second pair of hands is folded in front of his heart in the namaskāra mudrā. With his kind and compassionate eyes he looks down upon the six kinds of beings.

In the accompanying sketch of a maṇḍala of Avalokiteśvara (fig. 19) we see an arrangement of the six emanations in the form of the Buddhas. In the center of the lotus blossom is the Bodhisattva, and the six inner petals of the lotus bear the syllables of the mantric invocation Oṃ Ma Ṇi Pad Me Hūṃ, which is sacred to Avalokiteśvara. The six mantric syllables are at the same time associated with the six Buddhas and their realms of incarnation, which are to be seen on the corresponding outer lotus petals. These six worlds form the "wheel of life" of the sixfold world of suffering, in which the Buddhas spread to the inhabitants the law of liberation from the suffering of rebirth.

The realms of incarnation are those of the gods (T. Lha), the titans or demigods (T. Lha-ma-yin), human beings (T. Mi), animals (T. Byol-song), hungry ghosts or pretas (T. Yi-dvags), and denizens of hell (T. dMyal-ba). This comes from an old Buddhist classification familiar to us from Hīnayāna Buddhism, which is to be understood as a symbolic portrayal of human ways of behaving.[102] It concerns a world created by man's karmically unwholesome behavior, causing him to be reincarnated again and again in the cycle of existence. Rebirth in the six realms of existence as the consequence of ignorance is connected with the doctrine of the twelve conditioned dependencies (S. pratītya-samutpāda) which belongs to the core of Buddhist teachings about the inevitable

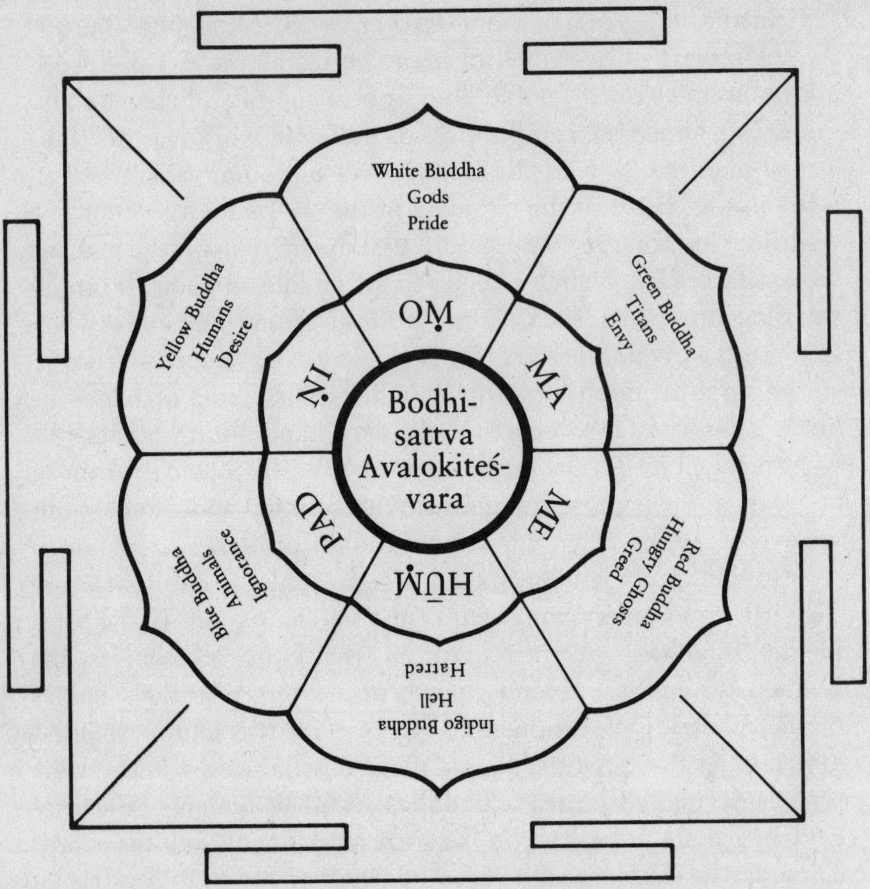

Fig. 19. The maṇḍala of the six emanations of Avalokiteśvara. In the inner lotus is the Bodhisattva with the six-syllable mantra; the outer lotus shows the six worlds of existence with the Buddhas.

conditioning of becoming and impermanence. As long as human life is attached to the world of impermanence through ignorance and delusion, hatred, and desire, liberation from the chains of rebirth in the six worlds of suffering is impossible. In order to communicate this fundamental knowledge to all six kinds of beings, Avalokiteśvara appears in the worlds of existence in the form of the six Buddhas.

In the world of the gods, whose heavenly existence can nevertheless not last eternally, the white Buddha brGya-byin appears as the Buddha of the realm of the gods (T. Lha'i thub-pa) with the melodious lute in his hands. This means that it is inappropriate for the gods to be proud of their serene existence in lofty spheres, since their sojourn in the heavens based upon good karmic deeds will at some time come to an end. The melodious tone of the lute (T. sGra-snyan) points to this impermanence. The mantric seed-syllable of the world of the gods, ĀḤ, is associated with the lotus center in the forehead, and the virtue of overcoming pride (T. Nga-rgyal) is the perfection of the meditation (S. dhyāna-pāramitā; T. bSam-gtan).

In the world of the quarrelsome demigods and titans there is great envy over the fruits of the tree of knowledge. The green Buddha Thag-bzang-ris appears there as the Buddha of the titans (T. Lha-min thub-pa), with his knight's armor and his sword, in order to settle the envy-inspired fighting. The mantric seed-syllable SU[103] of this world is assigned to the throat center. The green Buddha teaches the titans the perfection of moral education (S. śīla-pāramitā; T. Tshul-khrims), in order to overcome divisive envy (T. Phrag-dog).

In the realm of human earthly existence the yellow Buddha Śākyamuni appears with the alms bowl and beggar's staff in his hands. In the human world of birth, old age, and death, the earthly Buddha teaches men to overcome the principle passion of desire (T. 'Dod-chags), while striving after the perfection of the attainment of salvation (S. vīrya-pāramitā; T. brTson-'grus). The psychic lotus cakra of the yellow Buddha Śākyamuni with the mantric syllable NṚ is in the heart lotus as the place of the dharmakāya.

For the world of animals living in ignorance and stupidity, the blue Buddha Seng-ge rab-brtan appears carrying the book of wisdom. He teaches the animals to overcome ignorance (T. gTi-mug) by striving after the perfection of knowledge (S. prajñā-pāramitā; T. Shes-rab chos). The mantric syllable TRI[103] is assigned to the world of animals and is situated in the lotus of the navel center as the origin of the animalistic and instinctual world.

In the avarice- and greed-ridden world of the eternally thirsting hungry ghosts, or pretas (T. Yi-dvags), Avalokiteśvara appears as the red Buddha Kha-'bar-ma with the precious vessel of heavenly food (T. Rin-chen sgrom-bu). In order to overcome self-torturing greed, which prevents these beings from ever becoming satiated, the red Buddha teaches the pretas the perfection of generosity (S. dāna-pāramitā; T. sByin-pa'i chos). The psychic lotus for the world of the insatiable pretas is in the perineum and has the yellow mantric syllable PRE.

The lowest realm of existence is the world of hells with its eighteen cold and hot regions of hellish torments, into which the beings driven by hatred (T. Zhe-sdang) fall. The Bodhisattva in the

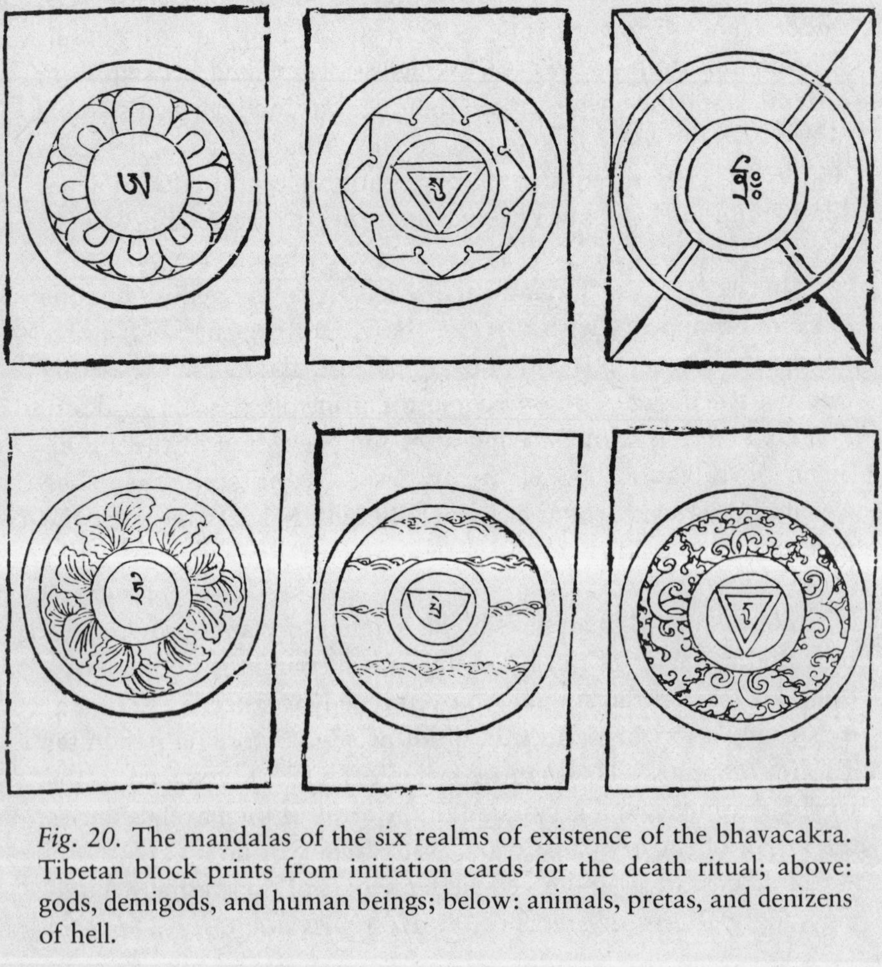

Fig. 20. The maṇḍalas of the six realms of existence of the bhavacakra. Tibetan block prints from initiation cards for the death ritual; above: gods, demigods, and human beings; below: animals, pretas, and denizens of hell.

The Six-Syllable Mantra of Avalokiteś-Vara	The Six Realms of Existence	The Six Seed-Syllables of the Realms	The Six Buddhas	Colors of the Buddhas	Symbols of the Buddhas	The Six Vices	The Six Wisdoms	The Six Lotus Centers	The Six Dim Lights of the Realms of Existence
OṂ	Gods	ĀḤ	brGya-byin	White	Lute	Pride	Dhyānapāramitā Meditation	Forehead	Whitish
MA	Titans or Demigods	SU	Thag-bzang-ris	Green	Armor and Sword	Envy	Śīlapāramitā Moral Education	Throat	Reddish
ṆI	Human Beings	NṚ	Śākyamuni	Yellow	Patra and Begging Staff	Passion and Desire	Vīryapāramitā Energy	Heart	Bluish
PAD	Animals	TRI	Seng-ge rab-brtan	Blue	Book of Wisdom	Ignorance	Prajñāpāramitā Knowledge	Navel	Greenish
ME	Pretas or Hungry Ghosts	PRE	Kha-'bar-ma	Red	Vessel with Amrita	Greed and Avarice	Dānapāramitā Generosity	Perineum	Yellowish
HŪṂ	Denizens of Hell	DU	Chos-kyi rgyal-po Dharmarāja	Indigo	Fire and Water	Hatred	Kṣāntipāramitā Equanimity	Soles of the Feet	Smoke-colored

TABLE 14: Overview of the symbolism of the six Buddhas of the Bhavacakra as emanations of the Bodhisattva Avalokiteśvara.

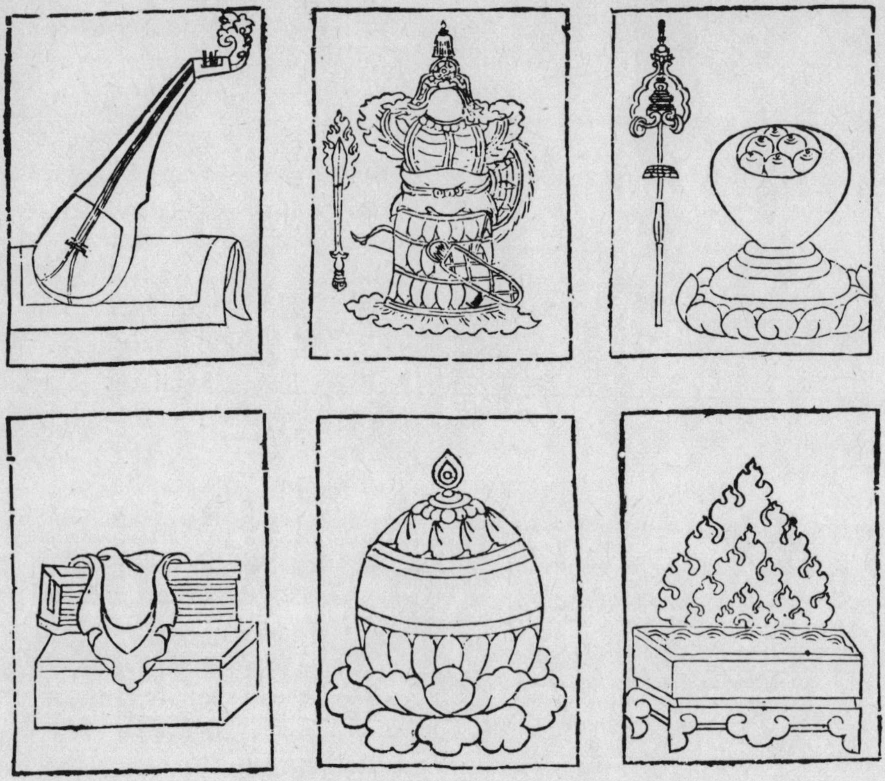

Fig. 21. The attributes of the six Buddhas of the worlds of existence.

form of the indigo Buddha Dharmarāja (T. Chos-kyi rgyal-po) descends into these hells carrying water and fire to alleviate the sufferings of the beings tormented by heat and cold. The symbolic lotus cakra of the worlds of hell with the mantric seed-syllable DU is situated on the soles of the feet (T. rKang-mthil rtsa-'khor). In order that the denizens of hell may overcome the opposites of passionate hatred, the indigo Buddha teaches them the perfection of equanimity (S. kṣāntipāramitā; T. bZod-pa'i chos).

We shall quote an excerpt from a Tibetan meditation text about the great Bodhisattva Avalokiteśvara[104] which will show the symbolism of the six syllables in relation to the worlds of existence.

From the invocations to the Bodhisattva Avalokiteśvara:

Oṃ maṇi padme hūṃ: The white syllable OṂ has appeared in the world of the gods in order to enlighten the suffering of becoming and passing away caused by pride. May the true wisdom of equality be perfected.
We call upon the lord of great compassion!

Oṃ maṇi padme hūṃ: The green syllable MA has appeared in the world of the titans in order to enlighten the suffering of struggle and strife caused by envy. May the true wisdom of the works be perfected.
We call upon the lord of great compassion!

Oṃ maṇi padme hūṃ: The yellow syllable ṆI has appeared in the world of human beings in order to enlighten suffering born of faint-hearted doubt. May the true and spontaneously-originated wisdom be perfected.
We call upon the lord of great compassion!

Oṃ maṇi padme hūṃ: The blue syllable PAD has appeared in the world of animals in order to enlighten the suffering of animal stupidity caused by ignorance. May the true dharmadhātu wisdom be perfected.
We call upon the lord of great compassion!

Oṃ maṇi padme hūṃ: The red syllable ME has appeared in the world of the pretas in order to enlighten the suffering of hunger and thirst born of the passions. May the true wisdom of discriminating clear sight be perfected.
We call upon the lord of great compassion!

Oṃ maṇi padme hūṃ:	The blue-black syllable HŪṂ has appeared in the world of hells in order to enlighten the suffering of heat and cold born of hate. May the true wisdom of the mirror be perfected. We call upon the lord of great compassion!

The symbolism of the six Buddhas and their mission as guides to salvation in the six realms of existence is dealt with by the Tibetan Book of the Dead in a particular ritual intended for the guidance of the dead person's awareness. The ritual portrays symbolically the path of the Bodhisattva Avalokiteśvara who appears in the form of the six Buddhas in the realms of existence in order to teach the Buddhist "perfections" (S. pāramitā) and wisdoms. A further significance of this ritual[105] lies in the "closing of the six gates of rebirth" (T. sKye-sgo) by the mantric syllables Oṃ ma ṇi pad me hūṃ of Avalokiteśvara, whereby the mission of the six Buddhas as emanations of the Bodhisattva is explained in detail. Moreover, in this central ceremony of the death recitations all the most important significations of the peaceful and wrathful deities are explained once again, above all the hand gestures and attributes (Phyag-mtshan) as well as the wisdoms of the Buddhas. For this purpose a series of painted cards, the Tsa-ka-li, is used, on

Fig. 22. Three initiation cards for the death ritual with vajra, ghaṇṭā, and buddha-crown. Tibetan block print.

which can be seen the attributes, the symbols, and the signs of the spiritual lineages of the deities. As an example we shall name here the two first series of symbols from the group of the six Buddhas:

For the yellow Buddha of the human world there is the series: pātra and begging-staff, karmakalaśa, dharmacakra, vajrasattva.

For the white Buddha of the world of the gods: lute, buddha-crown, vajra, three-footed kapāla.

Thus, for the symbolic portrayal of the six Buddhas and their realms and attributes alone, this requires a series of thirty cards, which during the ceremonies are shown simply in front of the image of the dead person and explained to it. The whole death ritual thereby becomes an initiatory succession of symbolic images connected with a precisely determined set of contents. It is therefore also to be understood as a technique of systematic image-meditation, in that the individual contents of the ritual process reveal themselves in the symbols. The dead person's awareness-principle embodied in the sByang-bu is called upon to concentrate on these images and to meditate upon their profound contents. Thereby the purification of the profane awareness is achieved.

The sByang-bu of the dead person occupies the central position in the ritual, and is addressed during the ceremony, admonished, guided, and imbued with spiritual powers by various abhiṣeka-consecrations, just as if it were an active participant. It is a question of the ability of the awareness-principle to find its way, spontaneously and with the guidance of the lamas, to liberation beyond the places of rebirth. The sByang-bu receives the place of honor in the view of the lama directing the ceremonies and is invited by him to take part in the ritual activity. The dead person's image represents him, and during the death ritual it travels in a symbolically ordered sequence on a specially prepared surface through all the various realms of incarnation that are possible places of rebirth. This surface as a cosmic plan of the six worlds of existence (T. 'Gro-ba'i khams drug) is placed on a rectangular wooden board (as in fig. 23) or on a kind of maṇḍala of the worlds. In the middle row of the rectangular field are six squares representing the six worlds. This row is bordered on either side by another row of six squares. Small bowls of sacrificial rice are placed on the squares of one row for the six Buddhas, and on the other row bowls with small cakes of dough (T. gTor-ma) are placed, which are offered to the inhabitants of the six worlds in the name of the dead person. These gTor-ma offerings are gifts for the evil and demonic spirits of the lower worlds which strive to harm the departed soul.

At the beginning of the ritual the dead person's awareness is summoned from the world beyond to appear and take up resi-

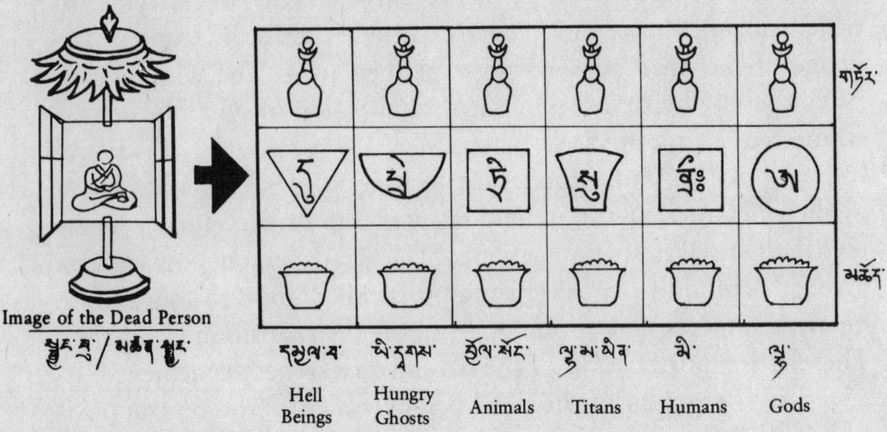

Fig. 23. Ritual plan for the ceremony of the guiding of the dead person through the six realms of existence.

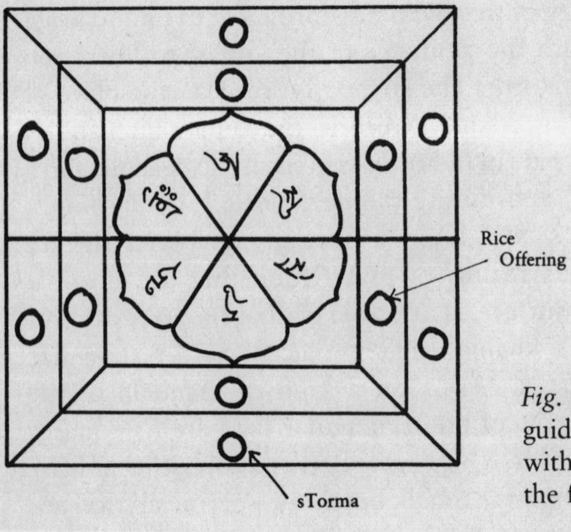

Fig. 24. Ritual plan for the guidance of the dead person with the six-fold division in the form of the maṇḍala.

dence in the sByang-bu or name-card (T. mTshan-sbyang). It should concentrate all its powers of awareness in this image and is admonished to recall the profound teachings and wisdom of its guru, to appropriate the wisdoms of the five Tathāgatas and to remind itself of its personal protective deity (T. Yi-dam).

The sByang-bu sits under a small canopy, and it is the name card of the dead person in that his name is inscribed under his image. This card is a symbol of the earthly body of the deceased. The stylized jewels on the card are a symbol of his spirit and the five-colored strips of silk hanging beside the canopy (see fig. 10) symbolize the five sensory components of his personality. After the summoning of the dead person comes the high point of the ritual, consisting of the instruction and guidance of the awareness by way of the sByang-bu, in order to lead it out of the six worlds of incarnation. The goal is the heavenly sphere of the great Bodhisattva Avalokiteśvara, or complete release in nirvāṇa.

The symbolic journey of the small image begins in the first square with the portrayal of the sufferings of the world of hells, which are caused by hatred. The sByang-bu is placed on this square, and the sufferings of this realm of incarnation are described to the image as the representative of the dead person. Now the deceased finds himself symbolically in hell; there he hears an account spoken by the lama of the appearance of Avalokiteśvara as Buddha Dharmarāja, who out of great compassion (S. mahākaruṇā) has descended as a savior into the world of hells. In the name of the dead person the small bowl of rice is offered to Buddha Dharmarāja who brings fire and water to alleviate the torments of heat and cold. Then the demonic beings of this realm are appeased with the gTor-ma offering, so that the awareness may leave the realm of hellish torments unhindered. At the end of this section of the ritual the gate to the world of hells is magically closed by means of mantras, and thereby rebirth in this realm is prevented.

Then the sByang-bu is placed on the square of the pretas, the sufferings of the hungry ghosts and their karmic causes are explained, and similar offerings of rice and gTor-ma are given to the Red Buddha and the harmful spirits. In corresponding sequence the sByang-bu is taken through the world of animals, titans, human beings, and gods. By the time this has been completed the six gates of rebirth have been ritually closed. Then the table of the six worlds is taken away, and the path of Avalokiteśvara leading to the spheres of enlightenment stands open to the deceased. The last earthly support of his awareness, the sByang-bu, is now no longer necessary and is burned over a light from the altar. The lama reciting the ritual speaks to the flames as follows:[106]

"May the triad of body, speech, and mind of the deceased transform itself into fire for the wisdom of the three bodies (T. sKu gsum); may he be purified of the three basic failings and burdens, and may the fruit of the trikāya be attained. Let the five components of the personality and the five principal failings of the deceased transform themselves in the fire into the wisdoms of the five bodies (T. sKu-lnga); may the five elemental realms be purified of stains and the five wisdoms of the five bodies (the five wisdoms of the Buddhas) be attained. Let ignorance and sinful failures transform themselves in the fire into the purest wisdom; may he be cleansed of all hindrances and defilements and reach the fields of the lofty Buddha Samantabhadra."

b. The Six Buddhas and the Great Image of the Realm of Hells

Another important section of the death ritual portraying the Srid-pa'i bardo is the detailed description of the worlds of hell with their wrathful ruler, Dharmarāja (T. gShin-rje chos-kyi rgyal-po). This theme has been taken up by many Tibetan artists who have treated it in vivid paintings which are to be found as murals or as scroll paintings in monasteries. In these pictures all imaginable sufferings of the eighteen hot and ice-cold hells are realistically portrayed, and in the center is the great court. Here the assistants of the judge of death assemble, and those beings burdened with bad karma are brought before Dharmarāja; the good and bad deeds are weighed and then the sentence of hellish torments is passed. In figure 25 we have a very fine Tibetan block print which depicts the realm of hells, the most important areas of which we shall now describe.

At the top we find the heavenly spheres of the five Tathāgatas (1), visible in the circular radiance of their transcendent world (T. Zhing-khams). At almost the same level we see two further heavenly realms: on the left is the palace of Guru Padmasambhava on the copper-colored mountain (T. Zangs-mdog dpal-gyi ri-bo), and there we see the tantric guru in his wrathful aspect as Guru bDud-dpung zil-gnon. He stands in front of an aureole of flames and is holding the vajra and the magic dagger. With him are his two female pupils, the Ḍākinī Mandārava and the Tibetan Ye-shes mtsho-rgyal (2). On the right side we recognize the turquoise palace in the heavenly realm of the goddess Tārā; she appears accompanied by two bodhisattvas and is the guide on the path to salvation (3).

Beneath these "heavenly spheres," which may be recognized during the meditative visions, extends saṃsāra, the sixfold world of suffering including hell. The Tibetans, on account of their mythical connection with nature and the gods, have long been accustomed to seeing all important events against their cosmic background. And so the world of hells portrayed here is transposed to the central and most holy place in Tibet, the mountain Kailāsa (T. Gangs-rin-po-che) in western Tibet. Kailāsa as the mountain sacred to the gods is the highest point in the land of snow, where, according to ancient belief, one could gain direct access to the heavenly worlds. For the Tibetans, Kailāsa is identical with the central cosmic mountain Sumeru, under the foundations of which are situated the hells of the god of death, Yama. In our picture (figs. 25 and 25a) we recognize the sacred mountain Kailāsa, in the center of which is a Buddhist stūpa, and to the side is the sacred lake Manasarovar (T. mTsho-ma-pham-pa), on the banks of which (5) stand ancient and venerable temples, monasteries, and places of pilgrimage. The sacred mountain is almost entirely taken up by the stūpa with a broad halo. The stūpa is a symbol of the Buddhist teachings and has been used since the times of the Buddha as a sepulcher for the ashes of monks and saints (4). On the sides of the mountain and below we see the six Buddhas of the realms of incarnation (a–f) amongst the inhabitants of the realms. On the side of the Buddha of the human world (c) we recognize the upward-leading illuminated path of wisdom, by way

Fig. 25. The great image of the realm of hells with the judge of death in the center. Tibetan block print.

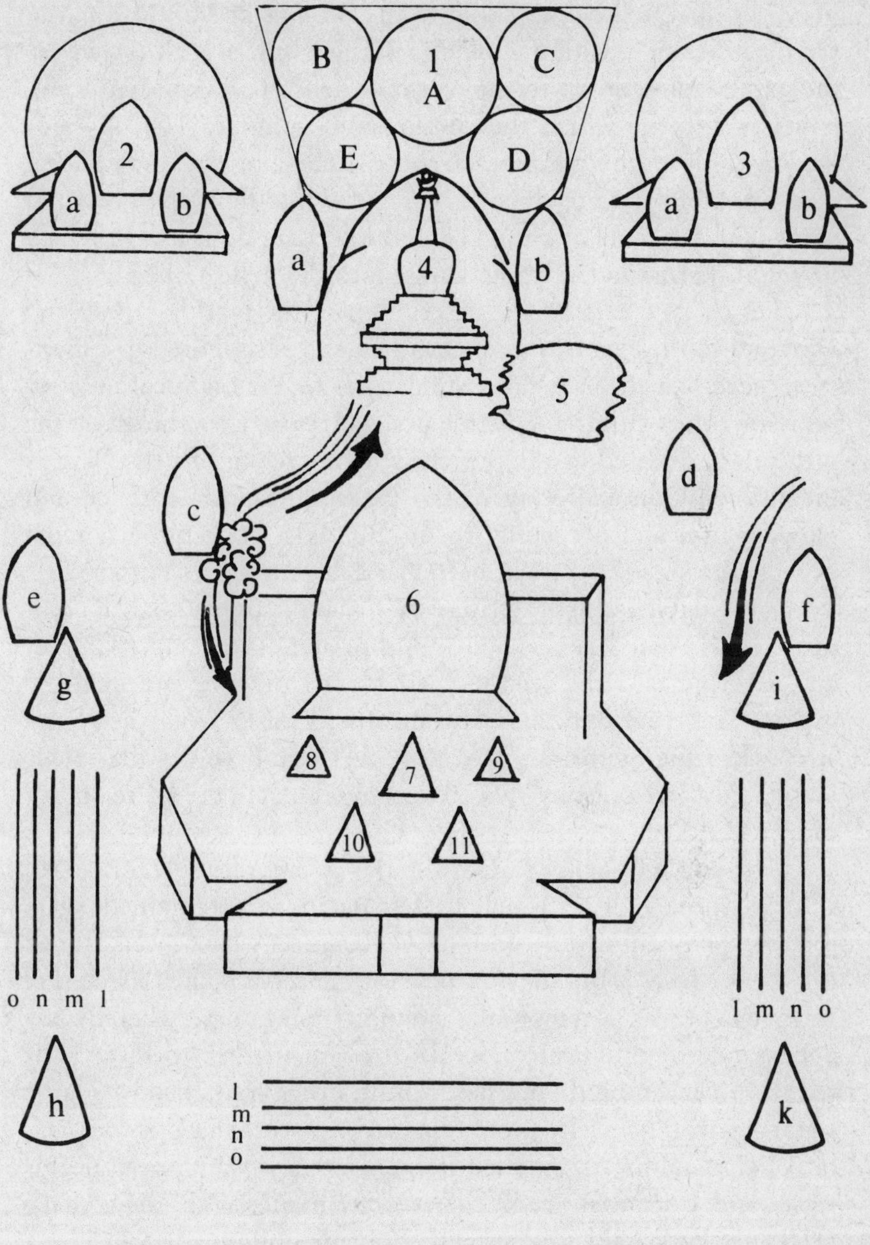

Fig. 25a. Diagrammatic representation of the Tibetan block print of the great image of the realm of hells.

of which liberated beings climb to the summit of Mount Kailāsa. On the other side, with the Buddha of the world of hells (f), we see the path leading down to the world of hells (T. dMyal-bar 'khig-pa'i lam), down which the sinful people plunge. The upward-leading path of liberation (T. mTho-ris thar-lam) shows the liberated beings in the upper part, but in the middle is the great red cloud with the wind of karma (T. Las-kyi rlung-dmar chen), which drives all karma-laden beings down into the hellish abyss.

Let us now turn to the description of the worlds of hell and above all to the events that the dead person is supposed to experience there, which bear many similarities to the mythical descriptions of other cultures and religions. Almost two thirds of the picture are devoted to the depiction of the realm of hells. This is the realm of the suffering of the extreme opposites of ice and glowing fire, and according to the Buddhist conception it must become through the vices of hatred and anger (S. dveṣa or krodha) the unavoidable place of retribution. From the psychological point of view this comparison is quite appropriate, in that anger, hatred, and aversion must be seen in their strictly divisive and dualistic aspect. To create opposites also means to suffer from the exclusiveness of the opposites. Therefore this vice occupies first place among the "five poisons" which lead to rebirth in the six realms of existence.

The world of hells (T. dMyal-ba) is an impregnable fortress of sufferings, the walls of which are festooned with so many dangers that escape is impossible until all wicked deeds have been atoned for. Nevertheless, Buddhism does not conceive of hell as eternal suffering, but as a temporally bounded purgatory, whereby the appearance of Bodhisattva Avalokiteśvara in the world of hells receives its meaning. In our block print, hell is contained by a large square with four rocky mountains strewn with sharp stones and peaks (T. Shal-ma-ri) situated in the southeast, southwest, northwest, and northeast (g–k). These mountains with their sharp ridges are impassable. Between the four mountains are four insurmountable walls of dangers: the innermost ring is fire, the second is a deep and treacherous morass of mud, and the third is a vast plain of knives (T. sPu-gri bye-thang chen-po), which is impossible to cross without being cut to shreds. Should someone manage to surmount these three hindrances (l–n), he will come to the treacherous hedge of sword leaves (T. Ral-gri lo-ma'i nag tshal), which immediately plunge down if anyone should try to break through (o). These four walls and the four mountains at the corners enclose the hell lying deep in the abyss.

In the center we see, standing in front of an aureole of flames, the judge of death, Dharmarāja (T. gShin-rje chos-kyi rgyal-po). His appearance is wrathful, with blazing hair and a crown of skulls (6). He has a third eye and carries the flaming sword of knowledge as well as the mirror in which all the good and bad deeds of the people who have died are reflected. In front of the judge of death sits one of Dharmarāja's retinue of eleven assistants who is the most important of the "counsels of karma" or "karma guides" (T. Las-mkhan), the ape-headed "karma guide" (T. sPre'u mgo-can) who carries the scales of justice (7). Two more assistants of Dharmarāja sit to the side at his feet: the scribe, Las-mkhan stag-gi mgo-can, with the head of a tiger, and the bird-headed prosecutor, Las-mkhan pu-shud mgo-can, who has the head of a hoopoe (8 and 9).

Beneath these are the dead people who have to account for themselves before the judge of death. The Tibetan Book of the Dead teaches that two spirits appear for every dead person who comes before the god of death, and these could be characterized as psychic aspects of the individual. They are considered to be good and bad spirits born simultaneously with the person. They appear together with the dead person before the judge of death; the "simultaneously born white genius" (T. Lhan-cig skyes-pa'i lha dkar-po) carries a sack of white stones, and the "simultaneously born black demon" (T. Lhan-cig skyes-pa'i 'dre nag-po), a sack with black stones. In calculating the karmic deeds of the dead person before the court, the white spirit lays the white stones for the good deeds on the scale, and the black demon puts down the black stones for the bad deeds. The relative weights of the stones determine the extent of the punishment of hellish torments (10 and 11). Dharmarāja has thirteen demonic assistants who help him make judgement over the dead person's individual karma:

1. Srin-po'i mgo-can	demon-headed deity
2. Glang-gi mgo-can	bull-headed deity
3. Srin-po'i gdong-can	second demon-headed deity
4. Las-mkhan spre'u mgo-can	ape-headed deity (with scales)
5. Las-mkhan stag-gi mgo-can	tiger-headed deity (with scroll)
6. Las-mkhan pu-shud mgo-can	hoopoe-headed deity
7. Las-mkhan sdig-mgo-can	scorpion-headed deity
8. Las-mkhan khyi-mgo-can	dog-headed deity
9. Las-mkhan send-dong-can	lion-headed deity
10. Las-mkhan phag-gdong-can	boar-headed deity
11. Las-mkhan dom-mgo-can	bear-headed deity
12. Las-mkhan dred-mgo-can	fury-headed deity
13. Las-mkhan sbrul-mgo-can	serpent-headed deity

These are the theriomorphic assistants of Yama Dharmarāja, who also guard the gates of the palace of hell, and from there they direct the sentenced beings into the eight hot and the eight cold hells. The two remaining realms of hell are situated at the bottom edge of the picture at the sides. Here the condemned beings find themselves surrounded by small biting vermin and in a lake of mud filled with snakes, worms, scorpions, and other small, tormenting animals.

We have now described the major areas of the great image of hell. We see how detailed the descriptions of the sufferings of the underworld are, which are to be seen as the consequences of karmically bad deeds. In some Tibetan collections, such as the "Kun-bzang bla-ma'i zhal-lung," individual bad deeds are described in detail together with the corresponding hellish tortures that can be expected to follow after death. These detailed descriptions are amplified by very appropriate psychological examples. It is of particular interest that, consciously or unconsciously, exactly those symbolic consequences are drawn which unconditionally correspond to individual complexes of action. Man knows his own failings, and the authors of the Tibetan Book of the Dead chose symbolic retributions for them that are by no means unfamiliar to us from dream-experience. The ancient knowledge of cause and effect here brought to light primordial symbolic images whose relation to the reality of human behavior makes valuable psychological comparisons possible. These will be more extensively confirmed when we come to consider portrayals of the world beyond from cultures like those of India, Greece, or ancient Egypt.

J. THE FOUR GUARDIANS OF THE MAṆḌALA (YAB-YUM)

On the sixth day of the visions of the peaceful deities, the four Guardians of the maṇḍala appear; these are protective deities of a semi-wrathful character who guard the four gates of the maṇḍala. Like all deities of the bardo visions they appear in tantric polarity with their female counterparts. They are of human form with wrathful faces, and they have the third eye of higher knowledge. With their wild hair and their crowns of five skulls, they guard the four cosmic directions of the maṇḍala and at the same time become the guides of the awareness-principle in the transcendent world. At the east gate the white Guardian Vijaya (T. rNam-par rgyal-ba) appears together with his Ḍākinī, Vajrāṅkuśī. The symbols carried by the wrathful Vijaya are a kapāla and a bell, and his female counterpart carries an iron hook.[107] The Guardian of the east gate appears in order to enlighten body-consciousness (T. Lus-kyi rnam-shes), and he effects the final physical dissolution of all beings. At the same time he represents one of the four divine boundless states (S. catur-pramāṇa; T. Tshad-med bzhi) and stands for the virtue of immeasurable kindness (S. mahāmaitrī; T. Byams-pa chen-po). With the appearance of the dynamic figure of Vijaya, flaming red upon a lotus, the doctrine of the immortality of things and of psycho-personal structure (T. rTag-par lta-ba) is overcome.

At the south gate of the maṇḍala the wrathful yellow Yamāntaka appears (T. gShim-rje gshed-po) with his Ḍākinī, Vajrapāśī, in red flames and standing on a lotus throne. Yamāntaka carries a sling and a bell. The Guardian of the south gate appears in order to dissolve the five corporeal senses, and he futher ensures that the "five poisons" (cardinal failings) are overcome by the five wisdoms. In addition he represents the divine state of great compassion (S. mahākaruṇā; T. sNying-rje chen-po) and leads the dead person's awareness beyond the doctrine of the boundedness of things. For neither thinking exclusively along the dimensions of bounded appearances nor thinking in terms of eternal conditions alone can ensure access to indescribable nirvāna, which lies beyond Being and non-Being. Thinking in mental conceptual constructions must be subjective and dualistic, and it thereby misses the experience of absolute reality (T. Don-dam-pa).

At the west gate of the maṇḍala is the red Guardian Hayagrīva (T. rTa-mgrin rgyal-po) with his female counterpart, the Ḍākinī Vajraśṛṅkhalā (T. rDo-rje lcags-sgrog-ma). Hayagrīva with the horse's head in his hair carries an iron chain (or else a club entwined with snakes) and a bell, and his Ḍākinī also has an iron chain. The wrathful Hayagrīva appears in order to dissolve all feeings and to ensure that the path of compassion is not abandoned. The deity is associated with the doctrine of self-contemplation and of reflective inner vision (T. bDag-tu lta-ba) and represents the divine virtue of sympathetic joy (S. muditā; T. dGa'-ba).

The Guardian of the north gate is the green Amṛtakuṇḍalin (T. bDud-rtsi 'kyil-ba) with his green Ḍākinī, Vajraghaṇṭā. He carries a crossed vajra and a bell and appears in order to enlighten the awareness of all bodily sensations. In addition he effects transcendence through infinite compassion. Amṛtakuṇḍalin represents the divine state of equanimity (S. upekṣā; T. bTang-snyoms) and overcomes all thinking in signs and forms. He stands to the north as the cosmic place of Buddha Amoghasiddhi, and thereby symbolizes the perfection of all earthly and karmically conditioned works. The four Ḍākinīs of the Guardians are also associated with the doctrine of the signs of the four boundaries (T. rTags-chad mu-bzhi), those boundaries within which alone all empirical experience of life can take place. These four boundaries of our physical and mental capabilities are birth and death (T. sKyed-'gag), immortality and dissolution (T. rTag-chad), existence and non-Being (T. Yod-med), and appearance and emptiness (T. sNang-stong).

We have now demonstrated some of the ethical and psychological symbolism. Various other texts give further and sometimes differing accounts of the meanings of the four Guardians. In conclusion we present an overview of these maṇḍala deities (table 15).

Direction	Bīja-Mantra	Guardian	Color	Ḍākinī	Bīja-Mantra	Catur-Pramāna
1. East	Hūṃ	Vijaya	White	Vajrāṅkuśī	Dzam	Maitrī-Kindness
2. South	Hūṃ	Yamāntaka	Yellow	Vajrapāśī	Hūṃ	Karuṇā-Compassion
3. West	Hūṃ	Hayagrīva	Red	Vajraśṛṅkhalā	Baṃ	Muditā-Joy
4. North	Hūṃ	Amṛtakuṇḍalin	Green	Vajraghaṇṭā	Ho	Upekṣā-Equanimity

TABLE 15

K. THE FIVE SECRET VIDYĀDHARAS (YAB-YUM)

On the seventh day of the bardo visions the last of the peaceful deities appear, namely, the five "knowledge-holding deities," or Vidyādharas (T. Rig-'dzin lnga), who occupy a special position within the bardo maṇḍala. Certain texts fail to consider them at all. The Vidyādharas are heroic tantric deities (S. vīra; T. dPa'-bo), and they form a maṇḍala in the sambhogakāyacakra of the throat center (T. Longs-spyod 'khor-lo). They stand at the place of the mystical mantric lute and are symbolic figures of the spiritually enlightened verbal plane of human activity. By way of their assignment to the cakra of the throat center, they belong neither to the sphere of the wrathful deities of the mental plane (the forehead center) nor to that of the peaceful spiritual plane of the heart lotus. Their position within the initiatory arrangement is special in that there is no particular initiation associated with them during the ritual, nor does their image appear on the consecration cards for the death ritual, which show the ritual sequence of the deities. Yet we often find the five Knowledge-holders in Tibetan paintings which depict the bardo deities.

The mantric path of the Mahāyāna (T. sNgags-kyi theg-pa) belongs to the secret paths of liberation through knowledge of the condensed meaning of the mantras and their recitation. Thus, the Vidyādharas, as deities on the mantric plane of pure speech (T. gSung-gi dkyil-'khor), even become guides on the path of liberation before the great cycle of wrathful deities dawns on the eighth day.

The first deity to appear from the heavenly spheres (T. mKha-spyod zhing-khams) in the fivefold radiant light of "simultaneously born wisdom" in the center of the lotus is the red Knowledge-holder, "Lotus Lord of the Dance" (T. Padma gar-gyi dbang-phyug), in tantric union with his red Ḍākinī. Like the other four knowledge-holding deities, he carries as symbols the tantric kapāla and the ritual sickle (T. Gri-gug). Then on the eastern lotus petal follows the white "Knowledge-Holder of the Earth" (T. Sa-la gnas-pa'i rig-'dzin), on the southern lotus petal the yellow "Life-Ruling Knowledge-Holder" (T. Tshe-la dbang-ba'i rig-'dzin), in the west the red "Knowledge-Holder of the Great Symbol" (T. Phyag-rgya chen-po'i rig-'dzin), and in the north the green "Spontaneously Arisen Knowledge-Holder" (T. Lhun-gyi grub-pa'i rig-'dzin). All have the same symbols and are accompanied by their mystical Ḍākinīs. Following the visions of these five deities are

Lotus Petal	Vidyādhara with Ḍākinī	Color	Symbols	Assignment to Psychic center
Center	Padma gar-gyi dbang-phyug	Red	Kapāla and Sickle	Kāya-Vidyādhara
East	Sa-la gnas pa'i rig-'dzin	White		Citta-Vidyādhara
South	Tshe-la dbang-ba'i rig-'dzin	Yellow		Guṇa-Vidyādhara
West	Phyag-rgya chen-po'i rig-'dzin	Red		Vāc-Vidyādhara
North	Lhun-gyi grub-pa'i rig-'dzin	Green		Karma-Vidyādhara

TABLE 16

many other ḍākinīs and protective deities, who are not, however, included in the maṇḍala of bardo deities proper. In conclusion we present a brief overview of the symbolism[108] of the Vidyādharas (table 16).

2. The Wrathful Deities

> The evil of the soul is ignorance, for whatever soul knows nothing of the nature of things or of the good itself, such a soul is blind and falls into the passion of the body, becomes an evil demon, does not recognize itself. . . .
>
> HERMES TRISMEGISTUS

THE SECOND cycle of bardo deities begins dramatically on the eighth day of the visions and lasts another seven days. From the depths of the abyss which opens up before the awareness-principle arise the wrathful deities. Yet this abyss is not to be found outside, but is rather a part of the human psyche itself, for according to the Tibetan Book of the Dead, the terrifying deities appear as emanations of the intellect from the four directions of one's own head (T. Klad-pa dung-khang). They are projections of the intellect, which through ignorance tries to overcome these images by rigid rejection, which causes the images to become all the more dangerous and overwhelming. Every reaction against the wrathful deities undertaken by awareness out of fear is, as a directed act of will on the part of the intellect, condemned to failure. The wrathful deities are the great counter-play—strengthened by demonic power—to the maṇḍala of the peaceful deities. In both cycles of the great maṇḍala, the wrathful and the peaceful, the awareness-principle experiences in itself the suffering of the self-posited dualism of acceptance and rejection. The Tibetan Book of the Dead repeatedly emphasizes this, in that the dead person is constantly exhorted to see through all kinds of visionary images with clear awareness, in order to recognize them as illusory. Liberation lies far behind these lofty radiances and beyond the terrifying apparitions. Every kind of clinging to the images is considered here, from the psychological point of view, as an impetus towards a new incarnation because of attachment that has not been overcome.

But since the awareness-body of the dead person is, according to the texts, equipped with all faculties of sense, he experiences in the full reality of the senses the dawning of the terrifying deities, their forms, the dim and smoky lights and flames, and their chilling cries which demand annihilation. This overwhelming aspect of the *numinosum tremendum* of the wrathful deities throws the awareness into various levels of unconsciousness, and the further along the descending path one goes, the more unconsciousness and the inability to liberate onself will spread. We called the path of awareness through the bardo a reversed path, since on it all events are the reverse of their counterparts in earthly life. In the bardo of the death experience, the 'Chi-kha'i bardo, the highest and most perfect awareness flashes for a moment, and there then begins the descent of awareness through the Chos-nyid bardo on the level of the sambhogakāya. Until the moment of the reincarnation of awareness at the end of the Srid-pa'i bardo, awareness has almost totally succumbed to unconsciousness. Thus, the Book of the Dead, in describing the visions of the wrathful deities and the hells, talks of the helpless awareness being driven to and fro and of the violent red wind of karma which drives beings down into the abyss.

The symbol of blood, well known in the Buddhist Tantras as the element of life, now receives its negative side, in that the wrathful blood-drinking deities (T. Khrag-'thung khro-bo) drink the blood, bearer of all desires and passions, of the dead person. With demonic energy they seize the dead person like Furies and drink his blood from the kapāla, the skull goblet. The awareness flees from this spectacle down into the lower realms of the bardo. It loses the ability to collect itself and succumbs to the demonic visions which are the only things it can focus upon. It is therefore considered necessary for a person to concern himself with the bardo deities during his life, so that afterwards he will not be deceived and fascinated by their appearance.

As with the peaceful deities, we find in the maṇḍala of the wrathful deities a series of psychological meanings, which were in the Tibetan Book of the Dead brought together inseparably with the doubtless extremely ancient theriomorphic deities. All the deities of the Book of the Dead, but above all the demonic emanations, are initiatory figures, as is the case with the Egyptian Book of the Dead. They are connected with a symbolism related to the human psyche and are amplified by a picture of Buddhist psychology, which presents itself before awareness in visions.

Let us follow the order of the deities of the second cycle according to the teachings of the Book of the Dead as taught, for example, on September 8 of the year of the bird (A.D. 1501) by the Tibetan treasure-discoverer Padma gling-pa before his students in the Kun-bzang-gling monastery in eastern Bhutan.[109] He emphasizes the psychological significance of the deities: "One's own body is the home of the peaceful and wrathful deities." Then from out of the powerful Mahāśrī-Heruka (T. Che-mchog Heruka), the wrathful manifestation of Ādibuddha Samantabhadra, there unfolds the group of the five blood-drinking deities in order to annihilate the five principal failings of human behavior (T. Khrag-'thung rigs-lnga). With them appear the five Heruka-Ḍākinīs to enlighten the five elemental realms (T. Khams-lnga kro-ti-shvari-ma). They are followed by the eight wrathful Keurima and the eight animal-headed Phra-men-ma for the enlightenment of the eight kinds of awareness and their realms of operation (T. gNas-brgyad yul-brgyad ke'u-ri bcu drug). These are the wrathful counterparts of the eight Bodhisattvas and Ḍākinīs from the maṇḍala of the peaceful deities. Then from the four cosmic directions of the visionary space follow the four theriomorphic female Guardians, whose purpose is to indicate to awareness its "four boundaries" (T. rTag-chad mu-bzhi sgo-ma bzhi). At the end there is a wild round-dance of animal-headed Furies who appear in groups of seven wrathful Ḍākinīs from each of the inner regions of the head, from its eastern, southern, western, and northern parts. They conquer all karmic hindrances in order to liberate the world of awareness from all passions and attachments. For only on the image-less level can the realm of transcendence be attained.[110]

We must indicate a further fundamental difference between the peaceful and wrathful deities that relates to the extensive cosmological and psychological physiology of tantric Yoga, which plays an important role in the picture of the universal man. These differences go back to the ancient Indian teachings of Buddhist Yoga, as handed down by the siddhas. They teach that there are three nāḍīs, or subtle channels of psychic energy, which run inside the length of the spine, and these are the moon-nāḍī, the sun-energy nāḍī, and the central avadhūtī nāḍī. The joining of the sun- and moon-energies in the central avadhūtī by means of physical and psychical yoga-techniques is said to lead to an intensification of awareness and enlightenment. The three nāḍīs in the profane and ignorant person are channels for the "three poisons," desire, hatred, and delusion, which are "the three evils of worldly existence."[111] They prevent the deities from having any influence in the three nāḍīs, for only through the "highest truth" can the nāḍīs be purified.

These generally secret teachings, transmitted in various traditions, in Kuṇḍalinī Yoga in particular, were transmitted to Tibet with the "Six Doctrines" of Nāropa. They are also the basis for the idea in Yoga that the appearance of deities is psychically conditioned, according to which the deities assume differing forms according to the state of awareness. Therefore, the peaceful deities are surrounded by an aureole of rays the colors of the five elements, and they always appear on a lotus-moon throne. This means that the top surface of the lotus is a horizontal crescent moon. All the heroic deities and the wrathful deities of the bardo appear in an aureole of flames and upon a sun-lotus throne. The inseparable unity of both of their ways of appearing, the peaceful and wrathful aspects, the male and the female emanations, leads to the totality of the experience of reality in the Chos-nyid bardo and to the recognition that all forms are images of one's own awareness, behind which "empty" and absolute reality is to be found.

A. THE GREAT HERUKA OF THE ĀDIBUDDHA (YAB-YUM)

Above the first maṇḍala of the five Buddha-Herukas, the Ādibuddha Samantabhadra appears in the form of the powerful and terrible red-brown Che-mchog Heruka (S. Mahāśrī-Heruka). The maṇḍala of the great wrathful blood-drinking deities is a fivefold lotus in the brain cakra, with a center and four petals.

"There first appears there from the center of the lotus and amidst the radiance of fiery light the great, wrathful blood-drinking Che-mchog Heruka," with three heads, nine eyes, six arms, and four legs, upon a lotus, and in a flaming aureole. His right face is the color of smoke, the middle white, and the left red. In his three right hands he carries the vajra, the trident (S. khaṭvāṅga), and a drum with a handle (T. rNga-chung), and in his left hands he carries the bell, the kapāla, and a sling made from innards. The powerful Heruka appears in inseparable union with his Ḍākinī Krodheśvarī, whose color is pure white.

Che-mchog Heruka appears as Ādi-Heruka outside the maṇḍala of the five Buddha-Herukas; he is the sixth Heruka and the unfolder of the great maṇḍala of the wrathful deities. He is the primary precondition for all other terrifying deities and in certain texts is not mentioned in the sequence of after-death visions. The best known texts of the Tibetan Book of the Dead usually begin with the maṇḍala of the five Buddha-Herukas. Like the Ādibuddha Samantabhadra, the great Mahāśrī-Heruka thus occupies a special position among the bardo deities.

B. THE FIVE WRATHFUL BUDDHA-HERUKAS (YAB-YUM)

On the eighth day (the first day of the wrathful deities) there appears in the center of the lotus cakra the Heruka of Buddha Vairocana in the form of the smoke-colored dPal-chen Buddha-Heruka with his white Ḍākinī, Buddha-Krodheśvarī. The central Heruka has three faces, six arms, and four legs. The right face is white, the middle smoke-black, and the left red. In his right hands he carries a long-handled axe, a flaming sword, and the wheel of the teachings; in his left, a kapāla, a ploughshare, and a bell. This wrathful Heruka is an emanation of Buddha Vairocana, manifesting himself in a terrifying flaming form.

His retinue then appears at the four cosmic directions, one of the remaining Buddha-Herukas on each day, as emanations of the peaceful meditation-Buddhas. They are the dark blue Vajra-Heruka with the Ḍākinī Vajra-Krodheśvarī in the east, the yellow Ratna-Heruka with his Ḍākinī Ratna-Krodheśvarī in the south, the red Padma-Heruka with the Ḍākinī Padma-Krodheśvarī in the west, and finally the green Karma-Heruka with his Ḍākinī Karma-Krodheśvarī in the north. All Herukas have three heads, six arms, and four legs and are adorned with the tantric buddha-crown of skulls and with skull-necklaces. These five Herukas in their terrifying numinosity vehemently set upon the "five poisons," with their seemingly ineradicable roots in ignorance, hatred, pride, passion, and envy.[112] It is explained to the awareness of the dead person in the ritual of the "confrontation with the wrathful deities" that these Herukas of the eighth to the twelfth day are nothing other than the emanations of one's own mind and that they should be recognized as forms of the Five Buddhas, one's own protective deities. This is a demand to integrate these visions into one's own awareness, whereby their psychically detrimental effect is dissolved. For the awareness-principle caught in the delusion of ignorance, or, psychologically speaking, in unconsciousness, these Herukas must constitute a great danger, since their true (psychologically conditioned) nature is not recognized. The wrathful Herukas are also to be understood as "guides on the illuminated path of the five wisdoms," just as the five Buddhas were addressed in the "prayer of liberation from the bardo" (T. Bar-do 'phrang-grol-gyi smon-lam). If the Herukas are seen in their true light, the danger dissolves, and the way to liberation in the sambhogakāya stands open.

Lotus Cakra	Heruka	Color	Heruka-Ḍākinī	Emanation of the Buddha
Center	Buddha-Heruka	Smoke-Brown	Buddha-Krodheśvarī	Vairocana
East	Vajra-Heruka	Blue-Black	Vajra-Krodheśvarī	Vajrasattva-Akṣobhya
South	Ratna-Heruka	Smoke-Yellow	Ratna-Krodheśvarī	Ratnasambhava
West	Padma-Heruka	Smoke-Red	Padma-Krodheśvarī	Amitābha
North	Karma-Heruka	Smoke-Green	Karma-Krodheśvarī	Amoghasiddhi

TABLE 17. The Five Buddha-Herukas.

A significant attribute of the Buddha-Herukas is that they generally have the wings of the garuḍa bird. The Herukas are magical apparitions, and they possess the power to overcome evil, which is symbolized in particular by the mythical bird, Garuḍa, the destroyer of the serpent-demons. Most paintings for the Tibetan Book of the Dead show the Herukas with wings, but there are also some in which only the central Che-mchog Heruka has wings. We also find many Tibetan pictures in which all six Buddha-Herukas are shown in the center of the maṇḍala of wrathful deities. More rare are versions which show only the five Buddha-Herukas. The different arrangements of the deities in the various paintings for the Book of the Dead reflect the different Tibetan texts upon which the paintings are based.

C. THE EIGHT KEURIMA

With the Fury-like eight wrathful female deities, called the Keurima, we encounter the terrifying aspects of the eight peaceful Bodhisattvas from the first cycle of bardo deities. As wrathful Ḍākinīs they have the same psychologically motivated task, the enlightenment of awareness, as the Bodhisattvas, but now considerably intensified by their powerful wrathful aspect (T. Drag-po). This becomes essential, as the awareness sinks deeper into unconsciousness and allows itself to be driven by fear of the terrifying figures which it does not properly recognize. The Keurima are called "Wisdom-Ḍākinīs of the eight kinds of awareness" (T. rNam-shes brgyad-kyi ye-shes mkha'-'gro bzhi).[113] These Ḍākinīs are also emanations from the cosmologically oriented portions of the head and are divided into two groups, that of the "inner four Ḍākinīs" (T. Nang-gi mkha'-'gro bzhi), of the cardinal directions with pure colors, and that of the "outer four Ḍākinīs" (T. Phyi-yi mkha'-'gro bzhi), of the intermediate directions with mixed colors. Once again the head is pictured as an eight-petalled lotus: from the east comes the white Keurima carrying a human corpse as a club in her right hand and a kapāla in her left; from the south comes the yellow Tseurima (Caurī-ma) with drawn bow and arrow (the tantric symbol for the unity of path and goal = Thabs-shes); from the west comes the red Pramohā with the makara sign of victory (which guarantees no further access to saṃsāra); and from the north comes the dark green Vaitālī (Petalī) who carries the vajra of eternal reality and a kapāla.[114]

The second group of ḍākinīs originates from the four intermediate directions: the reddish-yellow Pukkasī from the southeast, who pulls innards from the place of sinful misery; from the southwest, the greenish-black Ghasmarī, who stirs the skull-bowl with a vajra (or who drinks blood from the kapāla as a sacrifice to the giving up of saṃsāra); [115] from the northwest the pale-yellow Caṇḍālī, carrying a heart and a corpse (or who "is just tearing the head of false thinking from a corpse"); and finally from the northeast the blue-black Śmaśānī, who is twisting the head off a corpse. All eight terrible goddesses make wild gestures of threat, violence, and destruction and are surrounded by the raging flames of anger. They are followed by the eight theriomorphic Phra-men-ma Goddesses, who correspond to the peaceful Ḍākinīs of the Bodhisattvas.

D. THE EIGHT PHRA-MEN-MA

A second group of eight terrifying goddesses are the eight theriomorphic Ma-mo Goddesses or Phra-men-ma, who rule over the eight realms of awareness (T. Yul-gyi phra-men-brgyad). Like the Eight Keurima, they belong to the thirteenth day of the bardo visions, and they are the wrathful counterparts to the eight Ḍākinīs of the Bodhisattvas from the first cycle of peaceful deities.[115] In contrast to the Keurima, the eight Phra-men-ma goddesses, although of human form, have animal heads. Four of them have bird heads, and four animal heads: the animal-headed goddesses correspond to the four cardinal directions of the eight-petalled lotus, and the others to the intermediate directions.[116]

In the east appears the smoke-brown, lion-headed goddess Siṃhamukhī (T. Seng-mgo-can) amidst red flames. She holds her arms crossed in front of her breast in order to devour a corpse. The red Vyāghramukhī (T. sTag-gdong-can) appears from the south and has a terrible yellow tiger's-head. She holds both hands crossed below. From the west comes the black Śṛgālamukhī (T. Wa-mgo-can) with a red hyena's head (or fox's-head). In her right hand she brandishes a dagger, and in her left hands she grasps innards from which to drink the blood. From the north appears the dark-blue Śvamukhī (T. Spyang-mgo-can) with a grey wolf's-head, who carries a corpse in both hands and devours it. From the southeast comes the yellowish-white Gṛdhramukhī (T. Bya-rgod-mgo-can) with a vulture's head, and holding a corpse in her left hand, she tears innards out of it with her right. From the southwest appears the dark-red Kaṅkamukhī (T. Bya'i mgo-can) with the black death-bird's-head, who drags an enormous corpse on her shoulders. From the northwest comes the black Kākamukhī (T. Bya-rog mgo-can) with a raven's-head, who carries in her left hand a scimitar and in her right a kapāla. The last terrifying fury appears from the northeast and is the dark-blue ulūkamukhī (T. Ug-pa'i mgo-can), with the brown owl's-head, who carries in her right hand a vajra and in her left a kapāla (or else a sword). These are the eight flesh-eating demonic goddesses of the eight realms who, together with the five Herukas, originate from the various regions of one's own head. They should not be feared, but should rather be considered as emanations of one's own thinking. All theriomorphic goddesses as well as the eight Keurima wear leopard-skins and hover in empty space, surrounded by blazing flames. Psychologically, they perform the same functions as the eight Bodhisattvas and Ḍākinīs. The symbolism of the sixteen Fury-like goddesses as counterparts to the Bodhisattvas is of particular psychological interest, in that we find in the eight Phra-men-ma, groupings of mythological images of the negative mother and of the guidance of awareness which point to archetypal structures of mythically conditioned origination of images.

E. THE FOUR ANIMAL-HEADED FEMALE GUARDIANS OF THE MAṆḌALA

On the fourteenth day there appear from the four cosmic directions of the head the four animal-headed Ḍākinīs, followed by the 28 powerful and similarly animal-headed Ḍākinīs. The four Guardians (T. sGo-ma bzhi, or also sGo-skyong khro-mo bzhi) are fairly similar to the Phra-men-ma. As far as their buddhological significance is concerned, they again represent the "four divine boundless states" (T. Tshad-med bzhi). The four female Guardians are the four heralds of the 28 powerful goddesses and also count as members of this group, in which they appear again. But basically they also appear in the death ritual apart from the group as the guardians of the four gates of the maṇḍala. The 28 goddesses are subject to a cosmologically conditioned fourfold division into four groups of seven including the Guardians, or else the group of four Guardians can stand separately beside four groups of six goddesses.

At the east gate[117] the white rTa-gdong-ma appears with a horse's head,[118] holding in her right hand a kapāla and in her left a vajra iron hook (T. rDo-rje lcags-kyu). As the bearer of tantric symbols she teaches "boundless compassion" (T. sNying-rje tshad-med). At the south gate appears the yellow Phag-gdong-ma with the black boar's-head, carrying in her right hand a kapāla, and in her left a sling with which to pull the dead person out of the mire of saṃsāra. She announces the heavenly state of "boundless kindness" (T. Byams-pa tshad-med). From the west gate of the maṇḍala comes the red Seng-gdong-ma with the white lion's-head, carrying a kapāla in her right hand and an iron chain in her left. She is the herald of the state of "boundless sympathetic joy" (T. dGa'-ba tshad-med). At the north gate of the maṇḍala the green sBrul-gdong-ma appears with the grey serpent's-head, carrying the kapāla in her right hand and the bell in her left, the ringing of which fades away into emptiness. She announces the fourth divine boundless state of "infinite equanimity" (T. bTang-snyoms tshad-med). All four Guardians appear surrounded by flames and wearing tigers' skins.

F. THE 28 POWERFUL, ANIMAL-HEADED GODDESSES

On the fourteenth day the outer ring of the Maṇḍala of the Wrathful Deities produces the four times seven animal-headed goddesses, who originate from the cosmic directions. Some Tibetan paintings correspond exactly in their structure to the descriptions of the Tibetan Book of the Dead as translated by Evans-Wentz, and also to such descriptions as we have given.[119] In the central circle we recognize the five Buddha-Herukas and the Che-mchog Heruka, and in the first ring around the center are the eight Keurima and the eight Phra-men-ma as well as the four theriomorphic female Guardians. These are the thirty wrathful Herukas and deities (T.

Heruka drag-po'i lha bcu-sum tham-pa) referred to by the Tibetan Book of the Dead, without mention of the Heruka of the Ādibuddha. Then follow, in the four sectors of the outer ring, the 28 wrathful and powerful goddesses (T. dBang-phyug nyer-brgyad). They are also called the 28 flesh-eating Ḍākinīs (T. Sha-za mkha'-'gro).[120] First come the four groups of six Ḍākinīs from the four directions of one's own head and then the four female Guardians.

From the east comes the smoke-black Srin-mo goddess Rākṣasī with the head of a Tibetan yak (T. gYag-mgo-me), carrying a vajra. She is followed by the reddish-yellow Brāhmaṇī with a snake's-head (T. sBrul-gdong-ma) and the dharma wheel in her hand, the greenish-black Mahādevī with a leopard's-head (T. gZigs-mgo-ma) and the triśūla (trident) in her hand, the blue Vaisnavī with a mongoose's-head (T. Sre-mong mgo-ma)[121] and the dharma wheel in her hand, the red Kumārī with the head of a Tibetan snow-bear (T. Dred-mgo-ma) and a short spear in her hand, and, as the sixth goddess in this group, the white Indrāṇī with a bear's-head (T. Dom-mgo-ma), holding innards in her hand.[122]

Then from the south come the yellow Vajrī with a bat's-head (T. Pha-wang mgo-ma) and a knife in her hand, the red Śāntī with the makara-head of a water dragon (T. Chu-srin mgo-ma) and the kalaśa (the vessel of the water of life) in her hand, the red Amṛtā with a scorpion's-head (T. sDig-pa'i mgo-ma) and a lotus in her hand, the white Candrā with a falcon's-head (T. Khra'i mgo-ma) and the vajra in her right hand, the greenish-black Daṇḍā with a fox's-head (T. Wa'i mgo-ma) and a club in her right hand, and finally the yellowish-black Rākṣasī with a tiger's-head (T. sTag-gi mgo-ma) and a blood-filled kapāla in her left hand.

From the west appear the greenish-black Za-ba with a vulture's head (T. Bya-rgod mgo-ma) and a club in her hand, the red d'Ga'-ba with a horse's-head (T. rTa'i mgo-ma) and carrying the trunk of a huge corpse, the white Mahābalī with a garuḍa's-head (T. Khyung-gi mgo-ma) and holding a club in her hand, the red Rāksasī with a dog's-head (T. Khyi'i mgo-ma) and carrying a vajra-knife, the red Abhilāṣī with a hoopoe's-head (T. Pu-shud mgo-ma) and carrying a bow and arrow ready to shoot, and finally the greenish-red Nor-srung with a stag's head (T. Sha-ba'i mgo-ma) and carrying a kalaśa.

From the north appear the blue Vāyudevī with a wolf's-head (T. sPyang-ki'i mgo-ma) and a weathervane in her hand, the red Nārī with the head of an ibex (T. sKyin-gyi mgo-ma) and carrying a sling of strung teeth, the red Vajrī with a crow's-head (T. Khva-tva'i mgo-ma) with the corpse of a child in her right hand, the greenish-black sNa-chen with an elephant's-head (T. Glang-chen mgo-ma) carrying a huge corpse, and finally the blue Varuṇī with a snake's-head (T. sBrul-gyi mgo-ma) and carrying a sling wound around with snakes.

Now 24 of the 28 powerful goddesses have appeared and they are followed in the four gates of the maṇḍala by the four Guardians once again, who conclude the entire maṇḍala of the 58 terrible goddesses.

From the four directions of the head appear the four female Guardians who are similar to the goddesses of the maṇḍala gates mentioned above. In the east is the white Vajraḍākinī with a cuckoo's-head (T. Khu-dbyug mgo-ma) and an iron hook in her right hand. In the south is the yellow Ḍākinī with the antelope's-head (or goat's head) with spiralling horns (T. Ra-mgo-ma) and holding a sling in her hand, while in the west the red Ḍākinī with the lion's-head (T. Seng-mgo-ma) appears with an iron chain in her hand. At the north gate the greenish-black Ḍākinī with the snake's-head (T. sBrul-mgo-ma) appears and lets the bell (T. Dril-bu) in her hand ring into the emptiness.

All these deities should be recognized as manifestations of one's own mind. The 42 peaceful deities come from the radiance of the dharmakāya, and the 58 wrathful deities come from the radiance of the sambhogakāya.

The Tibetan Book of the Dead mentions another consequence of the transformations of the visionary deities in case one flees from these images out of fear. Then all the peaceful deities become forms of the protective deity Mahākāla, and all the wrathful deities change into the most extremely negative and threatening aspect of the god of death, Dharmarāja (T. Chos-kyi rgyal-po).

The peaceful deities assume the aspect of power which represents protection through wisdom and knowledge. Mahākāla, the great and powerful protective deity, is indeed a wrathful figure, but in the positive sense. Therefore he is also called Ye-shes mgon-po, the "protector of knowledge and wisdom." If, even under this positive aspect of the warding off of ignorance, the person does not become aware that all manifestations of the deities in the bardo are not external to his own mind, but rather are inherent in it, then the wrathful deities will suddenly all appear in the form of Yama or Dharmarāja, the god of death. For all manifestations of one's own thought, in the form of "images" of psychic projection, but not recognized as such or else they could be withdrawn, are now annihilated. The Tibetan symbolism has found in the intensification of the various aspects of the deities an appropriate psychological medium for the expression in such images of the psychic process of wisdom, knowledge, and enlightenment on the one hand, and of ignorance, delusion, and passion on the other. These of course come from an ancient mythical world, which always attains its own reality in high religions such as Buddhism. It is remarkable to see how, when such religions migrate to other countries, the high teachings are always expressed by ancient images in such a way that they are comprehensible to everyone.

For this reason the Tibetan Book of the Dead also says that one should regard the images as forms of manifestation of one's own awareness, i.e., the Buddhist doctrine is working here with realistic visions but is demanding their psychic dissolution and overcoming, since they would not be compatible with the doctrine of absolute liberation in imageless and purely transcendent nirvāṇa.

The lama or monk directing the whole death ritual and the recitations for the dead person admonishes the awareness "wandering through the bardo like a stray dog" to value properly his "spirit-body formed from karmically conditioned hindrances" (T. Bag-chags yid-kyi lus), in that, no matter how anxious it may be in the face of the threatening deities and furies, it cannot be destroyed and ultimately remains immortal in the bardo (T. 'Chi rgyu-med). For the person has no kind of embodiment and consists of pure awareness, even though this is seemingly capable of all sensation. The dead person is reminded, therefore, that his bardo body is in reality formed of emptiness (T. Stong-pa'i rang-gzugs). It was mentioned repeatedly during the earlier part of the ritual recitations that all the radiant and burning apparitions of the deities on the level of the sambhogakāya and of the highest dharmakāya are emanations from infinite emptiness. Or, according to Buddhist Vijñānavāda philosophy, all images and visions and also all objective things are emanations from the immeasurable ālayavijñāna, the universal-consciousness, which is capable of forming everything. Karma is characterized in the Book of the Dead as the wind from the red cloud which drives the dead beings into the abyss of reincarnation. But karma is also the wind which causes waves of thought on the surface of the ocean of awareness and the ten thousand created forms of mind which prevent a clear view into the depths of ground-consciousness.

Thus, at the end of the part of the Book of the Dead which presents the visions of the wrathful deities, it says that even the destructive forms of Dharmarāja are merely images of one's own thought forms, with no reality of their own. They are emptiness, and cannot harm the emptiness of a liberated awareness-principle. If the recognizing mind and the images mutually interpenetrate, then liberation on a higher level is attained, and this can no longer be described, since there is no kind of suffering of opposites. This is the meaning of the recognition of the "clear light," the highest experience of transcendence in the bardo.

G. THE FIVE JÑĀNA-ḌĀKINĪS AND THE POWERFUL VAJRAKUMĀRA-HERUKA

Certain ritual texts of the Tibetan Book of the Dead talk of some additional deities, which gives rise to an enlarged maṇḍala of 117 peaceful and wrathful deities.[123] We find this larger maṇḍala exclusively in the tradition of the rNying-ma-pa and the 'Brug-pa sects of Tibet, Ladakh, and Bhutan. The seven additional deities are situated in the two lowermost cakras, the mūlādhāra-cakra (T. gSang-gnas dkyil-'khor) and the maṇipūra-cakra (T. lTe-ba'i dkyil-'khor). In Chapter II (4E) we were introduced to the lowest cakra in the perineum as the location of the protective deity Vajrakumāra, or Vajrakīla-Heruka. This cakra is also associated with karmic activity (T. Phrin-las) and with Buddha Amoghasiddhi and is usually referred to in the bardo texts as the sukhapāla-cakra (T. bDe-skyong 'khor-lo). Here the powerful protective deity Vajrakīla-Heruka watches over the place of desire (kāma). Between this cakra and the heart-lotus is the maṇipūra-cakra, also called the nirmāṇacakra (T. sPrul-pa'i 'khor-lo). Here, in the place of karmic merit (S. guṇa) and of Buddha Ratnasambhava, appear the five "Wisdom-Ḍākinīs" (T. Ye-shes mkha'-'gro lnga).

They form a five-petalled lotus or a hexagram with the five mantric seed-syllables Bam, Ha, Ri, Ni, and Sa. In the center appears the white Buddha-Ḍākinī, in the east the blue Vajra-Ḍākinī, in the south the yellow Ratna-Ḍākinī, in the west the red Padma-Ḍākinī, and in the north the green Karma-Ḍākinī. They are initiation-goddesses, known in Buddhist symbolism also as emanations of the tantric Ḍākinī, Vajravārāhī (T. rDo-rje phag-mo).

In the lowermost lotus, the sukhapāla-cakra, the dark-blue Vajrakīla or Vajrakumāra-Heruka appears as a powerful personal protective deity. He has three heads, six arms, and four legs and stands on a lotus with his light-blue female counterpart. Vajrakumāra also has the wings of the garuḍa and wears the tantric death's-head buddha-crown. In his first pair of hands he holds a ninefold vajra (T. rDo-rje rtse-dgu) and a burning flame; in the second pair he carries a vajra and a long trident; in the third pair he holds a magic dagger and at the same time embraces his Prajñā. The magic dagger, also called a vajra dagger (S. vajrakīla; T. rDo-rje phur-pa), is an important ritual tool in the tantric rites of Tibet. Its handle is a vajra and it has a three-edged blade. The deity is himself named after this attribute. The dagger is used in Tibet for ritual exorcism and annihilation of harmful and demonic beings, and especially of serpent-spirits. According to the Tibetan Book of the Dead the magic dagger is associated with the sukhapāla-cakra in that it is the three-edged tool for annihilating the "three basic evils" or "three poisons" of all human activity, which continually lead to karma and attachment. These "three poisons" (T. Dug-gsum) are ignorance, hatred, and the passions. As long as they condition life and are continually set in motion by the desires, no exit can be found from the cycle of the worlds of suffering. Therefore the blue Vajrakumāra as the wrathful protective deity occupies the lowest cakra, in order to protect karma from these three failings. We have now become acquainted with all the deities of the Buddhist pantheon for the bardo visions, who symbolize in their individual meanings the total psychical and physical being of man.

Place	Visions	Lotus or Cakra	Five Buddhas
Forehead	Wrathful Deities	Mahāsukha-Cakra	Vairocana
Throat	Knowledge-holding Deities	Sambhoga-Cakra	Amitābha
Heart	Peaceful Deities	Dharma-Cakra	Vajrasattva-Akṣobhya
Navel	Wisdom-Ḍākinīs	Nirmāṇa-Cakra	Ratnasambhava
Perineum	Vajrakumāra-Heruka	Sukhapāla-Cakra	Amoghasiddhi

TABLE 18

3. From the Books of the Dead of the Pre-Buddhist Ancient Tibetan Bon Religion

> Then your heart is a dark valley; if you do not soon work for the birth of the light, he will then ignite the fire of anger in you . . . and you will be unable with your animal birth to reach the gates of heaven.
>
> JACOB BOEHME, *Aurora*

WE HAVE not yet considered in any depth the teachings of the ancient Tibetan Bon religion, which had been widespread in the high lands of Tibet before the arrival of Buddhism from India. We must of course distinguish between the various kinds of Tibetan folk-beliefs and the authentic Bon religion as such. Where the border between the two formerly lay cannot be stated categorically. What is certain is that with the propagation in Tibet of Buddhist teachings since the seventh century, we also know, from written evidence of the kings and early monks, of the existence of this religion whose adherents call themselves Bon-po. Tibetan folk-beliefs and local religious movements stem from essentially differentiated ideas of soul and spirit, woven into an ancient magical-mythical world view which exhibits ancient central Asiatic and shamanistic traits. This is a multi-layered realm of heterogeneous ideas about the essence and persistence of the soul after death, of its journey through the underworld and its return to the earthly world, and these ideas are clearly distinguishable from those teachings of the Bon religion with which we now want to deal. At first glance the systems of the Bon-po known to us today have such profound and well-ordered psychological and ethical foundations that they are hardly distinguishable from the Buddhist religion.

We also know, however, that in the course of the assimilation between Buddhism and the Bon religion on Tibetan soil which lasted many centuries, a transformation of the Bon religion took place, in which many forms of Buddhist thinking and categories were integrated. The Buddhist maṇḍala theory, for example, with its cosmology and the well-known fivefold symbolism, became an indispensable foundation of the Bon-po pantheon as in the extant writings of the Bar-do thos-grol. There were of course many demonstrable influences in the opposite direction, in the case of the symbolism of the "nine doctrinal systems" (T. Theg-pa dgu), for example. It is not our task here to engage in an historical and religious or philological comparison between the two religions, the problem being too complex and the subject not sufficiently researched. We can, however, apart from critical historical comparisons, deal with the Book of the Dead of the Bon religion, which exhibits a striking similarity to that of the Buddhist tradition.

If we consider that in the Bon religion there was the tradition, as in Tibetan Buddhism, of the "gTer-ma" scriptures which were found by the "treasure discoverers," we can then go fairly far back, historically speaking.

The work by the Bon-po gTer-ston 'Or-sgom phug-pa (12th–13th centuries) dealing with the Nāraka deities of the bardo worlds[124] bears a striking similarity to the Nāraka-cycles of the Buddhist writings from the Na-rag dong-sprugs genre. There are also manuscripts, which are perhaps three- to four-hundred years old, in which there is a systematic arrangement of the bardo deities, the peaceful and wrathful emanations, the six worlds of rebirth, and the six Buddhas of the wheel of life, which, even under other names, immediately display their relationship to the Buddhist tradition. Buddhist principles in the Bon religion are even clearer in the maṇḍala symbolism, the use of the elemental and psychological symbolism of the five skandhas, the five wisdoms and the "five poisons," which for the most part are applied in the Bon religion by means of the same concepts. We may also conclude that both these systems of organized religion could be of non-Tibetan origin, which has already been shown in the case of Buddhism.

Our historical knowledge indicates that important currents of the Bon religion came from western Tibet, perhaps even from beyond the western border (Kashmir to Iran). Also, the great founder or reorganizer of the Bon doctrine, gShen-rab myi-bo, is said to have come to western Tibet from the region of the west Himalayas.

His history is as much concealed behind fantastic legends as that of Padmasambhava, about whom we can at least establish a chronology of the few years of his stay in Tibet. Yet the influence of the teachings of gShen-rab was considerable, and many things and religious or spiritual stages were given his name (gShen), which is at the same time the principal concept of his doctrine.

Let us now come back to the Tibetan Book of the Dead and to that of the Bon religion. Even if we do not possess any translated works of this kind, there are nevertheless some Tibetan sources from which we can draw. The best known Tibetan Book of the Dead of the Bon-po is the Bar-do thos-grol gsal-sgron chen-mo, a work similar in many respects to the Buddhist version. Given certain differences in symbolism and in the various deities, which are generally more numerous and have individual personalities and different names, we could say that the course of the Bon-po Book of the Dead is more or less parallel in content to that of the

Buddhist version. Yet we must be careful not to oversimplify or to force any parallels. It is nevertheless helpful to the reader to have the schema of the Buddhist bardo visions in his mind's eye throughout the following presentation, since the structure in the Bon religion is somewhat similar.

In what follows we shall briefly describe the peaceful and wrathful deities according to certain bardo teachings of the Bon-po and describe their symbolism in outline, since we are unable here to present a more penetrating study or a more complete description of the very complex symbolism. Given a detailed presentation of the Bon-po traditions of the Tibetan Book of the Dead, the reader might become confused by the complexity of the symbols and colors of the deities and their attributes in the Bon religion.

Let us proceed from some basic premises common to the Bon religion and to Buddhism. We find similarities in the descriptions of the process of dying, the sinking of awareness through the elements, and in the division of the stages of the bardo. We again find the 'Chi-kha'i bardo, the Chos-nyid bardo, and the Srid-pa'i bardo. The number of deities in the visions is greater. The division into peaceful and wrathful deities with male and female aspects, the ḍākinīs, the buddhas, the theriomorphic deities, and the herukas are similar in both traditions.

A. THE PEACEFUL DEITIES

At the beginning stands another threefold invocation formula: Lha bon gshen dang gsum la phyag-'tshal-lo. Hereby the highest triad of the Bon-po religion is invoked: "I take refuge in the deities, the teaching, and the founder, gShen-rab." Whereas in the Buddhist Tibetan Book of the Dead we had the pure dharma-sphere of the Ādibuddha Samantabhadra as the transcendent and absolute origin, we have here the "swastika-sphere (T. gYung-drung-gi dbyings) of the unchanging Bon" (T. Mi-'gyur bon-nyid), from whose "radiant heaven of the light of wisdom" the highest deity Samantabhadra (T. mNga'-bdag kun-tu bzang-po) appears as the first figure.[125] It is remarkable that the dark-blue Samantabhadra is the highest deity of the Bon religion as well as of the ancient non-reformed rNying-ma-pa sect of Tibet. Samantabhadra is the perfected embodiment of Bon-reality and embraces all three worlds. From the absolute Bon-sphere, concretized in the blue Samantabhadra in the form of the true Bon (T. Bon-sku), there radiates from the heart-center the clear light of the highest wisdom. From this emanate all the deities, unfolding in luminous maṇḍalas, of the peaceful and wrathful orders (T. Zhi-khro lha-tshogs) of the Bon-po Book of the Dead, who appear in order to remove all impurities and hindrances on the path through the bardo. According to the sNyan-rgyud tradition of the Bar-do thos-grol[126] the first to appear from radiance and emptiness is the gShen deity "White Light" (T. gShen-lha 'od-dkar) on a magnificent sun-moon-lotus throne. His color is white and his hands lie in his lap in the dhyānamudrā. He is clothed in regal splendor and thereby manifests in the form of the sambhogakāya. In his heart-lotus there appears from the innermost essence of spirit (T. Sems-nyid ngo-bo) the luminous white mantric syllable A, which is the most important seed-formula of the Bon religion. From this syllable emanates the fivefold radiance of the elemental lights of the wisdoms, and from these come the peaceful and wrathful deities of the bardo visions. The swastika (T. gYung-drung) is an important symbol of the Bon religion. It is the left-pointing hooked cross found as an emblem of the throne of the deities, and carried, for example, as a swastika-scepter by the divine founder of Bon, gShen-rab myi-bo, in his right hands (fig. 26). The swastika also appears in Buddhist symbolism, but in that case is right-pointing. We find certain other symbols in the two religions that are distinguished only by their right- (Buddhism) or left- (Bon) orientation.

This is important in relation to the maṇḍala symbolism of the Bon religion, since this too is read in the opposite direction. From the center one proceeds to the east (below) and then by the north (right) to the south on the left side of the lotus-maṇḍala. Correspondingly, the holy circumambulation of a Bon-po stūpa takes place to the left, whereas in Buddhism it goes to the right.

After gShen-la 'od-dkar has initiated the bardo visions as the embodiment of the white light, the complex form of the peaceful

Fig. 26. The founder of the ancient Tibetan Bon religion, gShen-rab, seated on a lotus. In his right hand he holds the swastika-sceptre. Tibetan drawing by a Bon-po artist.

deity rGyal-ba 'dus-pa follows as an emanation of Samantabhadra. He sits in the middle of a blue heavenly sphere on a lotus-throne with the symbolic animals, the lion, the elephant, the horse, the dragon, and the garuḍa, supporting the lotus. The dragon is found as a symbolic animal only with the Bon-po deities. rGyal-ba 'dus-pa has a white body which radiates in crystal-clear light. He has five heads and ten arms and is adorned with the finery of the sambhogakāya. His five faces are white, yellow, red, green, and blue. As attributes he carries sun and moon in his first pair of hands, the victory-sign and bow and arrow in the second, swastika and sling in the third, and cakra and iron hook in the fourth, the fifth pair being empty. rGyal-ba 'dus-pa[127] rules over the maṇḍala of the peaceful deities and occupies a position equivalent to that of Buddha Vajrasattva in the emanation-schema of the bardo deities. His terrifying aspect among the wrathful deities is the powerful protective deity, dBal-gsas.

Then the indigo-blue Khri-bzhi nams-ting (or, Khri-bzhi nam-bting rig-pa'i lha) appears on a dragon-throne above the sun-moon-lotus, radiating in the white, unchangeable body of knowledge.[128] This deity appears in tantric union with his female counterpart, Thugs-rje byams-ma, also called Srid-pa'i rgyal-mo. Khri-bzhi nams-ting has four faces which look towards the four cosmic directions. He points towards the formation of the cosmic maṇḍala by the five bDe-shegs rigs-lnga, who now arise from the center.

In the center of the maṇḍala there appears from a heavenly sphere in the fivefold radiant light of the spirit the deity Kun-snang khyab-pa bDe-shegs Thugs-kyi lha. His color is white and he wears crystal-clear robes; in his right hand he holds a cakra and in his left the sling. Thugs-kyi lha, the deity of the essence of spirit in the heart, appears in tantric union with the Ḍākinī Nam-mkha lha-mo, the goddess of heaven, also known as "Great Mother of Wisdom" (T. Shes-rab yum-chen). The appearance of this deity overcomes the vice of hatred (T. Zhe-sdang), and the wisdom of emptiness (T. sTong-nyid ye-shes) is proclaimed.

From the east of the maṇḍala comes sKu'i lha on an elephant-throne, and he is associated with the plane of corporeality. His color and robes are yellow, and he appears in tantric union with his Ḍākinī Sa-yi lha-mo, the goddess of the element earth. He teaches the overcoming of ignorance by mirror-like wisdom (T. Me-long ye-shes). In the west we find the red Tathāgata gSung-gi lha upon a dragon-throne. His robes are red, and his female counterpart is Me'i lha-mo, the goddess of the element fire. gSung-gi lha is associated with the plane of pure speech and appears in order to overcome the passions, since he symbolizes the wisdom of clear sight (T. Sor-rtogs ye-shes). In the south of the maṇḍala, the fifth of the Bon-po Tathāgatas, the blue Phrin-las lha, appears on the plane of karmic activity. He wears a vaiḍūrya-jewel robe and appears in tantric union with his Ḍākinī Chu-yi lha-mo, ruler of the element water. Phrin-las lha overcomes the vices of greed and envy and symbolizes the wisdom of karmic perfection of action (T. Bya-grub ye-shes).

If we compare the symbolism of the five Tathāgatas from the Bon-po maṇḍala of peaceful deities with that of the Buddhist Books of the Dead, the similarities are immediately apparent. In the Bon teachings too, we have the five Tathāgatas with their Ḍākinīs, the five elements, the five basic evils, the five groups of the human personality (T. Phung-po lnga), and the five wisdoms, which are identical with those of Buddhism down to the first-mentioned wisdom of emptiness. Also the color symbolism of the Bon-po maṇḍala of peaceful deities is basically the same as in the Buddhist maṇḍalas. However, the leftwards progression alters the meaning-relations between the colors and the elements. The Ḍākinīs of the Tathāgatas stand for the five elements (T. Byung-ba lnga) and have the same color. We cannot here go into all the details of the deities of the Books of the Dead of the Bon religion, since this would require a book of its own. In addition, the same kinds of consecration-cards are used, which we encountered previously as Zhi-khro tsa-ka-li. They have the same names in the Bon-religion and show, divided into groups, all the deities of the peaceful and wrathful cycles, including their attributes and symbols. The five Tathāgatas of the Bon-po maṇḍala and their relations to the elements, symbols, and wisdoms are laid out in table 19.

Direction	Bija-Mantra	Tathāgata	Family	Color	Symbolic Animal Vāhana	Ḍākini and Element	Five Failings	Five Wisdoms
Center	A	Thugs-kyi lha (citta-deva) Spirit/Mind	Tathātā Suchness	White	Lion	Nam-mkha lha-mo Ether	Hatred	Wisdom of Emptiness
East	Oṃ	sKu-yi lha (kāya-deva) Body	Swastika Hooked Cross	Yellow	Elephant	Sa-yi lha-mo Earth	Ignorance	Mirror-like Wisdom
North	Hūṃ	Yon-tan lha (guṇa-deva) Merit	Cakra Wheel of the Bon Doctrine	Green	Horse	rLung-yi lha-mo Air	Pride	Wisdom of Equanimity
West	Raṃ	gSung-gi lha (vāc-deva) Speech	Padma Lotus	Red	Turquoise Dragon	Me'i lha-mo Fire	Passions and Desires	Wisdom of Clear Sight
South	Dzaṃ	Phrin-las lha (karma-deva) Karma	Ratna Jewel	Blue	Garuda	Chu-yi lha-mo Water	Envy	Wisdom of Perfected Activity

TABLE 19: Symbolism of the Five Tathāgatas from the Bar-do thos-grol of the Bon religion.

After the first maṇḍala, there follow the eight Ye-gshen sems-dpa' and their Ḍākinīs, who are known as Ye-sangs lcam-yum. We are immediately reminded of the eight Bodhisattvas and Ḍākinīs of the Buddhist Book of the Dead, who together form a group of sixteen deities. The significance of the Ye-gshen sems-dpa' is the same as that of the Bodhisattvas, and they are similarly associated with the eight functions of awareness and their realms of operation. Together with their Ḍākinīs they accompany the five Tathāgatas. Two of these deities are shown in plate 12; their colors and symbols are different from those of the Bodhisattvas, but they are otherwise quite similar.

In another text from the Bon-po tradition which deals with the meanings of the six worlds of incarnation,[129] we find an interesting indication of the relation between mind and the five basic failings with reference to the psychophysical organization of the human body. According to this idea, hatred arises out of the coming together of mind and ether; from breath, or prāṇa-energy, and mind comes pride; from mind and body-warmth comes envy; from mind and blood come the passions; and from mind and flesh comes ignorance.

The Tibetan Book of the Dead of the Bon religion also has a doctrine of the six realms of existence, into which one can be reborn as a result of karmic activity. Here we find the same division into the worlds of hells, pretas, animals, titans, gods, and human beings. The ruler of the dead souls in the terrible worlds of hells is Yama Khram-thogs rgyal-po. And again, the six worlds of existence have a savior figure who in various emanations enters these worlds in order to bring the teachings concerning liberation from suffering. Every existence is only a passing intermediate condition in one of the six realms (T. Rigs drug bar-do); to enlighten the six classes of beings gShen-rab himself appears, in various emanations in the forms of Buddhas. The six Buddhas of the Bon-po tradition (T. 'Dul-gshen drug) are very similar to the Buddhist forms, in that only the colors and hand-gestures are different (see plate 12). The six emanations of gShen-rab appear in the realms of incarnation in order to liberate the beings living there from the "five poisons" (T. Dug lnga). They therefore have the same task of moral enlightenment fulfilled in the Buddhist Book of the Dead by the great compassionate Bodhisattva Avalokiteśvara.

In a white light there appears in the realm of the gods the white Buddha Ye-gshen gtsug-phud (or Lha-yi gshen-rab) from the mantric syllable A, which arises from the forehead-center. Ye-gshen gtsug-phud teaches the beings residing in the transitory heaven the overcoming of all five evils and hindrances.

In a green light there appears from the throat-center the blue lCe-rgyal par-ti (or Lha-min gshen-rab) in the world of the warring titans. The seed-syllable of this realm is SU, and the blue Buddha teaches the overcoming of pride and egotism. In a red light from the heart-center the blue gSang-ba 'dus-pa (or Mi'i gshen-rab) appears with the syllable RNI for the world of human beings in order to overcome envy. In the animal world, which is permeated by ignorance, there appears in a blue light the green Ti-sangs rang-zhi from the lotus of the navel-center. For the eternally hungry and thirsty pretas there appears in a red light from the lotus of the perineum the white Mu-cho ldem-drug, whose function is to extinguish the passions and desires of these beings. In the sixth world of hellish torments there appears from the lotus-cakra of the soles of the feet in a smoke-black light the violet gSang-ba ngang-

Realm	gShen-rab	Color	Attributes	Lotus-center
Gods	Ye-gshen gtsug-phud	White	Mussel-Scepter and Iron Hook	Forehead
Titans	lCe-gryal par-ti	Blue	Hand-Drum and Amṛta-Vessel	Neck
Human Beings	gSang-ba 'dus-pa	Turquoise	Hand-Drum and Amṛta-Vessel	Heart Bon-nyid Cakra
Animals	Ti-sangs rang-zhi	Green	Radiant Wheel and Amṛta-Vessel	Navel
Pretas	Mu-cho ldem-drug	White	Iron Hook and Wheel	Perineum
Hells	gSang-ba ngang-ring	Violet	Iron Hook and Wheel	Soles of the Feet

TABLE 20. Symbolism of the six emanations of gShen-rab. From Bon-po Niṣpanna-Yoga (pp. 134–140) and Na-rag pang-'gong rgyal-po.

ring (T. dMyal-ba'i gshen-rab) in order to overcome the evil of hatred. These are the six emanations of gShen-rab, which are to be understood as bringers of salvation in the six worlds of existence.

It will not surprise us that the Bon-po tradition is similar to the Buddhist Tibetan Book of the Dead in that it also has in the maṇḍala of peaceful deities the four Guardians and their female counterparts. The four Guardians (T. Ye-shes sgo-bzhi or rNgam-chen khro-bo) have wrathful Ḍākinīs (T. Dus bzhi rgyal-mo), the goddesses of the four times. They each have one of the four colors of the maṇḍala and various gestures of the hand. They conclude the peaceful deities of the first seven days of the bardo visions, who are assembled in a group of at least 42 deities.

B. THE WRATHFUL DEITIES

Corresponding to the arrangement of the peaceful deities of the bardo visions, the wrathful emanations appear in the same sequence: Samantabhadra, the five-headed rGyal-ba 'dus-pa, the five Bon-po Tathāgatas, and the other deities. The schema, with the peaceful aspects of the heart-lotus and the wrathful apparitions of one's own thought-forms from the intellect, is in principle the same as in the Buddhist Book of the Dead. We shall therefore give only a brief overview of the most important figures of the Bon maṇḍala according to the Bar-do thos-grol and the Na-rag pang-'gong rgyal-pa.

From the wrathful and powerful sphere of Bon-reality, amidst a great space burning with raging fires, there appears as the first and highest deity in his terrifying aspect dBal-gsas rngam-pa khro-rgyal, in tantric union with his female counterpart, rNgam-mo bde-'gro yum. The wrathful dBal-gsas is blackish-blue in color, and has nine terrible, glaring faces, eighteen arms, and four legs. He carries various weapons and attributes, and is embraced by his greenish-black Ḍākinī. dBal-gsas is the wrathful emanation of rGyal-ba 'dus-pa and embodies the kāya-aspect in the trikāya schema.

There then follows as an emanation of the peaceful four-headed Khri-bzhi nams-ting on the wrathful plane of the vāc-aspect (sambhogakāya) the powerful Khro-bo lha-rgod thog-pa.

He is dark blue, and has four heads and eight arms. His female counterpart is the goddess Srid-pa'i rgyal-mo (or sNang-srid kun-grags dbang-mo), whose color is greenish-black and who is said to have a hundred heads and a thousand arms. While considering the wrathful deities of the Bon religion and of the Buddhist Books of the Dead we must bear in mind that the deities emanating from the awareness principle assume enormous dimensions, that they are "eighteen times larger" than the world-mountain Sumeru, for instance. This means that the terrifying nature of these threatening deities who appear surrounded by flames surpasses all human imagination. It is only in such dimensions as one encounters in the incorporeal space of the bardo after death that the many-limbed and many-headed figures of the wrathful deities can be comprehended.

After these two terrifying leaders of the wrathful deities, there unfolds the maṇḍala of the five Tathāgata-Herukas on the five planes of citta, kāya, guṇa, vāc, and karma. All five Herukas have three heads, six arms, and four legs and appear together with their female counterparts. Their heads all have three eyes and blazing hair; they carry various weapons of destruction, and wear tiger- or leopard-skins and ornamental chains of snakes or skulls.

After the Herukas of the Tathāgatas, who together form a group of seven wrathful deities, there appear the wrathful appari-

Place in the Maṇḍala	Wrathful Emanation	Female Counterpart	Color	Plane of Emanation
Center	Khro-gryal mkha-'gying-kha	mKha-la gdug-mo	Blue-Black	Citta Mind
East	gYung-drung khro-gsas	Ne-sla sra-brtan yum	Reddish-Yellow	Kāya Body
North	Khro-bo rngam-gsas	Li-mun lan-brgyad yum	Blue-Black	Guṇa Merit
West	Khro-bo dbal-gsas	Tshangs-ting dpal-mo yum	Reddish-Black	Vāc Speech
South	Khro-bo gtum gsas	Ting-nam rgyal-mo yum	Smoke-Black	Karma Action

TABLE 21. The five Tathāgata-Herukas and their Ḍākinīs.

tions corresponding to the eight Ye-gs-hen sems-dpa' and their Ḍākinīs. These are the eight Ha-la-khro-bo with their Ḍākinīs (T. Yum-chen khro-mo brgyad). They are followed by the four wrathful Guardians of the maṇḍala together with their Ḍākinīs, and then by a large group of theriomorphic figures, the 28 goddesses, seven for each of the four cosmic directions (T. dPal-mo nyi-shu rtsa-brgyad). This is however only a general arrangement of the bardo deities, corresponding to the groupings in the Tibetan Book of the Dead. The various texts of the Bon-po tradition name additional deities in the peaceful as well as in the wrathful cycle—the four karma-deities, for example, who appear in the form of the Buddha with a pātra in their hand. But we shall not go into any more detail and shall now conclude this preliminary look at the Book of the Dead of the Bon religion. It has sufficiently shown us the relationship between these two Tibetan religions as far as the after-death visions are concerned. We shall now turn to some more general comparative considerations.

IV
Psyche and Awareness

The most transitory, when it truly touches
us, awakes in us something everlasting.
FRIEDRICH HEBBEL, *Diaries*

AFTER reading the texts of the Tibetan Book of the Dead many readers will have asked, with justification, what exactly is it that is reborn—awareness, or the totality of the soul? With this question we touch on a fundamental problem, which we cannot even approximately solve in this chapter, in as far as there are infinitely many definitions of soul and of awareness, and the two concepts mutually interpenetrate and influence one another. Nevertheless, for thousands of years philosophies and religions—and today also psychology—have occupied themselves with this problem and will continue to do so, repeatedly bringing new knowledge to this old question.

Our aim here is simply to offer a few pointers towards a comprehensive understanding, and in this and the following chapters to extend the philosophical and eschatological meaning of the Tibetan Books of the Dead by adducing the thoughts and experiences of other spheres of culture. We shall thus gain a broader understanding by amplifying the significant statements of the Tibetan Book of the Dead with the contents of comparable writings. Only through the spiritual eyes of great thinkers and by drawing from the wealth of experience of other religions concerning soul, awareness, life and death, shall we be able to attain a more profound access to such an essential and, to us Westerners, extraordinary work as the Tibetan Book of the Dead.

A comparative study of the treatment of such questions shows to what extend the Tibetan Book of the Dead is a book that gives meaning to *life,* and that the world of its thought ultimately lies closer to us than we imagine, for it deals with Being or Non-being, with the transitoriness and permanence of the real. We do not wish to make any rigid evaluations, but one thing is certain—that we shall find in the Tibetan Book of the Dead an outstanding guide, capable of opening the gates to transcendence.

For the Tibetan, there exists already a complicated system of ideas about the soul and awareness that comes from two origins. Ancient Tibetan ideas stemming from folk religion and the older

Bon religion acknowledge a soul-principle or soul that has developed from a threefold function. *Bla* is the concept of the individual single-soul, which further has an energetic and a pneumatic aspect. The energetic component is *Srog,* life-energy, and the pneumatic ground or vital soul is the breath (S. prāṇa; T. dBugs). Ancient ideas from the magical-mythical era of Tibet are still active and are founded on the premise that the soul (T. Bla) is capable of being led astray by demons of illness, that it may even be totally abducted and must then be liberated from the clutches of the demons by means of certain rites. These dangerous spirits that harm the soul are primarily the *'Dre,* the *Lha,* the serpent demons (T. Klu) or the *Yakṣa*-spirits, and others.

At death the activity of psychic energy and of the life-force comes to an end. The soul is now free to wander about and is able to linger for some time in any kind of object. Through these resting places of the soul, which form its temporary support, it is possible to reach the soul by prayer. We see in this the foundation for the sByang-bu used in the Tibetan Book of the Dead, the image of the deceased, in which he is said to dwell for a time, in order to hear the instructions of the monks.

These ancient ideas of the soul have, of course, been long since superseded by Buddhism, which does not posit the existence of a personal soul. This is also the position of the Tibetan Book of the Dead. If anything survives death, it is the awareness-principle (S. vijñāna; T. rNam-shes) or something specifically spiritual (T. Yid-kyi lus) in the form of a spirit-body. It is then the task of the Book of the Dead to transform the spirit-body burdened by contaminations into a pure and knowing awareness (T. Ye-shes lus or rDo-rje lus). We have also mentioned the "clear light" at the beginning of death as a highly important stage of the spiritual experience. The spiritual-energetic principle (T. Sems) can, by means of procedures of knowledge and "enlightenments," be transformed into wisdom (T. Ye-shes). Wisdom as a purely spiritual "highly evolved form" of the spirit or as clear presence of the totality of awareness, is clear unadulterated light, or is of a luminous nature. In the visions of the Tibetan Book of the Dead the luminous character of the divine apparitions plays an important role. All visionary deities originate from a bundle of light composed of rays of five colors. This luminous source is, however, the light of one's own spirit, which becomes transformed into pure radiance by means of knowledge and wisdom. At first, all the deities appear from out of the same radiant light of the five wisdoms (T. Ye-shes lnga), and they then assume form. Since they are divine forms, they appear in the dual aspects of the numinous from the depths of primordial or universal awareness (T. Kun-gzhi rnam-shes). Seen from the standpoint of reality, all bardo visions are to be considered illusions of emptiness; they are conditioned forms of the constitution of awareness, which experiences all visionary images in the immaterial realm according to its karmic determination. For the Tibetans, influenced by Buddhist thought, there is no wandering and reincarnating soul with any personal connection, but only the idea that after death the awareness wanders through the bardo, and that it forms an awareness-body capable of experience, in which the stages of catharsis are undergone as images of awareness. The path through the bardo is determined by the karmic deeds of the previous life and by the ability of the awareness to achieve sublimation and encompassing awareness. The means to this are provided by Tibetan yoga and the various systems of spiritual education, such as the teachings of the "Great Symbol" (S. mahāmudrā) and of the Book of the Dead, which are an integration of many forms of knowledge.

Now what the devotee of Mahāyāna Buddhism in India and Tibet, and also in China and Japan, understands by transformation and enlightenment of awareness, and by liberation of consciousness from attachments to an earthly world full of suffering, has been seen by other people and cultures as transformation of the soul. This statement is admittedly a somewhat crude generalization, but it does in essence hit the mark.

It is therefore our task here to put forward some fundamental questions concerning the soul, awareness, life, and death, in order to recognize that in the final analysis it always comes down to the solution of the same eternal questions. But we shall now approach our topic from the Western conception of the soul. There is, however, a great similarity in descriptions of psychical phenomena and ultimate questions about the meaning of Being and possible transformation through death. Among the Greek philosophers, Plato offers fitting analogies to the structure of the soul; and all the examples we are about to consider can be related to corresponding levels in the psychological schema of the Tibetan Book of the Dead. Plato compares the soul to two steeds drawing a chariot: "Moreover one of them is noble and of good stock, whereas the other is of the opposite character and stock. Hence the task of our charioteer is difficult and troublesome" (Phaedrus 246b). This conception points to the dual nature of the psyche and corresponds to the nature of the peaceful and wrathful deities as described in the Tibetan Book of the Dead. The parallel becomes even clearer in the following passage from Plato: "And do we not see that opinion is opposed to desire, pleasure to anger, reason to pain, and that all these elements are opposed to one another in the souls of bad men?" (Sophist 228b). In this sense Hermes Trismegistos recognizes: "The human soul is nevertheless both demonic and divine." The recognition of the polarity and partially exclusive opposition of the soul or of psychical self-experience is to be found universally. From such statements one could develop a comparative phenomenology of the soul that would constitute a valuable adjunct to the psychology of the Tibetan Book of the Dead.

We also find in Plato appropriate points of comparison in his reflections on the relation between body and soul on the one hand and their unity with the world on the other. These ideas are very close to the Buddhist view of existence as being basically suffering. "For the body provides us with innumerable distractions . . . interrupting and disturbing and confusing us so that we are unable to see the truth. We are in fact convinced that if we are ever to have pure knowledge of anything, we must get rid of the body and contemplate things with the soul itself" (Phaedo 66b–e). It is not then a question of turning away from the world in a spirit of negation and one-sided introversion, but rather, as Buddhist teachings emphasize again and again, of the maintenance of a higher standpoint that cannot be found in this world of suffering as long as one is physically and psychically attached to it. Dissolving these attachments is liberation and freedom from all attachment, and only in this way can true insight be attained, in which one can recognize the essence of things and also of transcendence.

What is to be recognized, what we usually characterize as the upward path, is ultimately at the same time an inward path directed towards the intensification of awareness, towards knowledge of the self, or, in religious terms, towards the Divine or the Absolute. In the Tibetan Book of the Dead the way of ignorance turns out to be a precipitous path down to the torments of hell and the darkness of rebirth, but the way of knowledge is the penetrating power of awareness and union with the goal of liberation or of a divine condition *per se.* Wisdom and ignorance are symbolized in the Orient by light and darkness, which are the linguistic concepts adequate to the two opposing conditions of consciousness. According to the Chāndogya Upaniṣad: "Perceiving above the darkness the highest light, our own, we reach the radiant and divine source of energy, of the sun, of the highest lights" (III, 17.2). We find in this symbolism of opposites a number of indications that characterize the path of the soul or awareness towards the light as the divine path, seeing in the earthly changes of the body the path of death and the transitory. Man participates both in a transcendence that goes beyond him and in the transitory existence of earthly forms, or, as Plato puts it: the soul resembles the divine and the body the mortal.

A further universal way of thinking is to contrast darkness and ignorance with light and wisdom, or knowledge. This is a typical psychological symbolism found in all languages of cultured peoples. For every coming to light, every kind of enlightenment or knowledge, means a gain in awareness of previously unknown processes, in the becoming conscious of unconscious contents, which are characterized in the Indian religions as unknowing or ignorance. The cosmogonic and theogonic myths of the most ancient cultures already contain the symbolism of the opposites of light and dark in relation to the beginnings of creation, and this means nothing other than the opposition of complete unconsciousness and consciousness. One of the important Upaniṣads[130] offers the following definitions: "That which is even higher than this

"Totality" is without form and free from illness. Those who know this become immortal. The others, however, enter into suffering (that is, they are born again)." Wisdom is shown to be the way to immortality, (a characteristic Indian definition), whereas ignorance—and this is one of the fundamental tenets of Buddhism—leads to the psychical and physical conditions of rebirth. As long as ignorance reigns, karma is accumulated, and this obstructs the path to liberation. The Śvetāśvatara Upaniṣad states further: "Two, (that is) wisdom and ignorance, are set down in the unchanging, infinite stronghold of Brahman, where they are concealed. Ignorance is the changing, wisdom the immortal. But he who rules over wisdom and ignorance is another."

Pure wisdom as knowledge and intellectual wisdom as image-forms of the mind are two quite distinct things; the Tibetan would say: pure wisdom is of the heart, intellectual wisdom is in the head. It is integrated and sure knowledge that guides life and is confirmed by it; the other type constitutes things and is directed towards impermanent objects. In Western philosophy, in, for example, the great Christian thinker, Nicholas of Cusa,[131] we come across similar structures of thinking, which once again point to the central questions of wisdom and ignorance, and of life and death. "The highest bliss is the spiritual intuition of the Omnipotent itself, the fulfillment of our longing, in which we all demand to know. Therefore, the kind of reason that in all its wisdom knows nothing, will grieve away in the shadow of death in eternal privation." This is the question of the "noble forces in the soul, the lower as well as the higher," of which Meister Eckhart speaks. He too portrays the structure of the soul independently of the five senses, just as Buddhism has characterized them as the five skandhas or components of the human personality, for "in every person there are two kinds of person. One is the outer person, the person's sensory apparatus. The five senses serve this person, but these senses work by virtue of the power of the soul. The other person is the inner person, the person's inwardness."[132] With relation to the external world, the problem of psychic adaptation is of the first importance. Neither one-sided orientation towards the external world nor regression to an exclusive inwardness can be the proper way of actualization. The Indian Tantras above all, and in Buddhism the philosophy of the "Middle Way" (S. mādhyamika) of Nāgārjuna, offer various spiritual methods of completing the process of psychic adaptation to both worlds. For salvation by means of knowledge of reality is, according to the tantric conception, possible only through and with the body and through and with the spirit—i.e., the totality of the human being must participate in the process of transformation and enlightenment. Whoever believes that he is not of this world is precisely only in it; and whoever believes he can find liberation only in this world, is lacking all knowledge of transcendent realms of Being. The Christian mystic, Meister Eckhart, also proceeds from the recognition of the totality of the human being: "The purity of the soul depends on its being purified by a life that is divided, and on its entering a life that is unified."[133] The union mentioned here is the content of all the great teachings of Indian Yoga, it occupies a central position in Tibetan Atiyoga and in the teachings of the "Great Symbol" (S. mahāmudrā), and it constitutes the original condition at the onset of death in the 'Chi-kha'i bardo, where the unified light of all buddhas appears as the white clear light in awareness. Even at the end of the fourteenth day of the bardo visions, the dead person's awareness is told that now the unified light of all peaceful and wrathful deities is shining down upon the wanderer in the bardo. This single light as radiance from pure knowledge or from fully present awareness is a symbolic indication of the spontaneous functioning of a total psychic structure, which can in this life be experienced only by the mystic. This light is not objective in the sense of an external light source, but rather a highly subjective light as an inner experience. The Chāndogya Upaniṣad expresses this as follows: "Now, the light which beyond heaven shines on the backs of all, on the back of each one in the highest of high worlds, this is certainly the same light that is inside man" (III, 13.7).

Even if the world was a vale of suffering and of an impermanent nature for the ancient Egyptians, they nevertheless saw in the event of death the possibility of great progress for the individual, who would then be able to step into "the full light of day." At the moment of crossing the threshold of death the sun god Ra lets his rays illuminate the darkness of the realm of death, and the dead person steps into the full light of day. We find here a considerable similarity of psychological symbolism with the appearance of the "clear light" at the threshold of the bardo, as described in the Tibetan Book of the Dead. Even if the definitions of the presuppositions of the experience of light are different, they are still phenomenologically similar. Another text of the Egyptian scriptures of the dead[134] offers the following version: "O, mysterious land of silence . . . which fashions the figures (of the intermediate state), let (name) emerge so that he may see the sun and rejoice before the great god . . . and that I may praise the radiant sun thanks to the light of my eyes." Here is the human eye, which, if it were not sun-like, would not be able to see the sun.

The question of the transformation of the soul after death has long been pondered by the philosophical and religious thinkers of the West, in some of whom may be found a bridge to the understanding of oriental thought—of the Indian conception of karma in particular. Plato assumes that the soul of the perfect man is feathered like a bird, and the soul of the unliberated person unfeathered: "The perfect and winged soul soars on high and holds sway over the whole world; one that has shed its wings sinks until it reaches something solid, whereupon it settles down and assumes an earthly body . . ." (Phaedrus 246c). The feathered soul is borne by knowledge and perfect wisdom; the unfeathered is driven by ignorance, which inevitably leads it to a new incarnation in impermanent matter. Thomas Aquinas later goes into this problem intensively and comes to the conclusion: "It is therefore impossible that the understanding soul is mortal."[135] He considers the understanding to be part of what Eckhart calls the inner man, and this is immortal. "It is therefore impossible," says Aquinas, "that a self-perpetuating form of being ceases to exist."

Thomas Aquinas also poses the critical question of the meaning and purpose of psychic faculties and whether these come to an end at death or whether they can influence the continued existence of the departed soul. His point of view here can be considered an interesting Western contribution to the understanding of the Indian idea of karma. Aquinas proceeds from the question of whether all the faculties of the soul remain in the body after death. He comes to the following conclusion: "Since these faculties are parts of the soul or of the totality of soul and body, therefore, after the demise of the body, those faculties which were in the soul remain there, and those which were in the composite of soul and body remain only by virtue of their effects."[136] This conception of the efficacy of the psychic faculties after death is close to the Buddhist notion of karmic energy, which accumulates as a result of actions performed during life and then continues to be effective after death. According to the Indian doctrine it is not the same individual who is "reborn" as the continuation of his former existence, but rather, the degree of karmic accumulation determines the point of departure for a new incarnation. The karma becomes a directional condition for the new existence. But this should not be conceived rigidly or schematically, since the working of karma depends on the basic situation and the intentions of the individual concerned. In the Aṅguttara-Nikāya the Buddha gives a brief, basic account of the function of karma: "There is, O monks, the dark deed, whose fruit is dark; there is, O monks, the light deed, whose fruit is light; there is the deed that is partly dark and partly light, whose fruit is partly dark and partly light; there is the deed that is neither dark nor light, whose fruit is neither dark nor light: the deed that leads to the disappearance of effectual deeds" (IV 232).

We shall be reminded of the teachings of the Tibetan Book of the Dead concerning the path of the awareness-principle through the bardo and the chances of its rebirth if we consider a few more assertions of Thomas Aquinas. Aquinas arrived at the general idea that the wisdom acquired in the earthly world would also stay with the departed soul. His view is that the human soul is ultimately created for a better or higher determination, and that the earthly body as material support of the existence of the soul is only a tool on earth with which to prepare for a transformation of the soul. "It is therefore clear that the soul is for its improvement united with the body, in order that it may understand by turning towards ideas; but it may nevertheless continue to exist in a different way, after being separated from the body."[137] The notion of psychic predestination on the grounds of its earthly transformation, which we wish to compare with the concept of karma, becomes even clearer when we consider the following final passage: "The separated soul has awareness, although not of individual things, but rather only of that with which it has a particular affinity, either through previous acquintance or through inclination. . . ."[138]

In these remarkable quotations from the *Summa Theologica* of Aquinas, whole spiritual and intellectual epochs from ancient Greece until Christian mysticism converge; and we also find here the closest parallels to Buddhist forms of thinking in relation to the concept of karma. Of course, with this solution to the question of the condition of the soul in the world beyond, further problems are raised which touch the realms of genetics and of psychology. These statements have great significance for the validity of the theory of archetypes proposed by C. G. Jung. If we accept Aquinas's assertions and those of the Indian theory of karma as given, the theory of archetypes or primordial images, which can already be found in the Chinese I Ching, would have a broad foundation of justification.

Let us conclude by briefly referring to some extracts from the philosophy of Jean Gebser, who has recently grappled with some of the most ancient human problems. Gebser sees the soul in the aspect of polarity and justifiably names as one of its most meaningful symbols the Chinese t'ai-chi symbol (yin-yang). This is a symbol in which the day- and night-side of the soul are equally portrayed, the light part just as much as the dark. The advantage of such a symbol is that it applies equally to the soul in its present form and in the world beyond, and also equally to its conscious and unconscious components. Apart from this meaning, the t'ai-chi symbol stands for the whole Taoist world-view as the highest symbol of polarity, which knows only a mutual complementarity of opposites.

Gebser sees the dimension of the soul in the life- and death-pole of the same soul, standing in a vital relationship to one another. According to this view, death and life are polarities of the total energy of the soul, which are not fixable at any static point. The soul endures; it is only its state that changes. Each pole is in itself ambivalent, which is also expressed by the t'ai-chi symbol, and the ambivalent nature of one pole relates to the other in a complementary way. So on the side of night or death is already the seed of transformation into life, and *vice versa.* There is no absolute end-point of ultimate validity.

If we relate this to our discussion of the bardo as an intermediate state, we shall become aware of the dynamism of this conception. The bardo, the after-death state, is the energetic moment of transformation of awareness or the psyche (in the Western sense), in which the path towards a new existence is begun. The moment of transformation in the bardo is therefore, according to the teachings of the Tibetan Book of the Dead, the most important instant in the psychic existence. Upon it depends literally "life and death," if we attempt a spiritual solution to the problem. From this central point life decides itself as a path into the "concretion of the spiritual" (to use Gebser's formulation) or to the condensation of the merely physical and thereby to the propagation or prolongation of suffering on the karmically conditioned level of rebirth.

V

Some Comparisons with Ideas about Death and the After-Life in Other Cultures

> Concerning the freedom of the spirit mark this: The spirit is free as long as it is not attached to all nameable things, and they are not attached to it.
> MEISTER ECKHART, *On Self-Knowledge*

THE INSIGHTS of the Tibetan Book of the Dead have not only been of significance to the Tibetans themselves, but we find in it numerous symbols from the most ancient of man's ideas which we can partially recognize in the traditions of other religions and cultures. The authentic Buddhist-influenced doctrine of the Tibetan Book of the Dead with its highly developed ethics and psychology is a concern of Buddhism and its followers. But behind this we find an ancient symbolical structure to the problem of death, which has its roots in the images of mythology and in the psychic reality of the death experience. This symbolism, which engages the universal, fundamental questions of life and death, this world and the beyond, Being and Non-Being, the consciousness of life and the possible unconsciousness of death, is to be found throughout the world. These are primordial processes of human awareness, basic experiences of a similar kind, which according to the structure of the human psyche lead to related images. Man responds to the challenge of death in universally similar ways, by means of certain rituals, cults, and ways of behaving, whose purpose is defense against, or at least alleviation of, the problem. In his struggle with death, man generally begins to recognize his responsibility and the psychical powers which he needs to summon in order to recognize the dangers of the unknown world or to bolster his hopes.

Man has always conceived of the possible events to be expected after death in certain images or symbolical processes. If we briefly compare the images and descriptions of the realm of death and the worlds beyond from various spheres of culture, we will find certain points of similarity, which represent an archetypal basis of experience. Wherever man has pondered death and committed his reflections to writing, we find the idea of the continued existence of the soul or of some kind of awareness. And where the survival of the psyche is assumed, at least two kinds of existence are posited in the world beyond: the realm of light and bliss, and the realm of darkness and suffering. The ancient structures go back to a small number of images conceived as opposites, such as heaven and hell, a divine world and a demonic realm, light and dark, day and night, a return to human form or a departure into pure spirit, everlasting life or total annihilation. On the plane of advanced religious symbolism we are faced with the oppositions of man and world, man as an ensouled creature and man as a mortal shell. The same opposition is expressed in the question: to what extent is the soul divine or does it participate in transcendence and attain higher worlds, and why does the same soul participate in the mortal realm and the transitory material world? This is a primordial opposition which pervades all myth and legend, and all humanity's greatest writings, and which continually demands new solutions. In this context we shall present a few examples of the significance of death and of the worlds beyond, as treated in comparable non-Tibetan texts. Comparisons can be drawn only at a quite basic level, but these will nevertheless set the Tibetan Book of the Dead in a broader frame of understanding.

As already mentioned in the first chapter, the Vedic culture of India has some profound insights to offer. It is not impossible that some of these insights into life and death found their way into the Buddhist system, or that they constituted a general Indian wealth of wisdom about death.

1. Indian Insights in the Upaniṣads

> This thing about which there is so much doubt, O Death, what will befall us in the great crossing over—tell us that.
>
> *Kaṭha Upaniṣad,* I.29

ALREADY in the earliest Upaniṣads, in for example the Chāndogya Upaniṣad and in the Bṛhadāraṇyaka Upaniṣad, and in the Atharva-Veda as well as in the Aitareya-Āraṇyaka, we find detailed portrayals of the process of dying, of the signs of approaching death, and of the ritual forms of the funeral procession and of the burial. In the Atharva-Veda there is a self-contained Book of the Dead. We shall select only a few passages from the wealth of Indian sources, which will suffice to show the parallels with the portrayals of the corresponding processes in the Tibetan Book of the Dead. We shall then recognize the closeness of the relationship which justifies our assumption that insights about dying were part of a fund of knowledge common to the whole of ancient India, in which Buddhism also participated.

In the Bṛhadāraṇyaka Upaniṣad in particular, we find an extremely expressive symbolical description of the process of dying, which is quite similar to the account in the Tibetan Book of the Dead: "When the soul falls into unconsciousness and a weak and confused state, then the organs of life contract around it. The soul draws to itself these elements of energy and descends into the heart; but the spirit in the eye turns back out (to the sun), and then no longer recognizes forms" (IV. 4.1). And so we have first of all the concentration and drawing together of the physiological functions of the body, which now constantly concentrates on itself, as the outer functions are given up, and the heart is raised to the last island of earthly being. From there begins the transition of the psyche or awareness out of the body, after the last "glimmer" of the activity of the heart has been extinguished. The whole psychic organization of the "eight kinds of awareness," as described in the Buddhist Mahāyāna texts, have now become one, and all the senses and their functions are restricted to the center. There is therefore no longer any more sense-activity or perception related to the earthly world: "Then the point of his heart is illuminated, and by that light the soul (ātman) departs . . . and life then departs, taking all the life-organs with it. The soul is one with knowing, and all that is knowing departs with it" (IV. 4.2).

The same theme is treated in a similar, although shorter, form in the Chāndogya Upaniṣad. However symbolic the language used in such descriptions may be, the essential core of the problem still comes through to the "modern" and scientifically-minded person: "Then when his voice has gone into his thinking (manas), and his thinking into his prāṇa (breath—or vital-energy), his breath into the heat, the heat into the highest divinity—then he no longer recognizes them (his relatives sitting around him at his death)" (VI. 15.2). We find the same processes in the Tibetan Book of the Dead, and here too there is at first no more recognition, until later the awareness gradually re-enters its environment from the realm beyond. According to the view of the Chāndogya Upaniṣad, people are totally unaware that the entry into the world beyond is a most significant—*the* most significant—transformation. And so we find there the following poetical comparison: "Just as in this (the unity of the collected honey of the concentrated life-impulses) those juices do not retain any distinction of the particular trees they come from . . . in the same way these creatures, when (in death) they enter into Being, have no awareness that they are doing so" (VI. 9.2). There is a corresponding emphasis in the texts of the Tibetan Book of the Dead on the significance of the "clear light," to the effect that whoever lets this appearance slip away without being fully aware of it, remaining merely fascinated and spellbound, such a person will soon see the "secondary clear light" and then the whole pantheon of visionary deities in sequence. This means, however, that he is on the descending path that leads away from the highest reality of the dharmakāya, which previously radiated as "clear light" in pure absoluteness.

Various ancient Indian Veda texts similarly comment on the signs of approaching death. We find in them some remarkable material which could be of great heuristic value for contemporary psychology and for the study of precognitive dreams. We shall give a few examples to illustrate this point. In the Mokṣadharma we read: "Death will come within a year in the following cases: when poor vision occurs, and one does not see oneself in another's eye, when great wisdom is transformed into ignorance, when one sees the moon cracked like a spider's web, when the color of the face changes, and when one smells corpses instead of aromas" (11710–11723).

With respect to human responsibility and personal behavior which has its karmic effects on the form of transformation in the world beyond, the texts of the Upaniṣads are similar to those of the Buddhist tradition. The Bṛhadāraṇyaka Upaniṣad says the following about the problem of karmic character: "Man is made completely of desire; and according to his insight, such will be his actions, and according to his actions, such will be his fate" (IV 4.5). It is interesting that we find in these texts an abundance of passages which ascribe to human ignorance the fact that the sufferings of the abysses beyond are conditioned by this alone. "Many hells are established in response to lack of knowledge" (Mokṣadharma, 7186). This knowledge is as applicable to earthly life as to the world beyond. Seen psychologically, portrayals of the realms of death are simply faithful reflections of earthly life, except that they appear less refined and more mythical. And it must be this way, in order properly to emphasize the ethical responsibility of our present life on earth.

One's fate in the bardo remains uncertain, however many precise instructions and great speculations about the world beyond we may find in the scriptures of various peoples over the last few thousand years. They provide only portrayals and admonitions, possible images of unknown Being, which, even when taken together, fail to give the whole picture.

"The days do not come again, nor the months nor the nights, and man, uncertain as he is, walks endlessly along this path. The only meeting on the way is the connection with spouses and relatives, and there has never yet been one who could have lived with them eternally" (Mokṣadharma, 11834 and 11846).

Of great psychological interest in this context is the Anugītā (460–483), in which the false ways of behaving are described which are opposed to the principle of human life and lead to its ending. One could speak of a portrayal of self-destruction. The manifestations of regression are described here, which, through a misjudgement of life and its meaning, occur as man gets older, without attaining the corresponding wisdom about the ultimate things in life. We find further descriptions of the signs of approaching death in the Aitareya Āraṇyaka (III 2.4), and above all in the Śatapatha Brāhmaṇa. In the latter ancient Indian work we once again encounter the scales as a symbol of the weighing of good and bad deeds, as is familiar to us from the court of death in the Tibetan Book of the Dead, where the dead person is brought before the judge, Yamarāja, the ruler of the worlds of hell. The

Śatapatha Brāhmaṇa talks of the scales in the world beyond as follows: "The right hand of the vedi (fireplace) is the scales. The good that a person has done is inside the vedi, the bad is outside. Therefore one should sit touching the right edge of the vedi, since in that world they put (both) on one scale. Whichever of the two—whether the good or the bad—draws, he will follow. And so whoever knows (about this), he already in this world gets on the scales, and then in the world beyond gets around the weighing. His good works will draw, and his bad works not" (XI 2.7.33).

We find one of the most detailed portrayals of the events which befall the dead person in all their horrors and heavenly joys in the Pretakalpa of the Garuḍa Purāṇa, a Hindu text from the first century A.D. This is the Book of the Dead of the Indian tradition par excellence and many of its aspects are reminiscent of the visions of the Tibetan Book of the Dead.

In describing the process of dying it is explained that during the last moments of fading awareness, all subject-object relationships dissolve away and all objects retreat from awareness, and any consciousness of a personal soul or the external world becomes diffuse and dissolves away. The soul is the *puruṣa* of the dead person and contracts to the size of the human thumb. The soul of the bad person is led away by the executioners of Yama, the ruler of hell, while the good souls are directed by heavenly guides. On the tenth day after death, the piṇḍa body of the deceased, which is again the size of a thumb, arises from the rice-offerings (S. piṇḍa) of those present at the cremation, who bring them daily for the deceased. The person is also called preta, who will now in this form experience the fruits of his good and bad karma. The bad souls pass through many horrible tortures of thirst, hunger, and other suffering and arrive at the river Vaitaraṇi, which flows around the realm of hell. This river is crossed with torture and pain, and the soul arrives in the realm of Yama, with the hot and cold hells. There the dead person leaves the piṇḍa-body and assumes the form of a thumb-sized, subtle torment-body, called the yātanādeha. He thus comes before Yama, the terrifying 32-armed death-god of the hells, who appears on a buffalo. But the most horrible tortures of hell, which are then described, are meant only for the paying-off of bad karma, before the person can again achieve rebirth on the human level. The souls of the good people achieve rebirth either on the human or on the heavenly plane of the gods.

We cannot end our review of the Indian sources of the Hindu tradition without mentioning the important symbolism of Naciketas' fire which occurs in the Kaṭha Upaniṣad. There we have the famous dialogue between Yama, the ruler of the underworld, and Naciketas, the young son of a brahman. Naciketas was elected to inquire into the mystery of the underworld, and he descends to the realm of Yama to seek the law of karma and the true destiny of man. After Yama has offered him the fulfillment of three wishes, if he will only not ask after the ultimate things, Naciketas resists this very temptation and thus acquires the wisdom of immortality, by learning to penetrate all delusion. Yama concludes his speech by saying: "There are two things in the world, one of which is good and the other pleasant, . . . and these two bind the souls of mortals in various ways." The good thing is attachment to the path of liberation, that is, the path to release and perfection; the pleasant thing is great and limited self-deception. This path may perhaps appear to people on earth as the lesser evil, but the consequences of which in the world beyond are all the more dire.

Abhedānanda[139] sketches in a few clear words the whole problem of life and death, from a profound knowledge of Indian thought, which never held back from confronting ultimate questions with the strongest words: "Death means the transformation of our physical conditioning and not the extinction of our selves. Some people believe that death means annihilation. But death does not mean destruction and absolute dissolution, but the transformation of our life into its elemental conditions. That means coming and going. This realm is the sphere of birth and rebirth." Like so many Indian and Tibetan thinkers, Abhedānanda finally returns to the symbolism of the inner light, which as the light of knowledge has become the symbol of the experience of life and death: "Search for the inner light, and do not give up until this goal is achieved. When you have reached that light, you cross the boundaries of death."

2. Comparable Elements in the Religions of Persia, Babylon, and Egypt

A RECURRING symbol in various ancient religions is the dangerous narrow and forked path in the world beyond, which must be negotiated before the true path in the beyond can be taken. It is a kind of crossroads for the person's good and bad deeds, a deciding point for the heavenly or the hellish path, which is described in the Tibetan Book of the Dead as the threatening and terrifying defile of the bardo. Therefore there is a text in the Tibetan Book of the Dead with the title: "The prayers for salvation from the (abysmal) defile of the bardo" (T. Bar-do'i 'phrang-dol-gyi smon-lam), in which the Buddhas are beseeched to lead the dead person out of the horrors on to their illuminated path of wisdom.

In the religion of Zarathustra, the Zoroastrian religion of ancient Persia, we find in the Yasht (22) descriptions of the dead person's path. Immediately after death the soul of the believer stays with the body for three days and nights. During the first night "the soul experiences as much joy as in the whole night of life." It is called the night of life because the soul after death begins the ascent into the infinite realm of light, with which nothing during earthly life can be compared. In the morning after the third night comes the moment of reckoning with the arrival at the bridge of the judge, known as the Cinvat Bridge. This is the bridge where the good and the bad souls are separated. For non-believers and wicked people the bridge crosses over the abyss of hells like a fine silk thread. These souls, mortified with fear and terror, plunge down into the hells. The believing souls cross directly into the paradise of Garonmana, the home of the immortal saints. In Parseeism there also stand at the Cinvat Bridge the accusing demons, Mithra, Sraośa, and Raśnu. Raśnu carries the scales of justice and weighs the good and bad deeds. We recognize this symbol of the scales from the portrayal of the judge of death, Yamarāja, in the Tibetan Book of the Dead.

In the religions of Babylon and of ancient Assur we again find a striking symbol, which we shall meet again more often. It is the dark and seemingly unconquerable river of death. The dead person must cross the Hubur river in the underworld, in order to reach the mountain of justice. The water of death, which is familiar to us from mythology and psychological symbolism as the water of life and as the water of death, here forms the unknown depth of separation of the two forms of existence between life and death. On the far side of the Hubur river is also the realm of life, where the Anunnaki or (later also) Gilgamesh appear as judges of the dead. These death-deities are at the same time the rulers and guardians of the source of life. And in the religion of Ur we have the description of the path of Gilgamesh with the boatman Urshanabi, who guides the hero across the water of death. The simultaneity of the significant water-symbolism is striking here. Its life-aspect is inseparably connected with its death-aspect. What function water has depends upon which psychic state it appears under. In any case, water, as separating and as joining, plays an important role in the symbolism of death and rebirth.

In the ancient Egyptian religion we find in the Egyptian Books of the Dead of Amduat and in the even older "Book of the Two Paths" a wealth of mythical knowledge about the path of the dead person through the dangerous realm of the underworld, which is in many respects comparable with the visions of the Tibetan Book of the Dead.

We have already mentioned the striking similarity in the light-symbolism between the Tibetan and Egyptian Books of the Dead. In Egypt, the dead person immediately after death enters into "the full light of day," a remarkable piece of symbolism which in Tibet represents primary knowledge.

The ancient Egyptian realm of death is situated in the land of the setting sun, and the ancient cosmologically and mythically based path to rebirth in a world of light begins in the west and proceeds through the night of the rising sun of the east, which is the path of the sun-god Ra. The Egyptian realm of death is also divided into the two opposite regions of heaven and hell. Behind the passage lies the night, where the huge serpent-demon Aposis lurks, and then the field of the blessed, Iaru.

We find a further similarity to the Tibetan Book of the Dead in the ancient Egyptian doctrine of the structure of the soul and its transformation after death. The dead person appears in the underworld as a living soul-body being, the BA. Those beings who have been condemned to final death there attain total annihilation in the worlds of hell, while the blessed ones develop a "transfiguration-body" (called ACH) and arrive in the realm of the gods.

Before the deceased can reach the fields of Iaru, he must cross the treacherous narrows of the subterranean Nile, where the sandbanks of Apopis oppose the boat. The sun as bearer of light in the underworld is represented by the sun-bark of Ra with which the dead soul crosses the Nile and which is beset by many dangers. These can be overcome only by wisdom and by the knowledge of magic formulas which the dead person has to have learned during his life on earth. We have here again the idea that certain kinds of knowledge or wisdom are the only means with which to overcome the dangers of the world beyond. They become the actual preconditions for attaining rebirth in the realm of the blessed. In the fifth hour the lake of fire and the sandbank of the Apopis-demon must be overcome, as long as in the fourth hour of death the cavern of the Sokar has been negotiated successfully. In the dangerous seventh hour the power of the strongest magic incantations succeeds in exorcizing the Apopis-demon, who with a retinue of many other serpents, scorpions, and other evil creatures represents a dire threat to the crossing.

It is of critical importance that the dead person in the underworld know all the names of the demons there, so that he can render them harmless by means of the appropriate formulas. He must therefore possess magical-ritual knowledge to guide him through the straits of the intermediate realm. On reaching the far bank he arrives at the fields of Iaru, which are surrounded by the waters of life and have 15 or 21 gates, at which stand ferocious guardians with knives who guard the fields of the blessed. If the subterranean Nile was the water of death, it leads again to the waters of life which surround the fields of Iaru.

We find striking symbolism comparable to that of the animal-headed ḍākinīs of the wrathful deities of the Tibetan Book of the Dead in the many theriomorphic deities and demons to be found in the texts of the Egyptian Book of the Dead. Even if the meanings and psychological purpose of the deities of the Tibetan Book of the Dead have quite different foundations and roots, the morphological similarities to those of the Egyptians are nevertheless surprisingly great. We shall just mention Anubis with the jackal's-head, Chephri with the head of a beetle, Thoth with the head of an ibis, Hathor with the cow's-head, Sechmet with the lion's-head, Chnum with the head of a ram, Horus with the falcon's-head, and Selkis, the protective goddess of the dead with the head of a scorpion. These are all theriomorphic figures, with partly human bodies, who as initiation deities have a symbolic character. Like the animal-headed deities of the Tibetan Book of the Dead, they are also given certain attributes which are concealed under the symbol of the corresponding animal head.

We know from the visions of the Tibetan Book of the Dead that the animal-headed ḍākinīs of wrathful aspect are manifestations of the human intellect and that they appear in order to purify awareness of false thinking. These ḍākinīs are wrathful furies who combat ignorance and delusion. In the Egyptian Book of the Dead we can tentatively attribute a similar function to the theriomorphic deities who appear on the path to fields of eternal bliss. If the dead person is able to recognize them by name and to see through them as phantoms, they lose their danger for the individual. A similar element in the mantric texts of the Tibetan Book of the Dead is that all the deities are invoked by name and by the mantras sacred to them. Only one who knows these mantras is able to communicate with the bardo deities by reciting the sacred formulas. The mantras become bearers of divine energy and a medium for the wisdoms of the buddhas.

To conclude this account of Egyptian underworld symbolism we must mention the scales of justice which are to be found in the portrayal of the court of death. Together with 42 death-judges, the great god Osiris holds court in the great hall of the two justices. Osiris as god of the underworld sits on a throne surrounded by the waters of life, amidst the assembly of his 42 judges. Anubis, the jackal-headed god, and Horus with the falcon's head weigh the deeds of the soul on the scales of justice, while Thoth with the head of the ibis is the scribe who keeps the register of the life's deeds. This scene is so reminiscent of the court of Yama in the Tibetan Book of the Dead, who holds the mirror in his hand, with his animal-headed assistants and the scales of justice before him! It should be remembered, however, that the ancient Egyptians believed in a complete resurrection of the dead person in the world beyond, while in the Buddhist tradition a karmic transformation of the awareness occurs through various forms of earthly existence which are interrupted by the bardo state.

3. Comparable Elements with the Greeks, Romans, and Germans

In ancient Greek culture we again find the land of death in the most western part of Oceanus, and there lies Erelus, the underworld realm of the dead. Dark Erelus, where no ray of sun reaches, is the true location of Hades. Once again there are several treacherous underworld rivers, such as the Styx, Acheron, Cocytus, and the river of fire, Phlegethon. At the entrance to Hades stands the hell-hound Cerberus, the animal of the ancient god of death, Hades. This is where the souls of the dead arrive and lead a dreary and shadowy existence. In post-Homeric times the conception of Hades was broadened; there was a division between the blissful Elysian Fields for the good souls, and Tartarus, a place of torment for the bad souls. But on the outskirts of Hades were fields of asphodel where souls waited without shade in an intermediate state; these were the souls of those who had committed an equal number of good and bad deeds. The souls of the dead do not totally lose their existence, but lead a shadowy life as the psyche fluctuates between various levels of consciousness and unconsciousness.

There are various gods of death: Hades (or Aidoneus), Thanatos, and also Pluto, who keeps the register of the sins of the dead souls. Certain deities are associated with the sufferings in Tartarus, and they can be seen as figures symbolic of the failings of the soul. Of the three Furies, Tisiphone is the avenging killer, Alecto is the untiring pursuer, and Megaera the gruesome Gorgon-like goddess. The death-demon Thanatos wears black robes, has black wings, and holds a knife in his hand. The descriptions of the Furies and demons of Tartarus are quite reminiscent of the wrathful deities of the Tibetan Book of the Dead. Tityus appears as the pursuer of the opposites of desire and aversion, Tantalus punishes arrogance and anxiety, Sisyphus persecutes the inconstant human intellect and the turbulence of awareness which always strives in vain. Ixion punishes the desires of the soul, and the Danaids prosecute senseless beliefs and vain striving. Also among the host of tormenting spirits are the terrible Erinyes of Persephone, the Eumenides as goddesses of fate, the terrifying Chimaeras, the bird-like Harpies, and the Hydra with multiple snake's-heads. Thus, we find in Greek culture a wealth of ideas about the worlds beyond, even though no fixed meaning is assigned to the continued existence of the conscious soul. Death in Greek religion has essentially negative connotations, and this has prevented evolutionary thinking or genuine ideas of reincarnation from developing.

Similar principles are valid for the Roman ideas about death, and we shall only briefly mention the god of death Orcus, and Dis Pater, the ruler of the realm of death. The departed souls are the lemures or manes. These are ghost-like beings without a body, for return to the world is impossible. The manes are divided into two classes: the good and light souls were the lares, the bad and dark souls were the larvae. Their underworld was Orcus, which essentially corresponded to the Greek notion.

In the Germanic religions of the Nordic peoples and also among the Celts we again find water as the symbol of death. The dead were brought across water to the realm of death, which was called "Utgard" or by the Celts, "the House of the Donn." As death-deities we know Odin with the raven, and Thor, who is the ferryman of the dead across the river Wimur. Best known is the underworld called Hel, ruled over by Halja, the goddess of the underworld. It can in a certain sense be compared with hell; it was a hidden world of extreme cold in the dark north, around which was the bleak beach of corpses, Nastrandir, at which the dead arrived after crossing the water. In ancient England the dead souls had to cross the lake of terrifying skeletons and pass through the valley of death to the sea, on the shores of which the abyss of hell yawned. In the North of England people knew a bridge as thin as a thread, which crossed the abyss of hell into the realm of the dead. The image of the bridge as the narrow path leading to the world beyond is universally widespread.

4. The Soul and Death for the Manicheans and the Mandaeans

IN THE *Religion of Mani* there is a fundamental strict dualism between the irreconcilable opposites of light and dark, between a king of light in paradise and the Satan Iblis kadim of the deepest world of hells. Man is fatefully connected with the demonic powers, since a portion of his luminous nature was swallowed up by the world of darkness. The path of his life is a constant striving in the direction of re-acquiring his purely luminous nature, which must be wrested away from the powers of evil. Man strives for deliverance from the clutches of darkness. At death there appears to the Manichean soul the "guides" from the realm of light called Isa, and these are emissaries of the god of light and three other figures with a vessel of water, headband, crown, and radiant light. From the worlds of hell the emissaries of evil appear as demons, and yet they are overpowered by the helpful forces, and the soul is able to enter paradise. These helpful forces of the light are somewhat reminiscent of the radiant Buddha Amitābha (from the western paradise), who is portrayed in East-Asiatic art as descending from heaven with his assistants, in order to lead the believers among the dead to Sukhāvatī, the western paradise of light.

In pondering man's failings Manicheanism sees the problem clearly psychologically, as we find too in the Tibetan Book of the Dead. The human body is the "poisonous sea of fire," the "palace of the demons," the "fivefold pit of the realm of darkness," and in it are "the five poisonous places of darkness."[140] Man is "the root and origin of all evil" and "the gate of all hells," for the light portions of the soul have been "thrown into the jaws of all demons." Therefore we hear the plaint of the imprisoned souls, as preserved in a hymnal of the Manicheans of Turfan in central Asia: "Who will save me and take me away from the straits of hell? Who will save me from the jaws of all the wild animals . . . from those devouring depths, from the narrows of Hell?"[141]

We recognize here the psychological aspect of the problem of evil as a humanly conditioned way of being, which has its own responsibility. The light and the dark sides are aspects of the same soul, and to whichever one it leans, it will experience that aspect. Of the greatest interest to us is the symbolism of light in Manicheanism and the number five, for in the five Tathāgatas who radiate in the five lights of wisdom we find the five Buddhas as the basic structure of the maṇḍala. The light- and number-symbolism of Manicheanism, which was widespread throughout central Asia, may lead to the conclusion that certain forms of expression of Tibetan mysticism in the Buddhist and also the Bon-po tradition could have been influenced.

In the *Mandaean religion,* which is already a very complicated combination of Babylonian, Persian, Jewish, and Christian elements, we still encounter the same dualism of the worlds of light and darkness. Beneath the boundless spheres of light of heaven there stretched a great void, and beneath this, the dark waters of the underworld. The realm of human being also belonged to the underworld, since it is entwined with evil. Earthly existence with its sufferings and failings is the world of darkness. The king of light is the "great life," and the world of darkness and so also the earthly world, is of death. Therefore, according to the doctrine of Enoch: "There is life, and there is light; there is error, and there is truth." The path of man, who wishes to escape darkness (and therefore also ignorance), leads to light and life. Salvation leads out of the world of existence to eternal light and life. The abyss of sinful souls after death is called by the Mandaeans hell, or "the sea of the end." These are the inescapable "watched places," in which stand the guards of Mattarta, and as punishment there are hot and cold hells. In the mattarta of the Abatur are the scales of justice, in order to weigh "wages and work"; there spirit and soul are again united, before they reach the light. Only those who die "the second death" are totally damned, and these are the wicked souls who may not expect any resurrection after death and after the end of the world.

5. The Soul, Light, Life, and Death in Some Western Schools of Thought

IN THE preceding pages we have adduced certain comparisons which make possible some appropriate associations with the teachings of the Tibetan Book of the Dead. Our aim was to show some of the characteristic symbolism of opposites, and the alternative of the descent into the worlds of darkness or the ascent into the light. One is suffering, and the other is salvation or bliss, which are quite similarly characterized in the various religions. Precisely in the Tibetan Book of the Dead the whole doctrinal structure of the guidance of awareness rests upon the portrayal of the opposites, which result from the extremes of human behavior. Such patterns of behavior elicit correspondingly strong symbols. Yet the teachings of Buddhism have achieved a great development, namely the overcoming of the opposites and of the dualism between the heavenly and the hellish worlds, in as far as both aspects are united and portrayed as images of human being. Entelechy lies beyond the opposites which have in so many ancient cultures held sway over the questions of Being and Non-being. Herakleitos recognized this in his assertion: "Nature too strives for opposition, and brings forth harmony from this and not from similarity" (Fragment 10).

The process of transformation from life to death bears a considerable similarity to many processes of renunciation in life, or, as Lao Tse said: "Whoever lays no claims, therefore suffers no loss." The greatest Christian mystic of the Middle Ages, Meister Eckhart, offered many insights into this problem which are congruent with the central tenet of Buddhism of suffering through egocentricity. "All love in this world is founded upon self-love. If you can allow self-love, you can easily allow the whole world." Or, in other words: "If I throw out everything that is selfish, then I can be transposed into the pure nature of spirit." We can find in the language of the mystic the same primordial image of the overcoming of the world of darkness by means of the path of light. And if there is in this life the possibility of contact with the transcendent or the divine, which shows us that a timeless and deathless Absolute exists, it is then reasonable to transfer these paradigms to the "world beyond." The comparison with the positions of various great religions lets us recognize the extent to which the highest states of earthly knowledge or mystical insight are compared with the forms of pure release in death. In Buddhism there is samādhi as the highest form of unified and self-subsistent spirit in the light of knowledge during meditation, and at the moment of death this light can reappear as the clear light of self-composed spirit, which is similarly, although finally, separated from the body.

Light as wisdom and knowledge on the one hand, and darkness as deadly threat and unconsciousness on the other, are a primordial pair of symbols of psychic experience, perhaps the most ancient of humanity's images since spirit attained in matter the first sparks of self-consciousness. The Christian mystic, Hildegard von Bingen, asks herself the question: "I the pilgrim? Where am I? In the shadow of death. On what path am I travelling? On the path of error." In agreement with this she asserts: "For these evil spirits have . . . brought darkness in the place of bright wondrousness." We also find in the visions of Hildegard remarkable descriptions of the abysses of hell, which are similar to the experience in the bardo, when the dead person on the descending path encounters the apparitions of the wrathful deities. "Their jaws open up like a grave. They exhale fiery, stinking smoke. For the abyss devours the souls, offering them enticing delights and drawing them by godless deception down to the place of torment, where the fire burns and the smoke billows."[142]

Finally Hildegard recognizes in her visions of the world after death two different kinds of beings, which she characterized psychologically, just as in the Tibetan Book of the Dead, as figures from the deeds of human beings. "And therefore, as the soul releases itself, light and dark spirits rush by, the fellows of its transformation, according to the movements which it has completed in its home; for, when the human soul leaves its home, it then encounters . . . good and evil angels, the witnesses of its works . . ."[143]

If we look back to the descriptions of the visions of the Tibetan Book of the Dead, we then have the "witnesses of the works" in the figures of the peaceful and wrathful deities as forms of one's own awareness, and the witnesses of the works are laid before the Judge, Yama, in the form of the white and black stones on the scales. It is an eternal question, what really happens in the realm beyond. It is a crossing over into the unknown, which offers neither the conviction of total annihilation nor of everlasting Being. Here the experience of the transcendent, as already that of transcendence as knowledge of life, becomes a factor of the numinous, the reality of which we are no longer able to grasp by means of the intellect alone. The experience of death and every thought of it has something numinous about it, which seems to move between the extreme opposites of terror and eternal bliss.

If we think back to the visions of the Tibetan Book of the Dead, we then have on the one hand the transfigured luminous figures of the peaceful buddhas in their elemental radiance, and on the other, their counter-images of fear and terror. The former are the aspect of the *mysterium fascinans,* pleasing and attractive in appearance, and the quintessence of liberation. The latter are the terrifying herukas as aspects of the same *numinosum* in the *mysterium tremendum,* which cause human beings to tremble. It is for this reason that the texts say that one will feel simultaneously attracted to and repulsed by the deities. But both are simply opposing functions of one and the same ungraspable. This is characterized as the clear light and the great emptiness, which embraces everything. Rudolf Otto writes of the nature of the numinous as follows: "It has its wild and demonic forms . . . and it has its evolution into the fine, the clear, and the radiant."[144]

All the visions of the Tibetan Book of the Dead stand under the sign of the peaceful Tathāgatas and are therefore emanations from a primordial order of cosmic light. The highest visions are the luminous paths of wisdom of the buddhas as the aspect of the *mysterium fascinans;* they radiate in the light of the transfiguration of the psychic components as a spiritual cosmology of the five wisdoms. These lead over to the experience of the totally Other, which is circumscribed as the sphere of the world-order (S. dharmadhātu), as the diamond-clear wisdom, or as absolute emptiness (S. śūnyatā).

A. Metzger offers a valuable contribution to this basic problem of the demonic, which manifests as the world of hell, suffering, and persecution by the deities. For him, divinity "manifests in world-martyrdom." He puts forward the following proposition: "The demonic of earthly life is the necessity of the divine (of the 'absolute'): the necessity of untorn infinity in its dispersed tornness, to which it is exposed in matter, in *ens creatum.*"[145] We recognize beyond ourselves, beyond this cycle of earthly suffering and of unloosenable attachments, the one absolute, the place where "there is neither coming nor going," or, as the Buddha put it: "If there were not this uncreated that had not become, one could find no way out from the created realm of becoming." Yet we know that transcendence is possible in this world, that it appears here and can be intuited before being actually attained. So, however much life on earth remains a "world martyrdom," this is nevertheless only the demonic aspect of a greater whole. The one does not exclude the other, and the one is always a condition of knowledge of the completely Other. To this we shall add another of Metzger's definitions: "Transcendence and the demonic stand in an inseparable, *a priori* foundational relationship. They are . . . mutually supportive, powerful factors which constitute our transcendental creativity."

It is both natural and human that with the question of death there should arise the question of the meaning of life, for it is from this critical point that the past life gains a decisive and threatening dimension.

It is quite natural and justified if man with his advancing knowledge arrives at the conclusion that the many descriptions of after-death states, the journeys to heaven and to hell, ultimately portray a symbolic task of arriving at understanding through images and likenesses. It is above all on the magical-mythical plane that the image is one of the most effective forms of communication of contents that transcend rational comprehension. If in the Tibetan Book of the Dead the deities were recognized as figures symbolic of the psychic attributes of awareness, we then find in the Graeco-Roman tradition a transformation of the real image of the underworld or the world beyond. Many of the tormenting spirits of Hades, which arose in the post-Homeric era, were then understood as symbols of human behavior. Lucretius asserts in his third book: "In addition, all those fables about figures of the underworld without doubt apply to our earthly life" (980). He realizes that there were in actuality no such mythical figures as Tantalus, Tityus, and Sisyphus, but that "men are throughout their lives driven by a groundless fear of the gods." Lucretius relates the events in the underworld to intro-phychic processes, of which they are mythical images. "But that same Tityus lives within us: man, bound by the chains of love, is devoured by the vultures, anxiety gnaws away at him, or he is brought down by obsessive worries and desires" (1000). In the same way, the mythical images of Cerberus, the Furies, and the death-demons of Tartarus are seen by Lucretius as metaphors of psychic states as the result of personal behavior during life. Thereby Lucretius, as one of the first ancient writers, adopts a psychological point of view in recognizing that, even if these punishments may not appear in reality, man still subjects himself to the torments of his conscience—which comes to the same thing. "And so the spirit, who knows the transgression, who senses the punishments, itself applies the goad; it tortures itself . . . and does not see an end to all these tortures" (1020). It is earthly life itself that the unknowing ones form into their own hell.

We can establish that in general the Western sources continually emphasize the connection of wisdom with freedom and of ignorance with suffering and attachment. These are in themselves fundamental notions which have always formed a basic part of the teachings of Indian religions. We find, for example, in Hermes Trismegistos the assimilation of ignorance to suffering. "The evil of the soul is ignorance, for a soul which recognizes nothing about the essential things, or about nature itself, or about the good, such a soul is blind and falls into the passion of the body, becomes an evil demon and fails to recognize itself."[146] We see the extent to which this essential question relates to the ethical foundations of human life and how strongly it influences the question of the world beyond. Jacob Boehme approached the same question; for him the problem of the demonic and the divine was resolved by his alchemically conditioned polar thinking. He succeeded in synthesizing various opposing opinions and points of view into an impressive acknowledgement of the totality of man in unity with the creation.

He characterized the split psychic nature of man in the following terms: "You find . . . in the substance of the soul, eternal birth and in the inseparable eternal bond, the most terrifying, hostile torment, tantamount to the totality of devils, without the Light of God, in which its eternal torment subsists, warring in itself. . . ."[147] Boehme proceeds from the premise that the total universe of the spirit, all human strife, the divine and the demonic, are fundamentally inherent in the structure of the soul. "Nothing is closer to you than heaven, paradise, and hell: whatever you incline and strive towards is what you are now closest to. In this world you stand at both gates and you carry the births of both within you."[148] Thus, for Boehme, man carries his earthly and heavenly image within him, and on the other hand his hellish nature, from which all too easily the emanations of his vices unfold as terrible demons and threatening deities.

In Boehme too, existence is ultimately seen under the primordial schema of the images of light and dark, which we have characterized psychologically as the opposites of wisdom and ignorance. We see in the most philosophical writings, in Vedānta or in the Buddhist texts, for example, that the primordial form of division, that between light and dark, provides a foundation for a whole series of definitions that can be represented by these opposites. In Boehme, the symbolism that arises from this opposition takes many linguistic forms which are quite reminiscent of the visionary world of the bardo from the Tibetan Book of the Dead. "Your heart is then a dark valley; if you do not soon work towards the rebirth of the light, the fire of anger will be ignited in you . . . and with your animal birth you will be unable to reach the gates of heaven."[149] Another verse from Boehme reminds us of the experience of the "clear light" in the bardo, which is parallel with the knowledge of the highest divinity and its unity with the spirit. "The soul originates in the life of fire, for without the source of fire there is no spirit, and it goes of its own accord through death . . . and falls by its own will through the principles of fire into the luminous eye of God."[150]

We shall conclude this chapter by showing that important parallels in the experience of transformation, death, and salvation in the Tibetan Book of the Dead, are to be found in, for example, as famous a work as Goethe's *Faust.* With tremendously profound psychological insight in the character of Faust, Goethe has achieved a monumental classical study of tragic transformation, which has a validity that reaches far beyond its poetic effect. At the end of the second part of *Faust,* the four grey old women appear as fateful Eumenides. These are the inner doubts and torments which arise in Faust's soul—lack, guilt, care, and need. Just as the unknowing and therefore blind person always tries to avoid encountering and acknowledging his shadow-side, he thereby suffers actual blinding by "care." But what closes his eyes from outside, is capable of opening his inner eye.

> *The night seems to penetrate deeper and deeper,*
> *And only inside does bright light shine . . .* (11500)

And this light, which now like the "primordial clear light" becomes his guiding star in the realm beyond, appears to him as the descent of radiance.

> *Still he is blinded by the new day.*

Then Faust experiences the elemental transformation, represented similarly to the alchemical process, or to the descent through the elements as described in the Tibetan Book of the Dead. The purifying nature of the element fire is described in clear symbolic language. "Turn towards clarity, you loving flames!" (11800), and further:

Holy flames!
Whomever they surround
Feels in life
Blissful with the good.

In this elemental catharsis Faust experiences the necessary realization that all things which do not constitute the inner true self must be given up completely. Only if one holds back from outward and impermanent things can one open up the inner horizons; and it is here, within oneself, that truth is to be grounded. Thus the chorus sings (11745):

What does not belong to you
You must shun,
What disturbs your inner realm
You must not tolerate.

Finally Faust recognizes in the death experience the necessity of transformation, and he longs for it. The symbols that appear here are to be used to purify awareness; they are the strongest aspects of the spiritual power, of the self-destruction of the deceptive veil of the human intellect, which is always the greatest obstacle on the path to the integration and unification of the spirit.

Arrows, pierce me,
Lances, impale me,
Clubs, crush me,
Lightning, tear through me,
So that nothingness
Will volatilize everything . . . (11858)

In a vital symbolism reminiscent of the struggle of the forces of light against the demons of darkness from the Manichean-Gnostic doctrine, Goethe describes the radiant and peaceful heavenly emanations which appear to assist the soul, while evil dissolves into the fleeing horde of demons. For after Faust's death we see, before his soul leaves his earthly body, the visionary struggle of Mephistopheles and his satanic hordes for the possession of the soul, which is ultimately liberated for the realm of light by the heavenly armies. We are thereby reminded once again of Hildegard von Bingen: "For at death the good and bad angels are present as the 'witnesses of the works.'" The same image leads us again to the Tibetan Book of the Dead, where we have the host of the peaceful and wrathful deities as the "witnesses of the works," in order thus to effect the final purification of awareness of its karmic failings.

The indications of the meaning of life, of transformation, and also of the meaning of death are innumerable at the start of a new life. We have only considered a few of these indications in order to show that the relevance of the Tibetan Book of the Dead is not confined to its country of origin, but is universal. It is a book about death, dying, and rebirth, whose purpose is to invest the meaning of life with the proper worth and significance; for from the dividing path one gains an overview of past and future. There the ontological question of the psyche is raised to an intuited but unknown transcendence.

VI
Psychological Commentary to the Bar-do thos-grol

1. General Basic Thoughts from Buddhist Philosophy and Elements of Psychology

> First we must discern the nature of the soul, both divine and human, by considering its activities and its experiences.
>
> PLATO, *Phaedrus,* 245c

THE MOST important psychological task on the path of human individuation is the mastering of life as the great spiritual and conscious preparation for dying, which is held by the Tibetan Book of the Dead to be the most important moment of human life. At the center of the Tibetan teachings rightfully stands awareness and the intellect, those two manifestations of spirituality whose heights and depths make possible life in all its multiplicity and which introduce in the bardo the decisive vision of the peaceful and wrathful deities. The Tibetan Book of the Dead, in addition to its religious and philosophical content, is a thoroughly psychological work intended for the better understanding of and as a guide to psychic phenomena which are portrayed as after-death experiences and yet are actually images of psychic processes in daily life. Before turning to individual aspects and particular doctrines of the Tibetan Book of the Dead, let us again consider some basic premises of Mahāyāna Buddhism and relate them to certain concepts in Western psychology. We shall thereby recognize that many oriental ideas are not only genuinely psychological, but that they also have equivalents in our psychology. For one thing is common to both systems, Buddhism and psychology, namely, the analytical path towards expansion of awareness and of man's psychic structure.

A. SUFFERING AND THE PLEASURE-PAIN PRINCIPLE

The well known pleasure-pain principle in our psychology as an intra-psychic principle of opposites can also be taken as a fundamental premise of Buddhist philosophy, which is referred to again and again by the texts of Pāli Buddhism. In the religion as a doctrine of salvation, as in this principle, we have the opposition of suffering and nirvāṇa as a possible solution to the problem. In

Buddhism suffering is a fundamental inability of the psyche, conditioned by drives and desires, to attain any lasting fulfillment of its needs. Not only the external world, which is subject to the endless cycle of becoming and passing away, but also awareness itself is unsteady in relation to the external world. Thus man stands between love and hate, or, in other words, between the one-sided modes of behavior of acceptance and rejection. Both are individually effective attitudes of awareness, according to which man acts and structures his world-view. Acceptance and rejection come under the opposites of pleasure- and wish-fulfillment as well as unfulfillment, which produces negative psychic tension.

For the most part, however, the discrimination in the individual between what appears as good or evil, desirable or to be avoided, takes place unconsciously. That is, many of the inner levels of functioning of instinctual life, of the emotions, and of repressed and unconscious complexes determine conscious life and its decisions from this unconscious ground. The lack of consciousness of self-generated psychic processes prevents man from realizing that these realities of life which he has been ignoring could one day arise against him from out of the unconscious. This would be the confrontation with the unconscious, with the shadow, the hidden dark side of the personality, which attempts to penetrate consciousness. This is the essential point of all Buddhist teachings: only an increase in consciousness, an intensification of awareness, can eliminate unconscious and psychologically unhealthy processes. Therefore the symbol of Buddhism, as a religion of intensification of awareness, is enlightenment. Only when some degree of psychic adaptation and realization of awareness has been attained, does Buddhism pose the broader question of nirvāṇa as the goal of liberation. But nirvāṇa is attainable only by an overcoming of desire, the greatest attachment, with which "beings wander for ages through the cycle of rebirth." And so it says in the Majjhima-Nikāya: "To what extent is the non-attainment of that which one desires painful? The births of the fallen beings are prey to the wish: 'Oh, that we were not subject to birth, that no further birth stood before us!' But such a thing cannot be achieved merely by wishing, and precisely this non-attainment of what one desires is painful." Similarly with worry, pain, and despair, with old-age, sickness, and death, one can achieve no change through wishing. The great opposition, the freedom from suffering beyond all desire, opens up in nirvāṇa, which begins with enlightenment and inner stillness.

B. THE TWO STAGES OF LIBERATION

We come now to the question of liberation, which occupies a central position in Buddhism as in all high religions and also to quite an extent in Western psychology. If we wish to consider both of these last two, we must distinguish two categories of liberation, that of profane liberation (self-actualization) and that of sacred liberation, which ultimately includes a transcendent goal. Liberation in the profane and personal realm has as its goal the health and the liberation of the soul or the awareness. This health is psychologically oriented. We find it, for example, in the Vedas as the recognition of the inner puruṣa, the self, and this constitutes the precondition for any further form of liberation. If this becomes transparent, there then comes the great moment of the knowledge of sacred liberation as the absolute goal. This always has a transcendent character and is to be found beyond this profane world.

It is a psychological fact that man's sacred goal of liberation is congruent with his earthly goal. This is the transcending of the meaning of existence into the infinite, the timeless and deathless, which in religious imagery presents itself as the divine within the soul, as Brahman, as God, as pure light, as pure transcendental awareness, or as nirvāṇa. Sooner or later in the psychic process of individuation there arises the question of man's highest principles, which manifests in the confrontation with the problem of God and eternity. Therefore, what occurs quite necessarily in psychic life, in its transformation and maturation, is in the religions the *a priori* explicit goal of liberation. In the Buddhist and Hindu doctrines of liberation in particular, we find a great number of psychic techniques and psychological practices which are very closely connected with the religious doctrinal systems.

C. IGNORANCE AND WISDOM

We find in Buddhism as in all Indian religions that significant symbolism of the opposites of wisdom and ignorance. Ignorance is the failure to see the true background of the psychic relationships, the instinctual conditions and dependencies under which the "unenlightened person" lives and suffers. Wisdom is the illumination of all these generally unconscious fixations, where conscious illumination entails the disappearance of the hindrances (S. kleśa) which obstruct the path to liberation. The Asiatic understands by wisdom that kind of knowledge which serves the development of spiritual awareness and release. Rational wisdom is then of secondary importance and does not serve the true goal if it has merely been amassed by the intellect. Also unfamiliar to the Asiatic is the distinction—often too sharply drawn in the West—between consciousness and the unconscious. He rather sees the human person under the aspect of a totality of awareness. Certain Indian and Tibetan doctrines, for example, that of the "dream-state" (T. rMi-lam), which was handed down by Nāropa and Marpa, make this aspect quite clear. Their aim is to maintain a continuity of awareness throughout the sleep- and dream-state, capable of being controlled at all times. If we apply the characteristic function of Buddhist symbolism, which is informed by a deep knowledge of reality, to the psychological definition of the Western way of thinking, our model of consciousness and the unconscious could be used—provided that we clarify the borders between both ways of the manifestation of awareness and understand them dynamically.

Concerning ignorance (S. avidyā) we would want to say: it is the fundamental unconsciousness of an essential, personal portion of psychic processes which lie outside our conscious knowledge. We know that such processes take place from the psychology of the complexes, depressions, regressions, and suppressed contents and from the incongruence of individual psychic potential and its manifest actuality. The contents of dreams are only one example of this. Psychology has established a host of clear definitions for all those "sufferings" which ultimately have their cause in the "ignorance" of precisely these "sufferings" and their causes. Psychoanalysis is the uncovering and analyzing of psychic sufferings and their origins, in order to bring them to consciousness. If this succeeds, it becomes a psychological path to the "alleviation of suffering," in as far as consciousness gains knowledge of and power over hitherto "unconscious" or "unknown" contents. Then the obstructions can be overcome. We are here talking, of course, of the ideal case, which may be only partially attainable.

If we at this point look away from the highly complex theories of the structures of the unconscious in order to attain a more comprehensive view, a more dynamic conception of ignorance and unconsciousness would then seem appropriate. The more ignorance can be transformed into knowledge, the more wisdom and awareness can be actualized. This is the primary goal in Buddhism, prior to the asking of any transcendental question. The more unconscious contents can be raised from the unconscious, and the more consciousness can be increased, the more independence from the dangers of unconscious processes then develops, reducing dependence on drives and libidinous fixations. This is the task of Western psychology. There is, then, a path; if we call it philosophical, then it leads from ignorance to wisdom; if psychological, then from the unconscious to consciousness, which results from the potential of a possible evolution of awareness. We can also say then that the philosophical path towards knowledge rests upon the reality of the psyche and is one of its primary images. We could derive similar structures from the great symbolism of mythology which similarly constitutes a faithful image of the history of awareness, when looked at psychologically.

D. ON THE RELATION OF MIND AND BODY

The question concerning the fatefully determined attachment to the manifest world through desires and passions also touches upon a fundamental psychological problem which cannot be solved by mere theorizing but requires continual adaptation of life to reality. Man, because of the whole structure of his physical being, is a natural being and one therefore bound by natural instincts. This is the larger part of his being. His total corporeality occupies a position in the biological processes of instinctual life, which is common to all living organisms. But then man as a self-conscious and spiritual being was able to recognize another level of Being, which allowed him to set himself outside and beyond all purely natural events. That man exists within the cycle of nature cannot be doubted, but this fact is not problematic. The problem begins only when man's spiritual nature becomes autonomous and sets itself up against his earthly nature. This is the point of departure for the Buddhist doctrine of suffering, which it recognizes as a suffering of the world. Biologically and physiologically we are dependent on the world; but neither extreme asceticism nor total worldliness can be the right way to freedom from the opposites. To find the middle way between the divisive mind and physical existence inclined towards nature is a principal task of human life.

Buddhism thus has undergone transformation in various important schools, in order to dissolve this problem of "body alone on one side and mind alone on the other." In the Mahāyāna and Vajrayāna, methods centered around psychological techniques for achieving integration were developed to resolve this opposition. This is the task of psychology, to be concerned about accommodating the functions of instinctual life, and yet also to see behind this a life on a higher plane of awareness which is no longer in opposition to the physical constitution. The dualistic principle of spirit and matter is no longer applicable, but rather the integration of spirit as a power that pervades everything material. The Tibetan Book of the Dead is concerned with the opposition of awareness and intellect, because the intellect is the divisive function which creates the opposites.

E. KARMA AND SELF-RESPONSIBILITY

We have already discussed the problem of personal karma as a central idea in Buddhism. Karma is the personal experience of the fruits of one's own thoughts, intentions, and actions. It is the suffering of the working-out of previous actions and of the attitudes which led to them; the person is, so to speak, the sum of his doing. The notion of karma is certainly intelligible to the Westerner, even if he cannot quite grasp the incredibly strict consequences. There are many examples from the idiomatic uses of language which betray an underlying feeling for the law of karma—for example, the saying: "It all comes back on you."

Buddhism places this law concerning the consequences of one's actions in the realm of the absolute, which is to say that the law is effective beyond all boundaries of the individual life. It is the causal law of the world in itself. Only from this transcendence of time can the Buddhist theory be grasped, that man is also responsible for those so-called "acts of fate," which he cannot believe himself to have caused. According to the Buddhist conception, the events and sufferings of this life relate, not only to present activity, but also to earlier actions and their causes in an earlier life. In his present life man is therefore the sum and consequence of his previous deeds and decisions. The theory also presupposes that the future, including a later earthly existence, can be influenced positively or negatively by corresponding behavior. This is not a question of moral values in themselves but of behavior relating to the health of the total individual. Concerning the condition of human awareness, Buddhism talks of karmically favorable and unfavorable behavior; one furthers enlightenment and release, the other leads to attachment and ignorance.

In a certain sense we find in practical psychotherapy comparable points of contact, in its concern to achieve a comprehensive understanding of the meaning of being human. This is clear in the "analytical psychology" of C. G. Jung, which gives a central position to the total human being, also in the "Schicksalsanalyse" ("fate-analysis") of L. Szondi, and especially in the "Daseinsanalytic School" of L. Binswanger, M. Boss, and G. Condrau. In all of these, man's historicality plays an important role, from the "archetype" (Jung), to the "hereditarily conditioned compulsion of choice" of fate (Szondi), and the "fulfillment of Dasein" as the hanging-together of human experience.

The majority of people come into psychotherapy because they are no longer master of themselves owing to neuroses, anxieties, and depressions, and because a large portion of their psychic energy is so bound up with their "sufferings" that their freedom to act is significantly curtailed. They are always running into conflicts with their own complexes, which obstruct their path at every turn. These complexes also hinder the natural process of individuation, the psycho-spiritual perfection of man. These people even know, in part, that they are continually making the same mistakes, and it is remarkable that they are no longer able to remedy these failings by means of their own powers. Wrong behavior arises not only from ignorance and bad reasoning, but also from maladaptation, conditioned by neurotic complexes, to the natural structures of physical and psychical life, which are thereby thrown out of equilibrium.

Instinctual fixations arising from neuroses, deeply rooted complexes (which unconsciously lead to lasting delusions), and complex inhibitions and transformations of instincts lead to the formation of a second superstructure, which obstructs true knowledge, objective behavior, and the path to self-knowledge. The "picture of things" we individually construct, the object imago, is further pushed into unreality by the weight of the complexes. The ability to act responsibly from knowledge of one's own psychic capabilities is diminished. It is the task of psychotherapy to loosen these "attachments" of neurotic fixation, in order to achieve an increase in psychic energy, which then enables the person properly to relate to himself and his environment. Constricted awareness is then freed, and what was hitherto unconscious becomes conscious, which is why we talk of an expansion of consciousness.

Taking responsibility for one's thoughts and actions, as demanded by the Buddhist idea of karma, is also a goal of Western psychology, which seeks to return to man his full capabilities of acting. Freud was the first to discover the conclusions that can be drawn from dream-images. If a person believes that his behavior has no influence on his personally so loved and protected psychic existence, the psychology of dreams or the psychopathology of everyday life can show just the opposite. Therefore, the central task of psychology is to show man the path towards taking responsibility for himself. Common to the teachings of Buddhism and to psychology is the analytical path, the destruction of those psychically conditioned phenomena of a secondary character, that is, phenomena which can be led back to a deeper cause, which has become covered up or distorted. What has to become transparent is the psycho-energetic kernel and the pure center of awareness, so that free behavior can unfold.

F. ĀLAYAVIJÑĀNA AND ARCHETYPAL STRUCTURES

Another concept from Buddhist Mahāyāna philosophy, which was introduced in the second chapter, is that of the universal- or ground-consciousness, which we can translate exactly as "storehouse-consciousness" (S. ālayavijñāna; T. Kun-gzhi rnam-shes). From the Tibetan translation it is clearly a question of the "awareness of all causes" which lead to thinking and other intellectual activities. Yogācāra philosophy, the school of "mind-only doctrines" (S. vijñānavāda), proceeds from the premise that all things as objects, all images and appearances, are only mind or awareness. That is to say, we only recognize and know things as such in their multiplicity and individuality in as far as they are contents of consciousness. Consciousness is the presupposition of the process of "knowing." Thus everything that is not recognized in consciousness is therefore non-existent. The whole objective world is therefore ultimately consciousness, since this constitutes the presupposition for its being known. Mind, or pure awareness, is, according to the idealistic Vijñānavāda theory, the indispensable basis and essence of reality and is therefore absolute. Since nothing is imaginable without mind, it is called the absolute, or all-pervading emptiness, or simply nirvāṇa.

In man there are, according to this same theory, two levels of this storehouse- or ground-consciousness, which are distinguished only by their functions as static and maternal primordial ground and as activity. The ālayavijñāna forms the primordial ground or the inexhaustible potentiality for all conscious development. Its active form is the continuously self-generating and transforming thought-consciousness (S. manovijñāna; T. Yid-kyi rnam-shes). In the Buddhist texts the ālayavijñāna is compared with a vast ocean symbolizing the fullness and totality of all water. Ground-consciousness is, then, the storehouse of all impressions of awareness, which are communicated by the senses and by discriminating thought. However, all intellectual activities of discriminating thought-awareness occasion karmic consequences which impress themselves on the primordial ground and from there can again come to "maturation" in new thought-processes. Karma is then the personally occasioned "wind" of awareness-energy which blows over the surface of the ocean of ground-consciousness. It whips it up into a thousand waves and causes thoughts and associations in the depths of the storehouse-consciousness. Thinking is the dynamic process of the multiplication of contents immanent in consciousness, which is synthesized into the object. Karma, the causally conditioned, individual situation of man, causes the deepest personal and personally hitherto unrecognized images, ideas, and knowledge to well up into consciousness, since these are all contained in the universal potentiality of ground-consciousness as karmic seeds. In the latency of the storehouse-consciousness each individual image is there primordially, even though totally indistinguishable.

It is surely not "coincidence," but rather historically a psychic reality of great significance, that similar trains of thought are also to be found in the West since antiquity. They were first formed in Plato's Theory of Ideas, which talks of the eternal, intellectual, primordial images as Ideas. Plato saw these images of things as both personal and transpersonal, i.e., as existing before the individual's birth. In Plato the Ideas alone are truly real and are above all the primordial forms in which manifest things participate in a merely conditional way, for these are merely a limited expression of the totality of the Ideas. The Theory of Ideas runs through Socrates, Plotinus, and the Middle Ages and through the whole intellectual history of the West, although in the most varying forms. Perhaps we even find a version of it again in modern psychology, in as far as there must be something primordial in human awareness that from unknown depths influences human behavior in characteristic ways.

Freud was the first to recognize, from certain archaic and constantly returning dream-contents, that dreams produce seemingly "phylogenetically inherited" material reflecting functions and contents of consciousness more ancient than those of personal life. For Jung and his school this notion became the central doctrine, that in human consciousness primordial images, the archetypes, manifest, which are to be seen as structural dominants of the collective unconscious. Jung thereby conceives these archetypes in a way consonant with an energetic definition of the psychic, as preformative points of crystallization in the unconscious. The archetypes become psychically concretely visible and demonstrable through becoming conscious. We cannot therefore say that the primordial images as such are lying in readiness in the unconscious, but they exist rather as structural potentialities, which may under certain conditions be continually recognized as archetypes. Jung also calls them "self-reflections of the instincts," since they are identical with the primordial functions of the instincts.

If these archetypes are raised up into consciousness, they take on the characteristics of "discriminating" consciousness and therefore appear to be of ambivalent value or meaning. It is from this function that the systematic symbolism of opposites of the Tibetan Book of the Dead is to be understood, which is founded upon primordial symbols. But what we recognize in consciousness as "primordial images" has its invisible energetic preformation in the unconscious as structural dominants, or as a kind of primordial structure which can be described as an instinctual tendency. In biology and animal psychology such structures are known as inborn mechanisms which lead to the release of quite definite and consistent modes of behavior. The biologist A. Portmann sees things comparable to the archetypes of Jungian psychology in "the recognition of what-has-never-been-perceived by means of an inherited structure."[151] For Portmann they are "releasers," which release certain typical functions on the surface of visible behavior. These latter in turn point to the existence of primordial functions which preform the living organism in its behavior. We have touched upon these questions in psychology only in order to show that the question of a primordial consciousness and thereby the question of the transmission of contents of consciousness through generations is widespread. With the Buddhist concept of the ālayavijñāna we have a first Asian formulation of the problem, to which on the philosophical plane Plato's Theory of Ideas bears a certain relationship, and today psychology again poses the question of the permanence of human experiences which have been maintained in an archetypal collective unconscious.

2. Psychological Aspects of the Tibetan Book of the Dead

> There are many people who, at the moment of their death, have not only lagged behind their own possibilities, but also far behind those which had been made conscious in their lifetime by other people.
>
> C. G. JUNG
>
> *Memories, Dreams, Reflections*

ONE OF THE most remarkable things about the Buddhist philosophy in the Tibetan Book of the Dead is that the visionary deities can appear simultaneously as realities or as "illusory images." Or, in other words, they are on the one hand the highest reality and on the other, mere images of psychic projection. Yet both aspects are fully justified and in no way exclude one another. For Buddhist philosophy there exist no gods as absolute beings, for even their being is restricted to the time during which they are recognized as such by human beings. Nevertheless the Book of the Dead uses divine figures, the transcendent buddhas, in order to express certain spiritual and psychic qualities, or also their wrathful counter-images, in which the aspects of power and reaction manifest. But beyond all images and symbols, Buddhism has placed nirvāṇa, the imageless stage of liberation, which is therefore also called the great emptiness. In all-pervading emptiness, figures of reality and of mere appearance dissolve in their relativity, for here at the goal "nothing more is to be attained" which would have to be concretely made present.

The buddhas and bodhisattvas are considered a reality on the path of meditation in order that the adept may grasp philosophical and religious teachings. For the followers of the Mahāyāna they are the guiding symbols of the spiritual path, and thus these images are identical with the ethical contents of the teachings. As the Tathāgatas they point the way to higher awareness and to a life of metaphysical fulfillment of existence. Yet the Tibetan Book of the Dead teaches that the buddhas are only the visible forms of the inner, pure buddha-nature of awareness, representable manifestations of the enlightened nature of man which is always present in him.

We thereby reach the second level, that of the psychological knowledge that all images and visions, even the highest images and deities, are figures from one's own awareness. We thereby recognize them as projections, in which deep contents of consciousness are made accessible to us through images. The images of the Tathāgatas are nothing other than forms of expression of the contents of awareness.

Similarly, the projections of the visionary deities are logical extensions of Mahāyāna philosophy and its applications, in that it too teaches the psychological viewpoint that all images, forms, and thought-contents are ultimately to be understood as products of awareness. What on the side of reality are primordial images of spiritual actualities, become, from the psychological viewpoint, projections as imaginal contents of consciousness and symbolic figures representing psychic processes and concrete transformations of awareness. As long as the buddhas rest upon reality and their portrayal of spiritual contents, they are real, but as soon as they symbolically stand *for* anything, they are to be seen psychologically. What is metaphysically grounded upon the purely philosophical plane of Buddhist metaphysics, which is here represented in the most numinous images, appears on the psychological plane of projections of consciousness as a psychical and even metaphysical reality. Psychical because the visionary deities are recognized as symbols of the spirit, and because they are the archetypal symbolism of processes immanent in awareness. A metaphysical reality is thereby established, because the whole process of the existence of conscious and unconscious individuals is not yet transferred into the transcendence beyond earthly life. That is to say, the existence of the psychical is extended as a projection far beyond its earthly dimension.

The doctrines of Yogācāra philosophy, among which the Tibetan Book of the Dead can be counted, proceed from the premise that karmically laden awareness by far outlasts the earthly life-span of the individual. According to this view, psychic life lasts as long as the power of personal karma. Now, whether the buddhas represent the goal of the great perfection, or whether, after penetrating their imaginal nature we see them as stages on the path, as formed awareness, these are only two kinds of knowledge, two levels of spiritual practice. The philosophy of the Mahāyāna places above all conceptualization emptiness, suchness, pure buddha-nature, or the crystal clear diamond nature of human awareness, which is of imageless intensity. It is always there, it must simply be discovered. Therefore a question in Zen asks: "Why do you wish to go with the Buddha to look for the Buddha?" It is as if one wanted to use fire to look for fire. Self-knowledge is a spontaneous process of synchronicity between conscious and unconscious, between intellect or thought-consciousness and primordial ground or ālayavijñāna; here all images and visions are suddenly extinguished, curtailed by pure knowledge or enlightenment. This is the condition of "clear light" in the Tibetan Book of the Dead, in which only light itself is experienced as the dharmakāya. Therefore the Tibetan Book of the Dead can first proclaim the philosophical reality of the buddhas and their teachings, and after these have been grasped and penetrated, it can then say that these are only illusory images of one's own consciousness, for the pure world within needs no images of external form.

Whether man in his spiritual evolution, on the path of religious salvation, on the path of spiritual knowledge and liberation through philosophy and ethics, or else by the practice of Yoga and psychology, thereby discovers and perfects his individuation, each of these paths is nevertheless a self-contained symbol for the entelechy of the psychical in the totality of its earthly being and its transcendent possibilities. It is always a striving of spiritualization for knowledge, a turning of consciousness to metaphysical and irrational contents, a connecting with the purely divine, which can manifest already in this life.

If we consider the various accounts of the reality of the psychical, we find that there are various theories of the soul and awareness, but that the incredibly rich treasure of symbolism, concerning the great crossing over, formed by primordial human experience, is strikingly universal. Whether it is the path of the soul, the spirit-body, and the vital life-force of the ancient Egyptian into the realm of Osiris and then into the fields of Iaru, or the transformations and wanderings of the puruṣa in the pretakalpa of the Garuḍa-Purāṇa, or else the narrow path through the bardo for the "awareness-body" of the Tibetan, the path through the beyond is described by means of remarkably similar symbols. We recognize in this the phenomenology of a collective psychic faculty of expression, which archetypally revolves around more or less the same symbols. This is the recognizable law of the primordially conditioned reaction-formation of consciousness concerning the ontological problem of human hope and being.

Behind all these various descriptions, whether the soul is thought of concretely or as an amorphous structure of consciousness, lies the collective primordial ground of psychical notions and perhaps also genuine experiences. Who could draw the line here between reality and speculation? At least the dark region between the two is somewhat illuminated by the Tibetan Book of the Dead. We should also bear in mind that so many of the psychical situations in human life: the anxieties and needs of dreams, the true anxieties of life, the emergency situations of the greatest psychic tension and conflict, all these can evoke corresponding images of tension, demonism, solution, transcendence, and torments and sufferings of spiritual and earthly hells similar to those depicted in descriptions of the after-death world in mankind's wisest books. It is not mere coincidence that we find such parallel descriptions in the scriptures of the Old Testament, Judaic scriptures, and in the Egyptian, Greek, Indian, and Tibetan traditions.

Is the bardo or the intermediate state of the decisions and sufferings of consciousness between two forms of life merely a projection of basic anxiety in the face of death? The purely psychoanalytic point of view would like to define it as such. But does this do justice to the situation and to the lasting questions of thousands of years of human awareness? The answer lies between affirmation and denial, just as the Tibetan Book of the Dead makes possible simultaneously a philosophical and a psychological, a determinative and a relativizing judgement. Hence this emptiness, this "concept" beyond concepts. Or else, is it a question of transcendent experience, which dawns upon human existence as intuited reality? This question, as before, has to be pushed further. Metaphysics takes us into a realm beyond material or physical reality, and whether it is conducted empirically or ascertained through evidence, the ultimate proof of reality will always be lacking. Therefore its dimension may not be restricted by physical measures. Metaphysical events, if we proceed from a psyche bound to the individual, which yet reaches beyond this individual as a one-time being, necessarily lose for us their dimensions in a psychology related only to this world. If we know all too little about the psychical in man, about the true dimensions of consciousness, how can we hope to comprehend the worlds of the bardo? At this point a phenomenology of the possible conditions and speculations must begin. There is an abundance of evidence available, if we may call it that—the whole of intellectual history is proof that soul and awareness are more than just a once-only transitory embodiment. If we study the many writings about experiences of the world beyond, and also the Books of the Dead with their determinate statements, we could establish a "phenomenology of the beyond" utilizing definite statements and symbols. Yet the world beyond, as long as we are in this one, must remain a mystery. Even if it continues to remain so, the contents of the Tibetan Book of the Dead nevertheless constitute a rich fund of psychical treasure which serves to illuminate to some extent the phenomena of life, awareness, and the divine.

The Bar-do thos-grol, the Tibetan Book of the Dead in all its variations and independent of particular religious influences, offers us an instruction manual for the guidance of human awareness after death. All the events are described as psychic projections in the space of an already transcendent awareness, in such a way that they there underlie the same modes of reacting as previously on the earthly plane. To this extent the Tibetan Book of the Dead is primarily a book of life, for the knowledge of the path through the bardo must be gained "on this side" if it is to be put into practice "on the other side." This is the basis of the Buddhist way of life, which is set up as a model for the journey through the bardo. Without this basis a Book of the Dead that would communicate only knowledge for the beyond could not possibly be translated into our rational thinking. Therefore the ritual work for the Tibetan Book of the Dead is different, in that although it embraces the essential contents and philosophy of the Book of the Dead, it is substantially supplemented by ritual instructions for the performing of death-rites, consecrations, initiations, sacrifices, and supplications.

In the Buddhist trikāya doctrine, which forms the basis for understanding the transformations in the bardo, we can recognize three stages in the manifestation of awareness. The highest manifestation as the uppermost level of pure Being is that of radiant awareness as the self-illuminating clear light in the state of the dharmakāya. It is awareness *per se* and is therefore also equated with the great emptiness, which makes possible the plenitude of the spirit. The dharmakāya state, therefore, is symbolized by the unclothed deep blue Ādibuddha Samantabhadra. Deep blue is the color of intensive pure awareness, of the intellect sunk in meditation, and "without clothing" means "without any attributes" or "indescribable in his qualities." In the dharmakāya-state, pure awareness is in the realm of the primordial beginning, that is to say, that it subsists in an indivisible state of potentiality prior to all creation and all origination of contents of consciousness.

If something opposing appears, namely, an objective goal, then the activity of consciousness begins from its first self-positing and individuation, and then the emanations of awareness follow on the various levels. In the Tibetan Book of the Dead the symbolic opposite is the female counterpart of the buddhas, the prajñā or ḍākinī. Her inseparable union in the *unio mystica* with the buddha symbolizes the beginning of all maṇḍalas, of the structures of psychic totality and the unified symbols of Buddhism.

A second level of awareness is the visionary realm of visible transcendent figures, which manifests in the sambhogakāya, the plane of heavenly and divine visions. Looked at from the point of view of the physical body, the sambhogakāya is as a state of bliss an ecstatic projection which is experienced psychically, inwardly in awareness, or through visions in the most outward space. The meditation techniques of Vajrayāna Buddhism generally discuss two ways of psychic realization. The outer way consists of visualization and the active imagination of symbols, mantras, and images of the deities, which are imbued with meaning by means of various kinds of projection. The image recognized in outer projection by imaginative techniques, when united with consciousness, leads to ecstatic experience. The inner way as a complementary event at the center of awareness, without any influence from the external world, is a goal-directed and conscious introversion to the point that the again visionary events take place within the horizons of awareness. To unite these extremely inward visionary images with those most outward spheres of the external world is the goal of the tantric Buddhist psychic techniques, forming a great unity of immanent and transcendent visionary events. This visionary plane is comparable with the sambhogakāya, the "body of spiritual bliss" at the visionary level of the divine image. It manifests as a form of the numinous in its greatest opposition of the peaceful and liberation-bringing and of the wrathful, demonic, and threatening. Both these aspects are forms of awareness, which according to its situation expresses itself in one or the other of the opposites.

The third and general human level shows awareness in the nirmāṇakāya, the embodied consciousness in its mortal shell. In Buddhist philosophy this is the place of suffering, in which awareness experiences the nature of the impermanence in which it still participates. Here the total psyche is bound to impermanent form and suffers from the constant conflict of spirit and matter, between natural biological life and constantly evolving spirit, which extends its dominion in order to achieve independence and freedom. Yet this human life prefigures a path which begins in unconsciousness and yet can attain more mature and higher awareness, a life which is apparently capable of going beyond the earthly form. After the embodiment of awareness, the upward path to individuation begins, and according to the Tibetan Book of the Dead, awareness attains its highest moment at death. But there, the inverted path begins, from pure "liberated" awareness in the face of the dharmakāya, through the visionary state of the sambhogakāya, back down into unconsciousness, the resting of the activities of the spirit, before the beginning of a new life. These three levels are the 'Chi-kha'i bar-do, the Chos-nyid bar-do, and the Srid-pa'i bar-do. From the first life with minimal consciousness, man develops to the bright "daylight" of waking-consciousness, and thence to pure awareness at the crossing over into the bardo. Therefore the path to the next incarnation in the Tibetan Book of the Dead is called the descending path, because the power of awareness again sinks from its zenith down into union with the physical. The smaller the karmic accretions, the less effect they have in the bardo, and therefore, the higher the starting point for the new rebirth is, and so, the better the prospects for eventual liberation.

We have indicated that the Tibetan Book of the Dead is a self-contained work employing archetypal symbols, as are a few of the wisdom-books of the ancient world. We should like now to mention again some of these archetypal structures. First is the intensive light-symbolism as against the abysses of flaming and smoking darkness of the worlds of hell, which symbolize the opposition of the highest wisdom and the darkest unconsciousness. The five Tathāgatas appear in the radiant lights of the wisdoms, in cosmic colors, which denote a comprehensive intensification of awareness. If we think of the light-symbolism of the flames of the Holy Spirit, which appear at Whitsuntide above the heads of the disciples, then we have the same archetypal image of the birth of light in the spirit, which heralds a new awareness.

The bardo of reality-experience shows the visionary, imaginal, and also deceptive structure of the divine figures who arise as manifestations of awareness within the horizons of one's own mind. The more the luminous nature of awareness diminishes, the more powerful become the opposing forces, demonic, terrible, and arising out of the unknown depths, whence radiate the dim lights of the six lokas. These are the lights of the failing intellectual faculty, which has been dimmed by the instinctual worlds. The counter-images to great and peaceful wisdom are the herukas, the terrifying power-aspect which arises in the blazing figures when the human intellect has come away from the roots of consciousness. The archetypal symbolism of the theriomorphic deities is remarkable, who on the descending path towards the end of the visions announce a multiplication of the destructive aspect of the Great Mother. We shall return to this below.

Of great significance from the psychologico-religious point of view is the appearance of the peaceful and wrathful deities, who even in their great multiplicity are to be understood as aspects of the numinous. These are not only images and "manifestations" of awareness, but in them the presence of the divine is expressed, which can assume various forms in the psyche. Although Buddhism knows no relationship to a personal God or Creator, the nature of the divine is nevertheless in no way foreign to it, but rather an equally lofty ideal. The "four divine states" (S. caturapramāṇāni) of a disciple of the Buddhist teachings, which are similar to the virtues of Brahmā, may be an example. For the Tibetan Book of the Dead the buddhas and bodhisattvas are "deities," the highest metaphysical bearers of meaning, who appear as symbols of transformation on the path of enlightenment. They are not gods in the strict sense, although Buddhism knows such gods from the other Indian religions. These latter, however, have their place in the pantheon in one or other of the heavenly regions and are hardly of significance in Buddhist philosophy and ethics. The buddhas are deities in the sense of symbols of Buddhist wisdoms and virtues.

Their appearance in the symbolic world of the Book of the Dead corresponds to the archetypal structure of numinous contents of consciousness, in which the nature of the divine manifests as the ungraspable in twofold form. This numinosity was described by R. Otto under the two aspects of the *fascinans* and the *tremendum.* In a certain sense these primordial manifestations of the divine are also appropriate to the visions of the bardo. Corresponding to the self-reliant state of meditative awareness, the divine wisdoms appear as peaceful buddhas in the attractive and uplifting aspect of the *mysterium fascinans.* In their fivefold radiance they divert the gaze of consciousness upwards, and they are pictured "hovering in heavenly spheres." Their counter-aspect is the divine as *mysterium tremendum,* which appears in shattering, terrifying, threatening visions, when the intellect is in conflict with the ungraspable. The Tibetan Book of the Dead emphasizes again and again that the terrifying Buddha-Heruka is none other than the Ādibuddha Samantabhadra. And such great counter-images arise only when the absolute, the dharmakāya, and totally liberated awareness have not yet been attained in the first "clear light."

We have said that the bardo deities constitute a precisely ordered schema of psychological contents and relationships. Translation of the Tibetan scriptures taking account of the Buddhist symbolism makes it clear that the peaceful and wrathful deities are characterized as single structural elements of psychic organs and relationships. Therefore, according to the tantric scheme, all the deities are always connected with their opposing aspect, which is expressed in the conjunction of male and female or peaceful and wrathful components. We mentioned the remarkable theriomorphic deities, who are female and are called ḍākinīs. They appear first as anthropomorphized demonic goddesses, the eight Keurima, then as eight therianthropic goddesses in the form of the eight Phra-men-ma, and finally as the 28 animal-headed goddesses who initiate the dead person into the mystery of total self-dissolution, before a new life can begin.

These goddesses exhibit clear variations of the destructive and devouring aspect of the archetype of the Great Mother. They are at the same time images of the animal nature of the shadow-side of the human psyche. The animal-headed goddesses symbolize the aspect of annihilation by means of the Indian and Tibetan graveyard-symbolism, with which the ḍākinīs of annihilation are connected. The goddesses with the head of the serpent, the tiger, the leopard, the dog, the fox, the crow, or the vulture demonstrate the destructive function of the concluding bardo visions, which bring an end to the remnants of false thinking and illusion. The annihilation is carried out by the female aspect, in that the 28 goddesses appear from the "four directions" of one's own head, in order to effect a final catharsis of consciousness of all false identifications. It is striking that many Tibetan paintings for the Book of the Dead portray the terrifying deities with symbols of annihilation from the graveyard and that these almost always appear together with symbols of longevity.

Thereby the polar structure of the archetypal opposites is maintained; the symbolism designates, in spite of annihilation, the continuation of awareness in new forms of transformed existence. It is a basic function and characteristic of the archetype that it always appears on the level of consciousness in ambivalent images. There is not one image of an archetype but always several, whereby each differing aspect mirrors only one side of the primordial image. The forces "in the center of the heart" and the powers of the intellect must be brought into a functional unity, which makes possible a dynamic integration of the opposites. This is clearly portrayed in the fine Tibetan painting in plate 4, in which Buddha Vajrasattva unites both maṇḍalas, that of the peaceful deities in the heart center and of the wrathful deities in the head. This shows that the deities are projections of human awareness, which certainly form oppositions but which are yet one, namely Vajrasattva, or diamond-nature. This is buddha-nature, pure awareness, or the great emptiness.

Finally the Tibetan Book of the Dead is a treasure trove of maṇḍalas, which we know as the most important unifying symbols in psychology. The maṇḍalas of the five Tathāgatas and of the Herukas, their counter-images, reflect the polarity of the numinous aspect in the space of the greatest psychic order and unification, in which all the counter-images present in the psyche are again brought into unity. The structure of the maṇḍala consists of the square, as an ordering of the elements and of spiritual structures, and the circle, which expresses the cosmic and binding unity of the psychical. In the circle and the square the profane man and the sacred man are brought together in a spiritual symbol of unity. The earthly path is extended by means of transcendent and metaphysical meaning and placed into a cosmic and sacred order. The universality and totality from the individuation of a conscious person is represented in a psychologically related cosmic and divine world, in which a five-colored blazing circle of light surrounds the square. This is elemental luminous awareness, which encompasses the "heavenly sphere" and the plan of appearance of divine symbols. Thus the Buddhist maṇḍalas are visionary images and not yet ultimate realities, but as the archetypal structure of quaternity they symbolize those realms of the absolute, of the great light of the dharmakāya, which out of indescribable emptiness form the foundation of the manifold of all things.

In the two great maṇḍalas of the Tibetan Book of the Dead we recognize, from the psychological point of view, the portrayal of a double quaternity which brings together the manifestations of the numinous and of consciousness into a psychological and cosmological order. Each order has a polar structure, symbolizing the complementarity of the male and female aspects of awareness. Each brings a level of the numinous, one the peaceful and the other the wrathful. Both are dimensions of awareness and in the bardo state are to be interpenetrated by knowledge. Only then is the liberation through vision (T. mThong-grol) accomplished, which transcends the state of the merely symbolic in order to attain imageless reality.

Among the conditions laid down by the authors of the Tibetan Books of the Dead are progressive processes of knowledge beyond physical death. We ourselves have little opportunity to penetrate the realm of the unknown, yet our psychology knows an abundance of premonitions and dream visions which come true, and we also know synchronistic phenomena which point to the existence of other psychic dimensions than are normally acknowledged.

In Jung's analytical psychology there is the important definition of the transcendent function, which in the process of psychic individuation effects a synthesis between conscious and unconscious through the development of unifying symbolism. This constitutes significant knowledge about the nature of creativity, which like all conscious acts can take place only through the participation of a potential of the unconscious which is unknown to us. We thus recognize the extent to which our conscious functioning is conditioned by a much more complex unconscious, of whose dimensions and range we hardly have an idea. How far could the unconscious primordial ground of limited consciousness be effective beyond physical existence? Or is there a systolic contraction of the pure unconscious before new consciousness can arise out of primordial potentiality? Such speculations must not be indulged in, since they only serve to bind us to ideas instead of to realities.

The Books of the Dead of the Tibetans, the Indians, and the Egyptians, the myths of the eternal return of man, the abundance of prayers and songs of hope for a better life in a world to come or of the salvation of the soul, all these contribute to a theory of existence in the world beyond. If we call them such, whether in mythical image, in a metaphysical definition, or in psychological concepts, they are for us philosophically and psychologically real, however much we may use reason to put them in abeyance. The establishing of transcendent worlds, although only in theory, is nevertheless a reality which we cannot avoid as a problem of awareness. It is therefore worth concerning ourselves with these realms, at least for our own psychic development in "this world." Even if our evidence for the portrayal of other-worldly events or forms of existence is not conclusive, it still constitutes a rich harvest for the philosophy and psychology of this life, much of which remains to be gathered. For many questions remain open and retain their mystery, whether we now seek a philosophically exhaustive answer or a psychological solution.

The Tibetan Book of the Dead grew slowly, and for ages it occupied the living in establishing the meaning of the transformations in the beyond and in compiling this meaning in a book of wisdom. Actualization of life as psychic individuation and cultivation of awareness is demanded by man in his existence, if his transformation in the bardo is to fulfill the teleological meaning of his liberation. The Tibetan Book of the Dead was written for the spiritual guidance of the recently deceased, in order that he may grasp the new life awaiting him at the end of the 49 days in the bardo. The content of the Tibetan Book of the Dead consists of the most profound wisdom about life for the path through the uncertainties of the bardo, which is described by the Bar-do thos-grol with such assurance that it is as if premonitions of the unknown and beyond had become reality.

The question about what happens after the great transition can only be resolved by symbolic comparisons, which yet provide comprehensible evidence. Therefore we shall conclude this chapter with a comparison from the ancient Indian Chāndogya Upaniṣad (8.1.6):

> Therefore, those who depart from here without having recognized the soul and those real desires, they will lack freedom in whatever worlds they live; but those who depart from here after recognizing the soul and those real desires, they will find freedom in all worlds.

VII–VIII
Notes
Bibliography

VII. NOTES

1. W. Y. Evans-Wentz, *The Tibetan Book of the Dead,* Oxford, 1927. This work is indispensable for the interested reader, since it provides a translation of a considerable portion of the Book of the Dead. As mentioned in the introduction, our book sets itself another task as a comparative overview of the Tibetan Book of the Dead tradition and as a guide to the understanding of the initiations and visionary images, which in themselves portray an abundance of ancient life-experience. A new translation of *The Tibetan Book of the Dead* by Francesca Fremantle and Chögyam Trungpa has been published by Shambhala Publications, Inc., Berkeley and London 1975.

2. See Bibliography VIII, 1.A. No. 8.

3. Such texts are, for example, the *bTags-grol-gyi skor-rnams,* or the *sNying-thig-gi bshags-grol.*

4. A good example of this is figure 16 on p. 163 in D. I. Lauf, *Tibetan Sacred Art,* Berkeley & London 1976.

5. On the five Buddhas or Tathāgatas see pp. 135–146.

6. To these belong the texts in Biblio. VIII, 1.A. nos. 1,4,6,7,8.

7. Biblio. VIII, 1.A. no. 7.

8. 'Dzam-bu'i gling-du bstan-pa'i srog-shing btsugs.

9. Kha-ba-can-du chos-kyi sgron-me sbar.

10. bSam-yas was the first great Buddhist monastery, built according to maṇḍala-cosmology, located on the Tsang-po river south of Lhasa, and built around 780 by Padmasambhava and Śāntarakṣita during the reign of the Tibetan king Khri-srong lde-btsan.

11. On Samantabhadra and dharmakāya see chapter II.

12. On the sambhogakāya see chapter II.

13. The best known biographical work is the *O-gryan gu-ru padma 'byung-gnas-kyi skye-rabs rnam-thar padma 'bka'i thang-yig.*

14. Corresponding texts are in Biblio. VIII, 1.A. nos. 5, 10, 34.

15. See Biblio. VIII, 1.A. nos. 16 and 17, and the quotations from Mi-la in nos. 11 and 31.

16. Biblio VIII, 1.A. no. 29, written by 'Jigs-med gling-pa.

17. Biblio VIII, 1.A. no. 30.

18. Biblio VIII, 1.A. no. 31.

19. *bLa-ma'i thugs-grub rdo-rje drag-rtsal las / Zhal-gdams lam-rim ye-shes snying-po/Padma sam-bha'i snying-tig-go.*

20. *rDzogs-pa chen-po klong-chen snying-thig-gi sngon-'gro'i khrid-yig kun-bzang bla-ma'i zhal-lung.*

21. *Rig-'dzin padma gling-pa'i kha'-'bum yid-bzhin gter-mdzod.*

22. *rDo-rje theg-pa sngags-kyi gso-sbyong bdud-rtsi'i rol-mtsho.*

23. See note 27.

24. H. V. Guenther, *Life and Teaching of Nāropa,* Oxford 1963, p. XI–XII.

25. The spiritual teacher of the Indian siddha Nāropa was the Indian guru Tilopa; see also note 27.

26. The Shangs-pa sect, founded by Kyung-po rnal-'byor in the 11th century, is considered a subsect of the bKa'-brgyud-pa line of Tibet.

27. Biblio VIII, 1.A. nos. 13, 14, 15, and the smaller work, *Zab-lam su-kha chos-drug-gi brgyud-pa'i gsol-'debs.*

28. Biblio VIII, 1.A. nos. 14 and 16.

29. We find the more important writings on the Bon-po religion in the following titles: Tucci, G. / Heissig, W., *Die Religionen Tibets und der Mongolei* (The Religions of Tibet and of the Mongols), Stuttgart, 1970; H. Hoffman, *Quellen zur Geschichte der tibetischen Bon-Religion* (Historical sources of the Tibetan Bon religion), Mainz 1950; ———, *Die Religionen Tibets* (The Religions of Tibet), Freiburg 1956; S. Karmay, *The Treasury of Good Sayings: A Tibetan History of Bon,* Oxford 1972; Kvaerne, P., "The Canon of the Tibetan Bonpos I and II," *Indo-Iranian Journal* Vol. XVI, 1–2, the Hague 1974; ———, "Bon-po Studies, The A Khrid System of Meditation," in *Kailash, Journal of Himalayan Studies,* Vol. I, Kathmandu 1953; D. L. Snellgrove, *The Nine Ways of Bon,* Oxford 1967; ———, *Himalayan Pilgrimage,* Oxford 1961; Snellgrove/Richardson, *A Cultural History of Tibet,* Washington 1968; A. H. Francke, "gZer-myig, A Book of the Tibetan Bonpos," in *Asia Major* Vol. I (1924), Vol. 3 (1926), Vol. 4 (1927), Vol. 5 (1930), and Vol. 6 (1930); G. H. Roerich, *Trails to Inmost Asia,* New Haven 1931.

30. These texts are the Bon-po Book of the Dead *sNyan-brgyud bar-do thos-grol gsal-sgron chen-mo,* and the work of the Bon-po treasure discoverer, 'Or-sgom phug-pa, entitled *Na-rag pang-'gong rgyal-po.* Further texts, still unfamiliar to us, about the deities of the Bon-po Book of the Dead are: 1. *Na-rag gting-sbyongs,* 2. *Man-ngag 'khor-ba dong-sprugs,* 3. *Khams gsum sems-can skye-'chi'i mdo,* 4. *Zhi-khro rtsa-'grel chen-mo,* 5. *Zhi-khro yang-khol* and *Zhi-khro yongs-'dus,* 6. *Zhi-khro sbrag-sgrub* and *Zhi-khro spyi-bskul,* 7. *Zhi-khro yang-snying cha-lag dang-bcas-pa,* 8. *Zhi-khro yongs-rdzogs sku'i rgyud,* 9. *'Khor-ba dang dong sprug-gi mdo,* and 10. *Zhi-khro bcud-dril.* (According to the sources listed in S. Karmay, *Treasury,* Oxford 1972.)

31. Biblio VIII, 1.B. nos. 1–4.

32. S. Karmay: *The Treasury of Good Sayings,* Oxford 1972.

33. Although many of these texts are still located in unknown parts of Tibet and have not yet been discovered, many of them are at least known to us by their titles from our knowledge of the history of the Bon-po religion; they are listed in note 30.

34. The *Lam-mchog rin-chen 'phreng-ba* of the Tibetan sage, Dvags-po lha-rje, alias sGam-po-pa (1079–1153), Fol. 2 a–b. Dvags-po lha-rje was the most important pupil of the great yogi Mi-la ras-pa and a transmitter of the doctrine of the Great Symbol (T. Phyag-rgya chen-po), which is the ancient Indian mahāmudrā doctrine, of central importance in the bKa'-brgyud-pa sect.

35. This philosophical system originated in the 3rd or 4th century A.D. under the scholars Maitreyanātha, Asaṅga, and Vasubandhu. It teaches the practical and meditative "transformation on the path of yoga" (Yogācāra) or also the knowledge of universal awareness and other states of consciousness (vijñānavāda).

36. *Aṅguttara-Nikāya,* IV. 45 and *Saṃyutta-Nikāya* II, 3.6.

37. *Visuddhimagga,* VIII, 230, 239.

38. *Ye-shes bla-ma,* Vol. 68 a–b.

39. H. V. Guenther, *The Jewel Ornament of Liberation,* Berkeley 1971, p. 264, 265.

40. The ten perfections or stages of the bodhisattva path (S. daśabhūmi: T. Sa-bcu), on which beings proceed towards complete enlightenment, are an ideal image of the human progression from worldliness to transcendence of the world, or from profane life to the holy life of absolute spiritual release. The first group of six stages represents the possibilities of earthly life, while the last four are virtues of the bodhisattvas in transcendent space. We shall give a brief account of the ten stages: 1. The stage of "joyful" decision (S. pramuditā; T. Rab-tu dga'-ba); 2. From this follows the stage of perfect purity (S. vimalā; T. Dri-ma med-pa); 3. The stage of the "radiant" (S. prabhākarī; T. 'Od-byed-pa); 4. The stage of the "flaming" (S. arciṣmatī; T. 'Od-'phro-ba-can) as the burning of all vestiges of false ideas; 5. The stage "difficult to attain" (S. sudurjayā; T. Shin-tu sbyang-dka') of meditative knowledge, which leads to 6. the stage of "turning towards" (S. abhimukhī; T. mNgon-du gyur-pa) perfected wisdom; 7. the "far-reaching" stage (S. dūraṅgamā; T. Ring-du song-ba), which opens up transcendent space; 8. the stage of "unshakability" (S. acalā; T. Mi-gyo-ba); 9. the stage of "holy and pious" reflection (S. sādhumatī; T. Legs-pa'i blo-gros). The

10th and final stage is the "cloud of the doctrine" (S. dharmameghā; T. Chos-kyi sprin) in which the spiritual universality of the bodhisattva is achieved. Then the bodhisattvas in the radiant form of the sambhogakāya partake in the existence of the buddhas in the Tuṣita heaven.

41. *Bar-do thos-grol chen-mo,* Biblio. VIII, 1.A. no. 4.

42. I.e., beginning from the forehead, we have the order sKu, gSung, Thugs, Ye-shes, or kāya, vāc, citta, jñāna.

43. Biblio. VIII, 1.A. no. 37.

44. Biblio. VIII, 1.A. no. 7, Fol. 48 b; no. 11, Fol. 3 b, and no. 6 part d; *Bar-do'i rtsa-tshig.*

45. Biblio. VIII, 1.A. no. 15, fol. 12 a.

46. Biblio. VIII, 1.A., *Mi-la mgur-'bum,* Fol. 147a.

47. Translated by Evans-Wentz: *The Tibetan Book of the Dead,* pp. 202–204; and Biblio. VIII, 1.A. no. 6, part d: *Bar-do'i rtsa-tshig.*

48. See note 45.

49. On the doctrine of the dream-state see Evans-Wentz, *Tibetan Yoga and Secret Doctrines,* pp. 215–22, Oxford 1967, or in the *Na-ro chos-drug,* Biblio. VIII, 1.A. no. 13, which offers a different version of this doctrine.

50. Biblio. VIII, 1.A. no. 15, Fol. 46b.

51. Biblio. VIII, 1.A. no. 15, Fol. 47a–48b.

52. Biblio. VIII, 1.A. no. 16, Fol. 147a–b.

53. Evans-Wentz: *The Tibetan Book of the Dead,* pp. 183–193 and also *Yoga and Secret Doctrines,* p. 242.

54. Biblio. VIII, 1.A. no. 16, Fol. 144b.

55. Tshe-ring mched-lnga, which is the group of five ancient Tibetan mountain-goddesses, of whom Tshe-ring-ma is the leader and the best known. The five mountain-goddesses were considered, after conversion by Mi-la ras-pa, to be the protective-goddesses of all Tibetan yogis. See also, D. I. Lauf, "Tshe-ring-ma, the Mountain-Goddess of Long Life and Her Retinue," in *Ethnd. Zeitschrift Zurich,* Vol. I, Bern 1972.

56. Biblio. VIII, 1.A. no. 16, Fol. 146a.

57. Biblio. VIII, 1.A. no. 7, Fol. 46b.

58. Biblio. VIII, 1.A. no. 16, Fol. 92b–93a.

59. Biblio. VIII, 1.A. no. 16, Fol. 213a–b.

60. Evans-Wentz: *Yoga and Secret Doctrines,* pp. 246–50.

61. Such protective deities called yidams are, for example, Hevajra, Cakrasaṃvara, the eight-armed and eleven-headed Bodhisattva Avalokiteśvara, or protective deities of the teachings such as Mahākāla, Lha-mo, or Vajrakīla.

62. The ḍākinī as mystical partner is, for example, the red Vajravārāhī, the white Lab-sgron-ma, Siṃhavaktrā, or Tshe-ring-ma.

63. The cakkhu-āyatana are 1. the realm of infinite space (P. ākāsānañcāyatana); 2. the realm of infinite awareness (P. viññāṇañcāyatana); 3. the realm of nothingness (P. ākiñcaññāyatana); and 4. the realm of neither-perception-nor-non-perception (P. neva-saññānāsaññāyatana).

64. Zab-chos zhi-khro nges-don snying-po, Biblio. VIII, 1.A. Fol. 12b–13a.

65. See G. Tucci, *Geheimnis des Maṇḍala,* and D. I. Lauf, *Tibetan Sacred Art,* pp. 117–61, as well as L. Govinda, *Foundations of Tibetan Mysticism.*

66. *Zab-chos zhi-khro nges-don snying-po.*

67. *Maṇi bka'-'bum,* Part Vam, Fol. 32a–b.

68. *Zab-chos zhi-khro dgongs-pa rang-grol las/dBang-bskur 'bring-po 'gro-drug rang-grol* and *Rigs-drug gnas-'dren,* Biblio. VIII, 1.A. no. 8.

69. The five senses, in the form of symbolic offerings (S. pañcakāmaguṇāh), are among the most important symbols for the overcoming of attachments to the impermanent world of the senses; they are shown as a mirror for the emptiness of corporeal form, cymbals for the impermanence of sound, a filled spiral horn for deception through fragrance, fruit for the sense of taste, and a silk shawl for the overcoming of sensations of touch.

70. The eight Buddhist sacred signs are: 1. the wheel of the teachings; 2. the vessel of the water of long life; 3. the two fishes; 4. the lotus; 5. the eightfold knot of eternity; 6. the Buddhist sign of victory; 7. the Buddha's canopy of honor; and 8. the white conch.

71. The eight sacrifice-symbols (S. aṣṭadravyaka; T. rDzas-brgyad), which refer to the life of the Buddha, are the mirror, the Gi-vang, yoghurt or sour milk, the dūrvā grass, fruit, the white conch, red cinnabar powder, and white mustard seeds.

72. The seven insignia of the true ruler (S. sapta-ratnāni; T. Rin-chen sna-bdun) are the wheel of the law, the wishing jewel, the queen, the minister, the elephant, the horse, and the warrior.

73. Evans-Wentz, *The Tibetan Book of the Dead,* p. 21.

74. L. A. Waddell, *The Buddhism of Tibet,* Cambridge 1959, p. 469; also E. Schlagintweit, *Buddhism in Tibet,* London 1968, where on p. 253 an east-Tibetan sByang-bu is shown, which is described as Me-

lha'i rgyal-po. This picture is, like the ones shown in our book, also used for the death ritual and has the same symbols.

75. sGyu-'phrul zhi-khro rab-'byams-kyi dkyil-'khor.

76. *dBang-bskur 'bring-po 'gro-drug rang-grol.*

77. See Biblio. VIII, 1.a. nos. 9 and 38.

78. See note 76.

79. Tibetan: Phyi bum-pa'i dbyibs la nang lha'i gzhal-yas-khang chen-po.

80. *Na'ro chos-drug* and also *Ye-shes bla-ma,* Fol. 58a–59b.

81. *Na'-ro chos-drug,* part III, Fol. 26a–b and 27a.

82. Biblio. VIII, 1.B. nos. 4, Fol. 28b–29a.

83. *Zab-lam sukha chos-drug,* Part I, Fol. 2a and 7a.

84. We learn about the "clear light" in more detail in the *Ye-shes bla-ma,* fol. 24a.

85. Biblio. VIII, 1.A. no. 7, Fol. 47a.

86. Biblio. VIII, 1.A. no. 11, Fol. 18a.

87. *Ye-shes bla-ma,* Fol. 22b.

88. From a fragment from the texts of the Na-rag dong-sprugs genre, from an ancient manuscript from Bum-thang, Vol. K, a, Fol. 22b–23a.

89. Biblio. VIII, 1.A. no. 7, Fol. 23a.

90. This arrangement of the often complex symbolism in the iconography of the five Tathāgatas follows the texts in Biblio. VIII, 1.A. nos. 2, 3, 5, 6 part b, 7 and 4.

91. On the five Tathāgatas see also G. Tucci, *Indo-Tibetan III, 1;* D. L. Snellgrove, *Buddhist Himalaya;* D. I. Lauf, *Tibetan Sacred Art;* B. C. Olschak: *Mystic Art of Ancient Tibet;* L. Govinda, *Foundations of Tibetan Mysticism;* and H. W. Schumann, *Buddhismus,* Dusseldorf 1971.

92. This may vary: so according to the texts in Biblio. VIII, 1.A. no. 6 part b and no. 4, the Tathāgata Vairocana is assigned to the realm of consciousness (S. vijñāna; T. rNam-par shes-pa'i phung-po), while Akṣobhya appears as lord of the element of body.

93. According to the work *Shes-rig rdo-rje rnon-po* the dharmadhātujñāna is a motionless wisdom resting in concentration and pure vision (T. dMigs-bsam spros-bral-ba'i chos-dbyings ye-shes).

94. According to the sNying-thig tradition of the rNying-ma-pa schools the Buddha Vairocana can also appear as a Tathāgata with four heads in the cosmic directions in the aspect of the Sarvavid-Vairocana (T. Kun-rig rnam-par snang-mdzad), whereby the universality of the omniscience of the Buddha is emphasized.

95. According to *Shes-rig rdo-rje rnon-po* the "wisdom of the mirror" is: Gsal la grub-pa med-pa'i me-long ye-shes.

96. According to *Shes-rig rdo-rje rnon-po* the "wisdom of equality" is: Ro-mnyam ngang la gnas-pa mnyam-nyid ye-shes.

97. According to *Shes-rig rdo-rje rnon-po* the "wisdom of discrimination" is: sNang-ba 'od-lnga ma-'dres kun-rtogs ye-shes.

98. According to *Shes-rig rdo-rje rnon-po* the "wisdom of (karmically conditioned) action" is: gZung-'dzin gnyis snang sgrol-ba bya-grub ye-shes.

99. Bodhisattva, an enlightened being who can be effectual in worldly and trans-worldly realms in working towards the well-being of sentient creatures. The bodhisattva finally, when all beings have attained liberation, reaches the state of buddhahood.

100. Biblio. VIII, 1.A. no. 9.

101. *Maṇi-bka'-'bum,* Part Vam, Fol. 8b.

102. In ancient Pāli Buddhism we find as characterizations of the six realms of existence: deva, asuranikāya, manussa, tiracchānayoni, peta, and niraya.

103. The assignment of the mantric syllables of the worlds of the titans and animals frequently varies. We find the syllables SU or TRI given for the titans as well as for the animals. This disparity in the texts seems to go back to very ancient confusions. Our arrangement follows *Ye-shes bla-ma,* Fol. 6b–7a.

104. Biblio. no. 22, Fol. 3b–4a.

105. The most important ritual work here is the *gNas-'dren 'gro-drug rang-grol khrigs-su bkod-pa* from the collection *Kar-gling zhi-khro.*

106. *Rigs-drug gnas-'dren,* Fol. 9a–b.

107. The symbolism of the four Guardians follows the texts in Biblio. VIII, 1.A. nos. 2 and 5.

108. Biblio. VIII, 1.A. no. 1.

109. See *Pad-gling gsung-'bum,* Vol. Cha, Fol. 44b–45a.

110. Biblio. VIII, 1.A. nos. 1 and 7.

111. Biblio. VIII, 1.A. no. 7, Fol. 20b.

112. Biblio. VIII, 1.A. no. 5, a work from the Vimalamitra tradition in which there are ten Herukas in the bardo, called the ten dPal-chen Herukas. They appear in the following order: dPal-chen-po che-mchog Heruka, Vajra-, Buddha-, Ratna-, Padma-, and Karma-Heruka; then follow the Rakṣa-Heruka, Sānu-Heruka, Guhya-Heruka, and Yakṣa-Heruka.

113. Biblio. VIII, 1.A. nos. 5 and 7.

114. A further description of the symbolism of the eight Keurima can be found in Biblio. VIII, 1.A. nos. 2 and 7.

115. See table, p. 183, in D. I. Lauf, *Tibetan Sacred Art,* Berkeley 1976.

116. The description of the eight Phra-men-ma deities follows Biblio. VIII, 1.A. nos. 2 and 7.

117. Biblio. VIII, 1.A. nos. 1, 2, and 7.

118. Evans-Wentz names a tiger-headed deity in place of this horse-headed Ḍākinī. Our description has been compared with several texts, and it is possible that in the text on which Evans-Wentz's translation was based there was a confusion between the similar words rTa-gdong (horse-headed) and sTag-gdong (tiger-headed). Printing errors in Tibetan block prints and errors in manuscripts are often confusing, especially in relation to names from the Sanskrit; the various scripts also vary considerably and are used differently in different Tibetan dialects. Many such errors are handed down in the copying of texts over centuries.

119. Biblio. VIII, 1.A. nos. 1 and 2, and well as no. 7, Fol. 60a–71b.

120. Biblio. VIII, 1.A. no. 5.

121. Evans-Wentz mentions an ape-headed goddess here, which does not appear in our texts. This is probably owing to an orthographic deviation in the Tibetan text: sPre = ape, Sre = mongoose.

122. The colors of the 28 goddesses as well as their attributes are described differently in different texts. For example, in the *Na-rag dong-sprugs* text we find the colors of the first six goddesses to be: reddish-yellow, pale red, yellowish-black, whitish-red, yellow, and pale red. According to the text in Biblio. VIII, 1.A. no. 1, the colors are: off-white, yellowish-white, greenish-white, bluish-white, reddish-white, and white. In fact these variations are not irrelevant, since they indicate differing points of departure in relation to Tibetan maṇḍala-cosmology. It is possible to tell precisely from Tibetan paintings which texts they are based on. Connected with this are the references to the particular traditions and sects with which the scriptures as well as the paintings are connected.

123. Biblio. VIII, 1.A. no. 9.

124. Biblio. VIII, 1.B. no. 2.

125. Biblio. VIII, 1.B. no. 2, Fol. 2a–b.

126. Biblio. VIII, 1.B. no. 1.

127. Biblio. VIII, 1.B. no. 1, Fol. 10b.

128. The deity Khri-bzhi nams-ting can be portrayed as white or indigo-blue. According to text no. 2 in Biblio. VIII, 1.B., this deity appears after the five bDe-shegs rigs-lnga.

129. Biblio. VIII, 1.B. no. 5, Fol. 2a–5b.

130. W. Rau, *Śvetāśvatara Upaniṣad,* III, 10 and V, 1.

131. Nicholas of Cusa, *Gesprache uber das Seinkonnen* (Conversations on Being-Possible), Stuttgart 1963, p. 30.

132. Eckhart, "Von der Selbsterkenntuis" (On Self-Knowledge) and "Von der Abgeschiedenheit" (On Detachment) in *Wunder der Seele* (Wonder of the Soul), Stuttgart 1971.

133. Eckhart, "On Death" in *Wunder der Seele.*

134. Thausing, G., *Der Auferstehungsgedanke in agyptischen religiosen Texten,* (The idea of resurrection in Egyptian religious texts), Leipzig 1943, p. 169.

135. Thomas Aquinas, *Summe der Theologie* (Summa Theologica), Stuttgart 1938, chapter I, 76.6.

136. Thomas Aquinas, *Summe der Theologie,* I.77.8.

137. Ibid., chapter I.89.4.

138. Ibid., chapter I.89.4.

139. Abhedānanda, *Mystery of Death,* pp. 47–48.

140. Kroll, J. *Gott und Holle* (God and Hell), Darmstadt 1963, p. 310.

141. Ibid., p. 311.

142. Hildegard von Bingen, *Scivias,* Berlin 1928, pp. 66 and 38.

143. Ibid., p. 37.

144. W. F. Otto, *Das Heilige* (The Idea of the Sacred), Munich 1964, p. 14.

145. A. Metzger, *Dämonie und Transzendenz* (Daemonia and Transcendence), pp. 204–5.

146. Hermes Trismegistus, Munich 1964, p. 52.

147. J. Boehme, *Seraphinisch Blumengärtlein* (The Seraphinic Flower Garden); ——————, *Die drei Prinzipien des gottlichen Wesens,* 5.3 (The Three Principles of the Divine Nature).

148. Ibid., 9.27.

149. J. Boehme, *Aurora,* 21.47.

150. J. Boehme, *Vierzig Fragen von der Seele* (Forty Questions of the Soul), 1.185.

151. A. Portmann, *Biologie und Geist* (Biology and Spirit), Zurich 1956, p. 142.

VIII. BIBLIOGRAPHY

1. Tibetan Original Sources

Manuscripts, block prints, and more recent editions. The works cited are various versions of the Tibetan Books of the Dead, commentaries, and texts which contain explanations of certain contents of the Books of the Dead and of their iconography.

A. TIBETAN BUDDHIST TEXTS

1. *Bar-do thos-grol-gyi yang snying chos-spyod bag-chags rang-grol.*
2. *Zab-chos zhi-khro dgongs-pa rang-grol las/Chos-spyod brgya-phyag sdig-sgrib rang-grol.*
3. *Zab-chos zhi-khro dgongs-pa rang-grol las / Zhing-khams snga'i smon-lam thos-pa rang-grol* (gTer-ma scripture).
4. *Bar-do thos-grol chen-mo/* and *Khro-bo bar-do ngo-sprod gsol'-debs thos-grol.*
5. *Dam-tshig thams-cad-kyi nyams-chags skong-ba'i lung-lnga.* Text from the tradition of the Indian sage Vimalamitra.
6. *Zab-chos zhi-khro dgongs-pa rang-grol las thos-grol chen-mo.* Block print from sPa-gro chos-ldan skyed-chu lha-dbang.
7. *Zab-chos zhi-khro dgongs-pa rang-grol las/Bar-do'i gsol-'debs thos-grol chen-mo bklag-chog-tu bkod-pa 'khrul-snang rang-grol.* Block print from Bum-thang bkra-shis chos-gling.
8. *Zab-chos zhi-khro dgongs-pa rang-grol las/Kar-gling zhi-khro.* Collection of 38 various primary texts, ritual texts, and supplications for the recitation of the Book of the Dead.
9. *Zan-chos zhi-khro nges-don snying-po sgo-nas rang dang gzhan-gyi don-mchog-tu sgrub-pa'i las-rim 'khor-ba'i mun-gzhoms kun-bzang thugs-rje'i snang-mdzod.*
10. *Zhi-khro na-rag dong-sprugs rnal-'byor-gyi spyi khrus 'gyod-tshangs-kyi cho-ga dri-med bzhang-rgyud.*
11. *Bar-do'i spyi'i don thams-cad rnam-pa gsal-bar byed-pa dran-pa'i me-long.*
12. *Bar-do'i rtsa-tshig.*
13. *Zab-mo na'-ro'i chos-drug-gi nyams-len thun chos bdud-rtsi'i nying-khu zhes-bya-ba sgrub-brgyud karma kaṃ-tshang-gi don khrid.*

14. *Zab-mo ni-gi chos-drug-gi khrid-yig zab-don thad-mar brdal-ba zhes-bya-ba dklags-chog-ma.*
15. *dPal-ldan na'-ro chos-drug-gi khrid-yig mchog-gi gra-chen dang gsan-spyod zlog sgom-gyi khrid-yig zil-non seng-ge'i nga-ro.*
16. *rJe-btsun mi-la ras-pa'i rnam-thar rgyas-par phye-ba mgur-'bum.*
17. *rJe-btsun mi-la ras-pa'i rdo-rje'i mgur-drug sogs gsung-rgyum thor-bu 'ga'.*
18. *bLa-ma mchod-pa'i cho-ga yon-tan kun-'byung,* Fol. 11a–12b.
19. *Bar-do thos-grol/The Tibetan Book of the Dead,* by the great Ācārya Śrī-Siṅg-ha, Varanasi 1969, Tibetan text.
20. *Kun-gzang bla-ma'i zhal-lung.* This compendium of Mahāyāna Buddhism gives detailed descriptions of the kinds of suffering in the various hells and of the six worlds of existence, and in addition contains a description of the process of dying. Fol. 7b, 11a–13a, 50a–80a, and 295a–b.
21. *Lam-rim ye-shes snying-po.* An important standard text with detailed commentary from the tradition of Padmasambhava.
22. *Thugs-rje chen-po yi-ge drug-pa'i gsol-'debs-kyi sgrub-thabs byin-rlabs-can,* Fol. 3b–4a.
23. From the collection of the *Klong-chen snying-thig: Bar-do' 'smon-lam dgongs-gcig rgya-mtsho,* Fol. 2b.
24. *bTags-grol-gyi skor-rnams.*
25. *bTags-grol stong-gsal til-mtha' dbus-bral.*
26. *sNying-thig-gi bshags-grol.*
27. *Zhi-khro ngan-song sbyong-ba'i chog-sgribs khrom-dkrugs gsal-ba'i rgyan bklags-chogs-mar bkod-pa.* From the *sNying-thig.*
28. *rDo-rje theg-pa sngags-kyi gso-sbyong bdud-rtsi'i rol-mtsho.*
29. *rDzogs-pa chen-po klong-chen snying-thig-gi gdod-ma'i mgon-po'i lam-gyi rim-pa'i khrid-yig ye-shes bla-ma,* Fol. 6b–7a.
30. *kLong-chen snying-gi thig-le las bskyed-rim lha-khrid 'og-min bgrod-pa'i them-skas.*
31. *Shes-rig rdo-rje rnon-po'i 'grel-ba/Yang-zab kun-bzang bla-ma'i gsang-mdzod/Legs-bshad 'phrul-gyi lde'u-mig,* Fol. 45b–46a and 97a–98b.
32. *Rig-'dzin padma gling-pa'i bka'-'bum yid-bzhin gter-mdzod las/*Part *'Cha,* Fol. 13a, 35b–36b, 38b, 45a, 55b–56a; Part *Ja,* Fol. 7a; Part *Nga,* Fol. 12a.

33. *Maṇi bka'-'bum.*
34. *Na-rag dong-sprug phyag-rgya gcig-pa'i rgyun-khyer yang-zab snying-po.*
35. *rJe-sgam-po rin-po che'i lam-mchog rin-chen 'phreng-ba.*
36. *Na'-ro gsang-spyod-kyi dmigs-rim.*
37. *rDo-rje theg-pa'i chos-spyod thun bzhi'i rnal-'byor-gyi rim-pa.*
38. *bKa' rdzogs-pa chen-po yang-zab dkon-mchog spyi 'dus-kyi las-byang khrigs-su bkod-pa 'khrul-med rab-gsal dngos-grub mchog-ster.*
39. *Bar-do'i gsol-'debs-kyi mchan-'grel nyung-bsdus thar-lam shing-rta.*

B. TIBETAN TEXTS OF THE BON-PO RELIGION

1. *sNyan-brgyud bar-do thos-grol gsal-sgron chen-mo.*
2. *Na-rag pang-'gong rgyal-po.*
3. *Pad-ma klong-yangs-kyi mdo.*
4. *Theg-pa chen-po'i mdo.*

From the Bon-po Nispanna-Yoga of the rDzogs-chen zhang-zhung tradition:

5. *rDzogs-pa chen-po zhang-zhung snyan-rgyud las rigs-drug rang-sbyong-gi gdams-pa.*
6. *rDzogs-pa chen-po zhang-zhung snyan-rgyud las phyi lta-ba spyi gcod-kyi man-ngag le'u bcu-gnyis-pa.*
7. *rDzogs-pa chen-po zhang-zhung snyan-rgyud las sgron-ma drug-gi dgongs don 'grel-pa.* Published by L. Chandra and Tenzin Namdak, New Delhi 1968.

2. Secondary Literature

Abegg, E. *Der Pretakalpa des Garuḍa-Purāṇa.* Berlin 1956.
Abhedānanda, Swami. *The Mystery of Death.* Calcutta 1967.
Bromage, B. *Tibetan Yoga.* London 1959.
Chāndogya-Upaniṣad. Mylapore, Madras 1965.
Chos-kyi grags-pa, Tibetan Dictionary. India, n.d.
Chandra, L. *Tibetan-Sanskrit Dictionary, Vols. 1–12.* New Delhi 1959.

Das, S. C. *Tibetan-English Dictionary.* Alipore 1960.
Deussen, P. *Sechzig Upanishad's des Veda.* Leipzig 1905.
——. *Vier philosophische Texte des Mahābhāratam.* Leipzig 1922.
Evans-Wentz, W. Y. *The Tibetan Book of the Dead.* Oxford 1927.
——. *Tibetan Yoga and Secret Doctrines.* Oxford 1958.
Geldner, K. F. *Vedismus und Brahamanismus, Religionsgeschichtiches Lesebuch.* Tubingen 1928.
Guenther, H. V. *Life and Teaching of Nāropa.* Oxford 1963.
——. *The Jewel Ornament of Liberation.* Berkeley and London 1971.
Joshi, L. M. *Studies in the Buddhistic Culture of India.* Varanasi 1967.
Karmay, S. F. *The Treasury of Good Sayings: A Tibetan History of Bon.* Oxford 1972.
Kvaerne, P. "The Canon of the Tibetan Bonpos I. and II." *Indo-Iranian Journal,* Vol. XVI, 1–2. The Hague 1974.
Lauf, D. I. "Initiationsrituale des tibetischen Totenbüches." In *Asiatische Studien,* Vol. XXIV, 1–2. Bern 1970.
——. *Tibetan Sacred Art: The Heritage of Tantra.* Berkeley and London 1976.
——. *Das Bild als Symbol des Tantrismus.* Munich 1973.
——. "Nachtodzustand und Wiedergeburt nach den Traditionen des tibetischen Totenbüches." In *Leben nach dem Sterben.* Published by A. Rosenberg, Munich 1974.
Muses, C. A. *Esoteric Teachings of the Tibetan Tantra.* New York 1961.
Nyanatiloka. *Visuddhimagga: Der Weg zur Reinheit.* Konstanz 1952.
Rau, W. "Versuch einer deutschen Ubersetzung der Śvetāśvatara-Upaniṣad." In *Asiatische Studien,* Vol. 1–2. Bern 1964.
Ribbach, S. H. *Drogpa Namgyal, A Tibetan Life.* Munich-Planegg 1940.
Roerich, G. N. *The Blue Annals, Part II.* Calcutta 1953.
Schumann, H. W. *Buddhismus, ein Leitfaden durch seine Lehren und Schulen.* Dusseldorf 1971.
Schlagintweit, E. *Buddhism in Tibet.* London 1968.
Seidenstucker, K. *Pāli-Buddhismus.* Munich 1923.
Snellgrove, D. L. *Buddhist Himalaya.* Oxford 1957.
Tucci, G. *Indo-Tibetica,* Vol. III, 1. Spiti e Kunavar, Rome 1934.
——. *Tibetan Painted Scrolls.* Rome 1949.
Tucci, G. / Heissig, W. *Die Religionen Tibets und der Mongolei.* Stuttgart 1970.
Wayman, A. *The Buddhist Tantras.* New York 1974.
Waddel, L. A. *The Buddhism of Tibet or Lamaism.* Cambridge 1959.

3. Comparative Literature

Bingen, Hildegard von. *Scivias-Wisse die Wege.* Berlin 1928.

Boehme, J. *Seraphinisch-Blumengärtlein.* Berlin 1918.

Brandt, W. *Das Schicksal der Seele nach dem Tode.* Darmstadt 1967.

Chantepie de la Saussaye. *Lehrbuch der Religionsgeschichte, Bd I und II.* Freiburg 1897.

Cues, Nikolaus V. *Gespräche über das Seinkönnen.* Stuttgart 1963.

Eckehart. *Vom Wunder der Seele.* Stuttgart 1971.

Gebser, J. *Ursprung und Gegenwart, Fundamente und Manifestationen der aperspektivischen Welt.* Stuttgart 1966.

Hornung, E. *Ägyptische Unterweltsbucher.* Zurich 1972.

Herzog, E. *Psyche und Tod.* Zurich 1960.

Jeremias, A. *Allgemeine Religionsgeschichte.* Munich 1924.

Jung, C. G. "Über die Archetypen des Kollektiven Unbewubten." In *Eranos-Jahrbuch* 1934.

_____. *Psychologie und Religion, Gesammelte Werke Bank II.* Zurich.

_____. *Psychologie und Alchemie.* Zurich 1952.

Kolpaktchy, G. *Das Ägyptische Totenbüch.* Weilheim 1970.

Kroll, J. *Gott und Hölle, der Mythus vom Descensuskampfe.* Darmstadt 1963.

Lübker, F. *Reallexikon des classischen Alterthums.* Leipzig 1874.

Lucretius. *Über die Seele und den Tod.* Translated by G. Sprandel. Darmstadt 1963.

Metzger, A. *Dämonie und Transzendenz.* Pfullingen 1964.

Orelli, C. *Allgemeine Religionsgeschichte, Bd. I und II.* Bonn 1913.

Otto, R. *Das Heilige.* Munich 1971.

Otto, W. F. *Die Manen.* Darmstadt 1962.

Plotinus. *Schriften, Bd. la.* Translated by R. Harder. Hamburg 1956.

Preller, L. *Griechische Mythologie.* Leipzig 1854.

_____. *Römische Mythologie.* Bonn 1878.

Rohde, E. *Psyche.* Tübingen 1925.

Simrock, K. *Handbuch der deutschen Mythologie.* Bonn 1878.

Spiegel, J. *Das Werden der altägyptischen Hochkultur.* Heidelberg 1953.

Thausing, G. *Der Auferstehungsgedanke in ägyptischen religiosen Texten.* Leipzig 1943.

Thomas von Aquino. *Summe der Theologie* (Summa Theologica). Stuttgart 1938.